John Gregory Country

Team and wagon near the top of Junction Hill, the old name for the W side of Michigan Hill. The men are unidentified. Notice the blanket drawn over their knees.

Charlie and May Barstella
July 2000

Dedicated to Marcetta Lutz,
who threw down the gauntlet

John Gregory Country

PLACE NAMES AND HISTORY OF RALSTON BUTTES QUADRANGLE

Jefferson County, Colorado

Charles and Mary Ramstetter, Editors

C Lazy Three
PRESS

GOLDEN, COLORADO

John Gregory Country
Place Names and History of Ralston Buttes Quadrangle
Jefferson County, Colorado

Ramstetter, Charles and Mary, eds.
ISBN 0-9643283-2-1
Library of Congress Catalog Card Number 96-96350

Cover and interior by Troy Scott Parker, Cimarron Design

Cover illustration: From Harper's Weekly, February 8, 1868. The caption on the pen-and-ink sketch reads, "Overland Mail-Coach Crossing the Rocky Mountains—Scene in Guy's Gulch.—Sketched by Theodore R. Davis."

Printed in the United States of America by Thomson-Shore
First printing, November 1999

Published by C Lazy Three Press
5957 Crawford Gulch
Golden, CO 80403

Contents

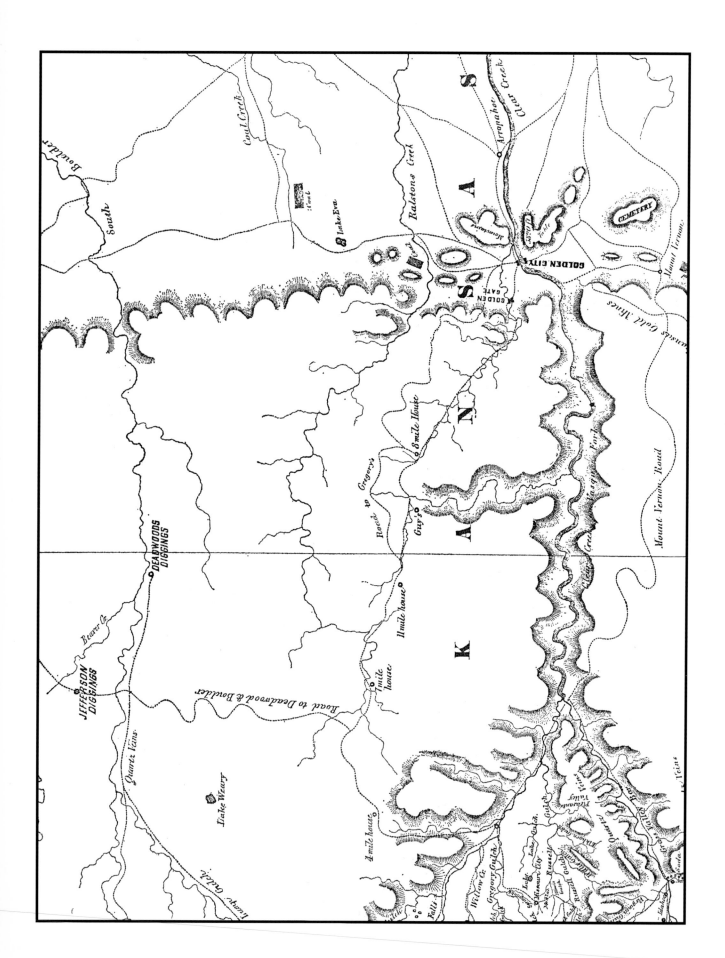

Introduction

What follows is a modest attempt to locate both geological and historical reference points in and adjacent to the Ralston Buttes Quadrangle of Jefferson County, Colorado. And to hear what they have to say.

The Ralston Buttes Quad is 57.36 square miles—6.65 miles wide and 8.62 miles deep. Rocky Flats, Blue Mountain, Centennial Cone and Indian Gulch (U.S. Geological Survey designation) anchor the quad. To position the Ralston Buttes Quad with regard to its neighbors, the adjoining edges of adjacent quads are included. Included too are stage stops eastward on the Cheyenne Road which entwine with this history, as well as the Burt and Berthoud map of 1860 which takes us west all the way to Black Hawk.

The year of the quad used to locate the place name does not limit the information to that quad. It may, however, limit the elevation to that quad as elevation figures can vary from edition to edition.

Black Hawk, a.k.a. Blackhawk, is shown as recorded.

Early place names reflect a tendency for literalness. Clear Creek is a good example. The river has been called Cannon Ball Creek for the large fields of boulders in its bed, Vasquez Fork for the fort located at the river's confluence with the South Platte, Long's Creek by the Long Expedition, Toughcuss for the tough

FACING PAGE AND LEFT
A portion of the Burt & Berthoud map of 1860. The smaller print in the map header reads:

including the adjacent country with the principal roads, streams & towns
BY
S.W. Burt & E.L. Berthoud,
Civil & Mining Engrs.
Central City & Golden City
1860.

Rocky Mountain News Printing Co. Denver City.

terrain, and Clear Creek for the clearness of the water that flows into the muddy South Platte.

Many place names do not appear on known maps but persist in being handed down. Sheep Mountain, officially known as Centennial Cone, is a good example. Some names appear on early maps only to be cast aside later. Dry Creek is one of these. That drainage is now known as Van Bibber. The name *Dry Creek,* however, continues in common use.

Another name that stubbornly refuses to die is Mt. Tom. Although replaced from time to time with Golden Peak, the original name is holding its own on more recent quads. Then there's Indian Gulch and the unfortunate mix-up that resulted in the near loss of that important piece of Indian history.

A big chunk of missing information is in the dearth of Indian and Spanish names. These appellations did not survive the high tides of European gold seeker and settler long enough to be handed over to the archivist.

To those dusty sojourners of bygone days who called it as they saw it, and to today's collectors of maps and stories, keepers of the flame, we are deeply indebted. Information gathered from a garden variety of common knowledge is presented at face value. Published sources are listed. Special thanks are extended to Richard Van Horn, Geological Engineer with the U.S. Geological Survey, whose generous gift of the 1906 Blackhawk Quad solved many mysteries.

For questions on USGS place names, contact USGS Earth Science Information, 507 National Center, Reston, VA 22092, telephone 703-648-6045. For inexpensive aerial views of the region, contact the Mapping Department of Jefferson County. For assistance in researching county records, contact Duncan McCollum, Director, Archives and Records Management, Jefferson County, telephone 303-271-8448. For permission to explore a site, contact the relevant county assessor's office to determine current ownership.

May you be entertained and prompted to further investigation by this meager beginning. Additions and corrections are earnestly solicited for a second edition. If you have a photograph or information which we use in the second edition, it's worth a free book.

Charles and Mary Ramstetter
C Lazy Three Press
5957 Crawford Gulch
Golden, Colorado 80403
Telephone and fax (303) 277-0134

Maps

The following nine pages show the U.S. Geological Survey Ralston Buttes Quadrangle with the adjacent edges and corners of all the neighboring quads. The scale is 80% of the original maps. To quickly find a location using the USGS section, township, and range numbers provided in this book, use the diagram below to find the appropriate page number.

Map Pages

NW	NC	NE
WC	C	EC
SW	SC	SE

Example

The location
*Black Hawk Quad
S25, T3S, R72W*
is Section 25
in Township 3S
and Range 72W
of the USGS
Black Hawk
Quadrangle.
It can be seen
in detail on the
Southwest (SW)
map on page 16.

◀R72W R71W▶   ◀R71W R70W▶   ◀R70W

T2S

12	TUNGSTEN 7	8	9	10	11	12	7	8	LOUISVILLE 9

ELDORADO SPRINGS

NW   NC   NE

13	18	17	16	15	14	13	18	17	16
24	19	20	21	22	23	24	19	20	21
25	30	29	28	27	26	25	30	29	28
16	31	32	33	34	35	36	31	32	33

RALSTON BUTTES

WC   C   EC

1 BLACK HAWK	6	5	4	3	2	1	6	5	GOLDEN 4
12	7	8	9	10	11	12	7	8	9
13	18	17	16	15	14	13	18	17	16
24	19	20	21	22	23	24	19	20	21

SW   SC   SE

| 25 | 30 | 29 | 28 | 27 | 26 | 25 | 30 | 29 | 28 |
| 36 | SQUAW PASS 31 | 32 | 33 | 34 | 35 | 36 | 31 | 32 | MORRISON 33 |

EVERGREEN

| 1 | 6 | 5 | 4 | 3 | 2 | 1 | 6 | 5 | 4 |

◀R72W R71W▶   ◀R71W R70W▶   ◀R70W

NW	NC	NE
WC	C	EC
SW	SC	SE

Northwest
T2S, R72W • T2S, R71W

QUADS SHOWN ON THIS PAGE
Tungsten
Black Hawk
Eldorado Springs
Ralston Buttes

◄R72W │ R71W ► ◄TUNGSTEN QUAD │ ELDORADO SPRINGS QUAD ►

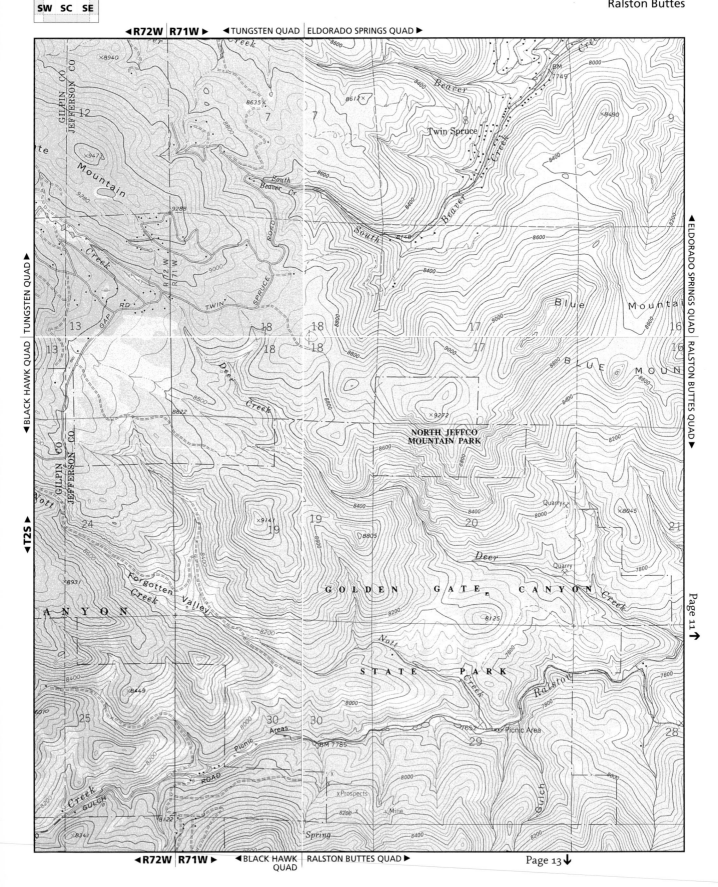

◄R72W │ R71W ► ◄BLACK HAWK QUAD │ RALSTON BUTTES QUAD ►

Page 11 →

Page 13 ↓

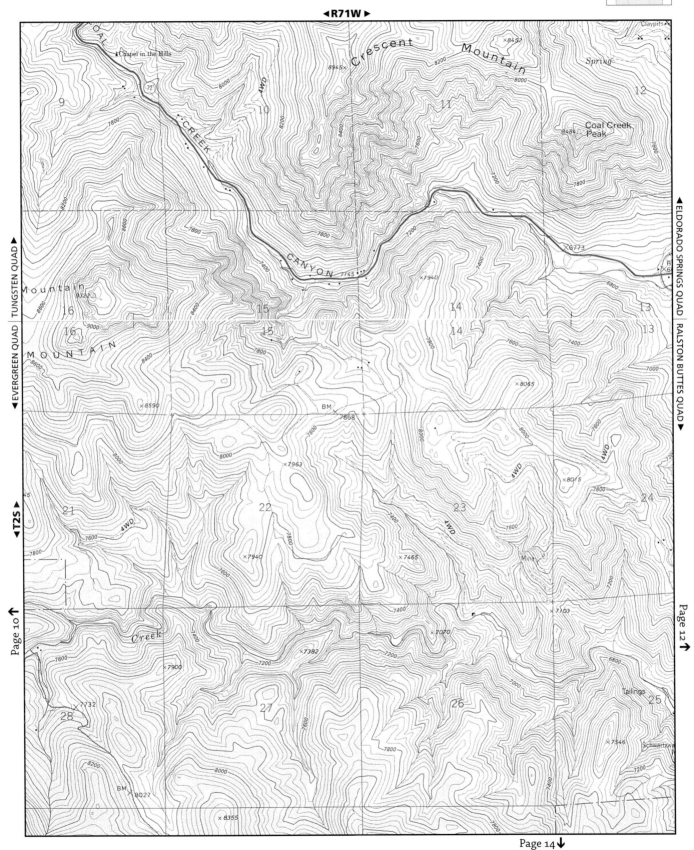

NW NC **NE**
WC C EC
SW SC SE

Northeast
T2S, R71W • T2S, R70W

QUADS SHOWN ON THIS PAGE
Eldorado Springs
Louisville
Golden
Ralston Buttes

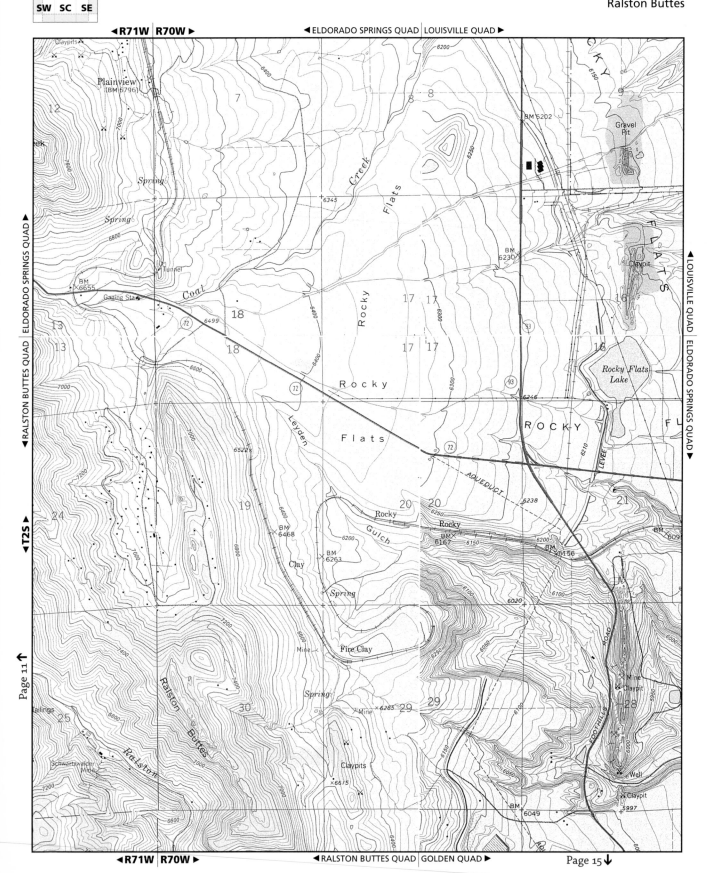

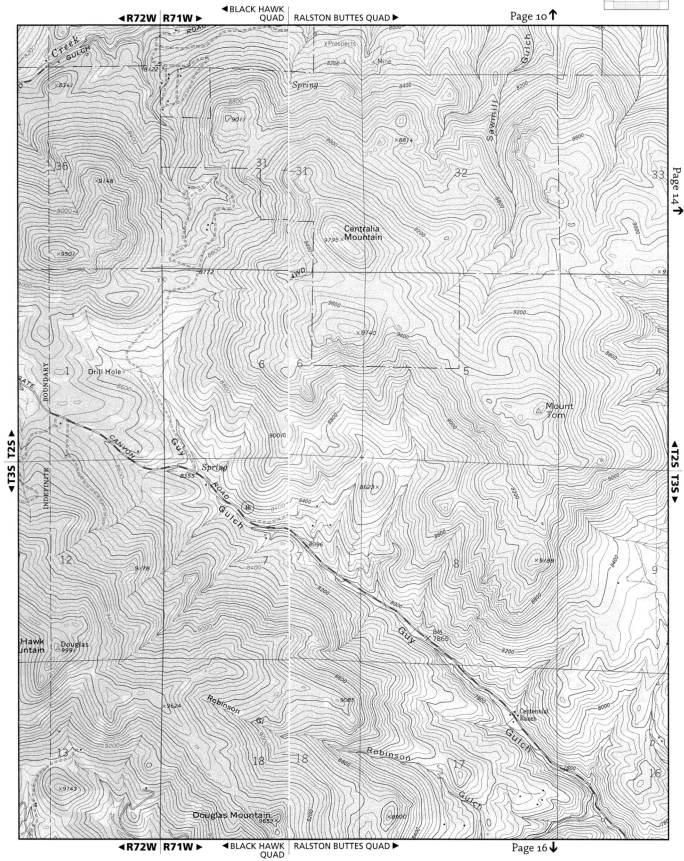

NW NC NE
WC C EC
SW SC SE

Central
T2S, R71W • T3S, R71W

QUAD SHOWN ON THIS PAGE
Ralston Buttes

◄R71W ►

Page 11 ↑

Page 13 ↑

Page 15 ↑

◄T3S | T2S ►

◄T2S | T3S ►

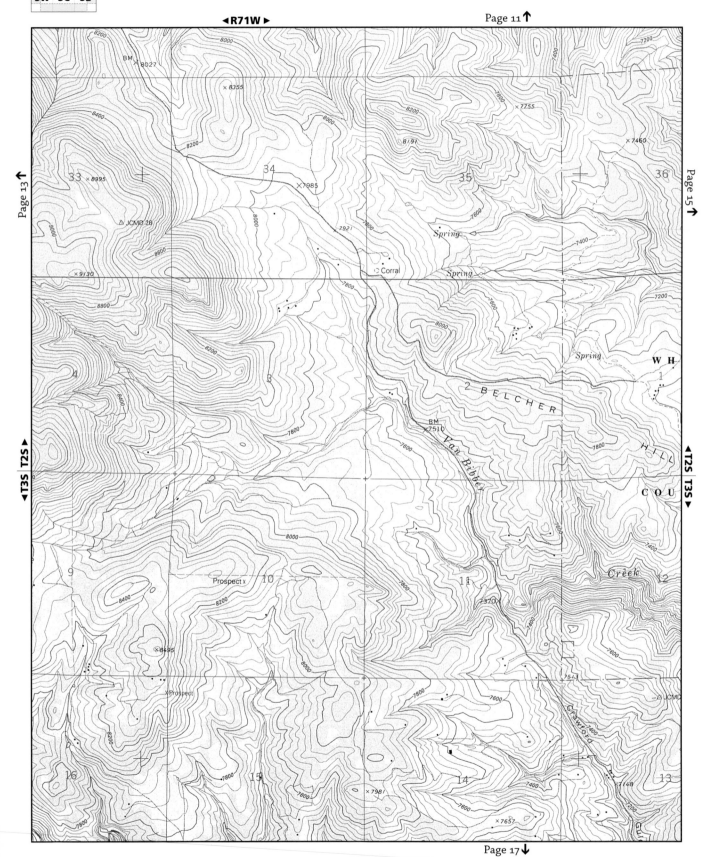

Page 17 ↓

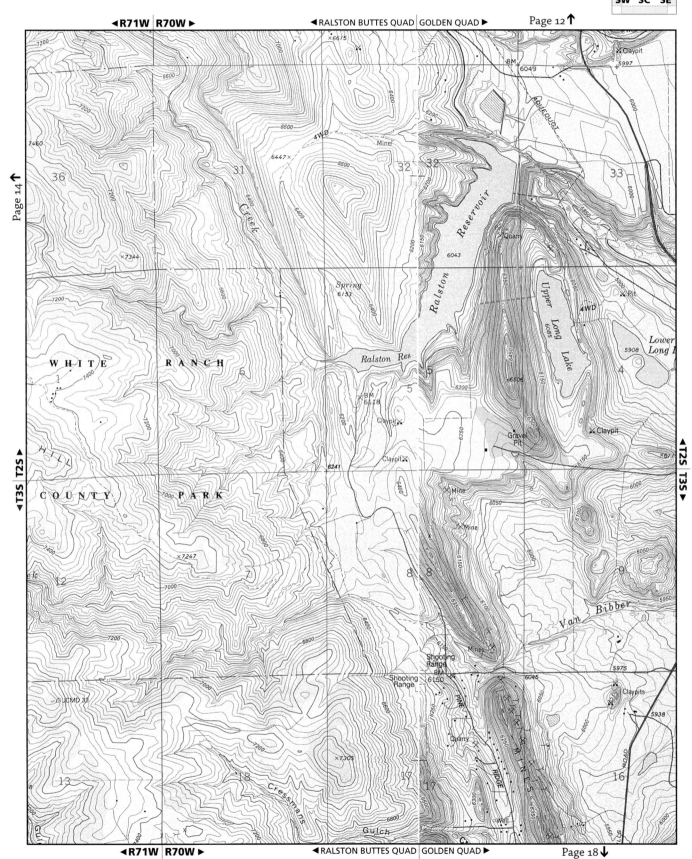

Southwest
T3S, R72W • T3S, R71W • T4S, R72W • T4S, R71W

◄R72W R71W►   ◄BLACK HAWK QUAD   RALSTON BUTTES QUAD►   Page 13 ↑

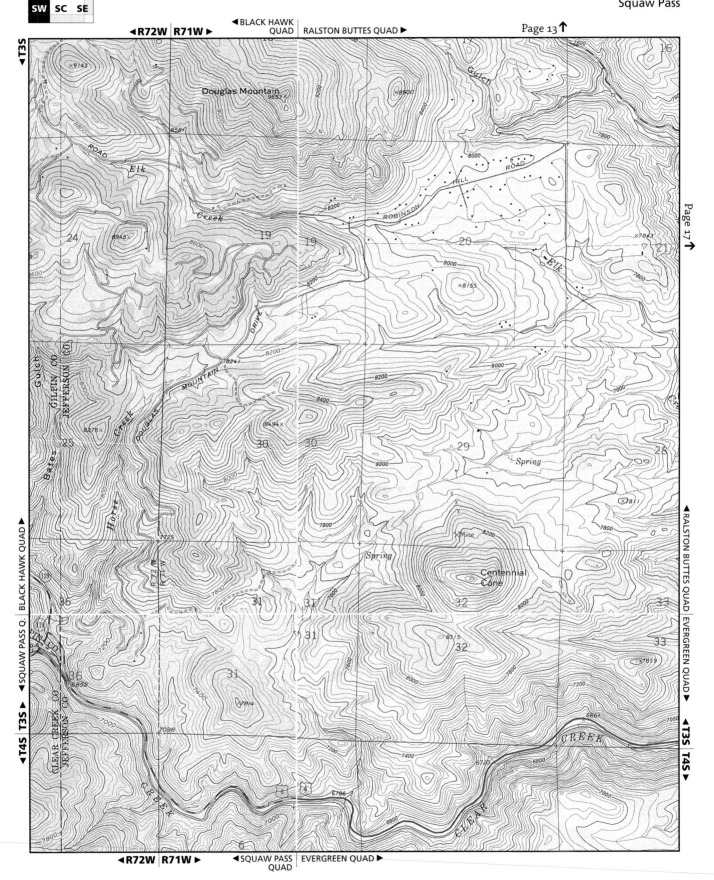

◄R72W R71W►   ◄SQUAW PASS QUAD   EVERGREEN QUAD►

South Central

T3S, R71W • T4S, R71W

◀R71W▶   Page 14↑   Page 16↑   Page 18↑

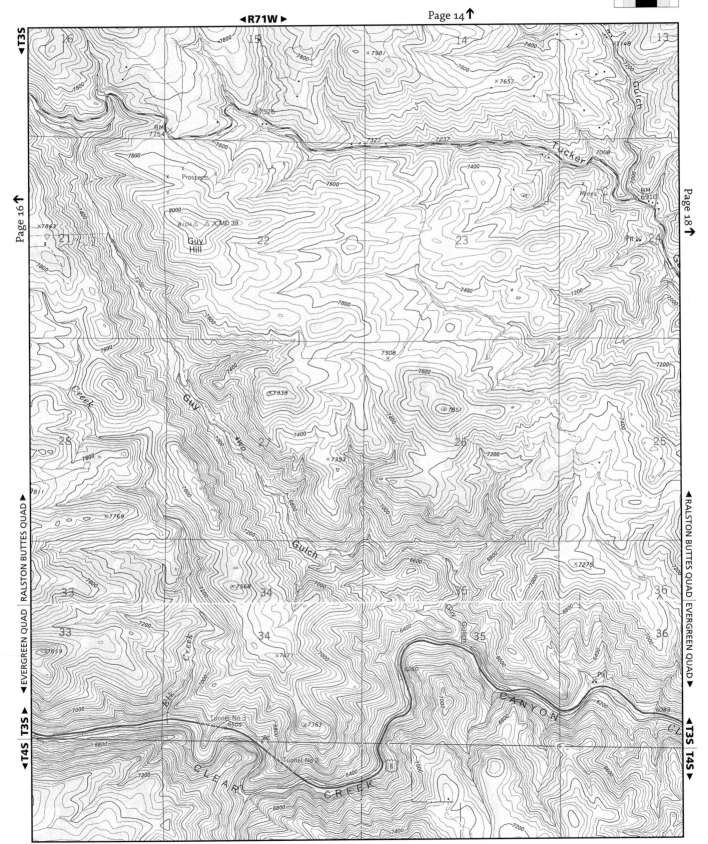

NW	NC	NE
WC	C	EC
SW	SC	SE

Southeast
T3S, R71W • T3S, R70W • T4S, R71W • T4S, R70W

QUADS SHOWN ON THIS PAGE
Evergreen
Golden
Morrison
Ralston Buttes

◀ R71W R70W ▶   ◀ RALSTON BUTTES QUAD GOLDEN QUAD ▶   Page 15 ↑

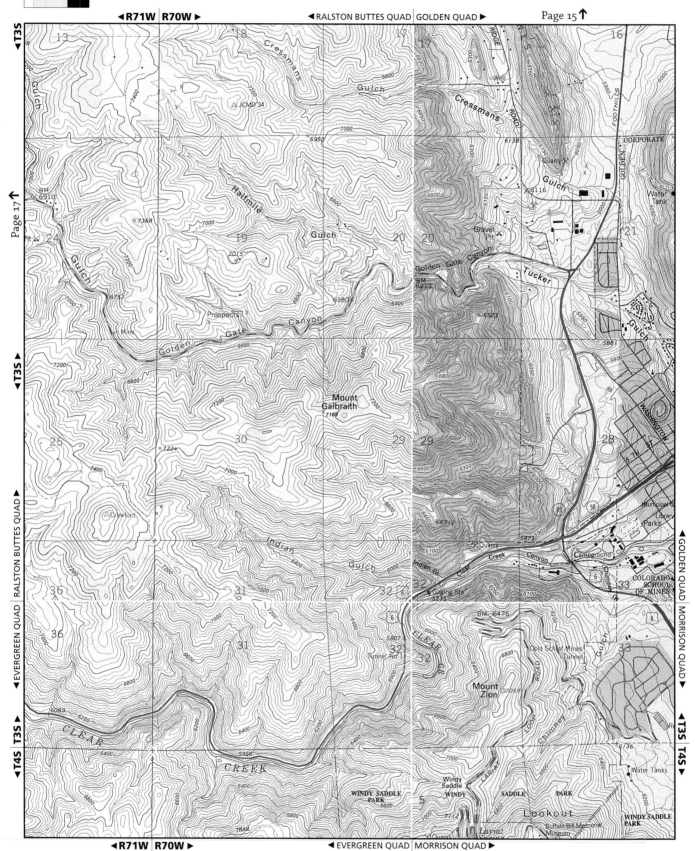

◀ R71W R70W ▶   ◀ EVERGREEN QUAD MORRISON QUAD ▶

Abbreviations

ab.	about		**NW**	northwest
a.k.a.	also known as		**quad**	quadrangle—a tract of country represented by one of a series of map sheets
BQ	Black Hawk a.k.a. Blackhawk Quad		**RBQ**	Ralston Buttes Quad
butte	an isolated hill or mountain with steep or precipitous sides		**R**	range—a north-south row of townships referred to collectively
c.	at, in, or of approximately		**S/b**	should be—used when the place name cannot be located on a quad
CCC	Coal Creek Canyon		**S**	section—one square mile
CCRR	Colorado Central Railroad		**S**	south
E	east		**SE**	southeast
elv.	elevation		**SH**	state highway
ESQ	Eldorado Springs Quad		**SW**	southwest
EQ	Evergreen Quad		**T**	township—a territorial division containing 36 square miles
GQ	Golden Quad		**TQ**	Tungsten Quad
GGC	Golden Gate Canyon		**var.**	variant
Ibid.	cited above		**W**	west
N	north			
NE	northeast			

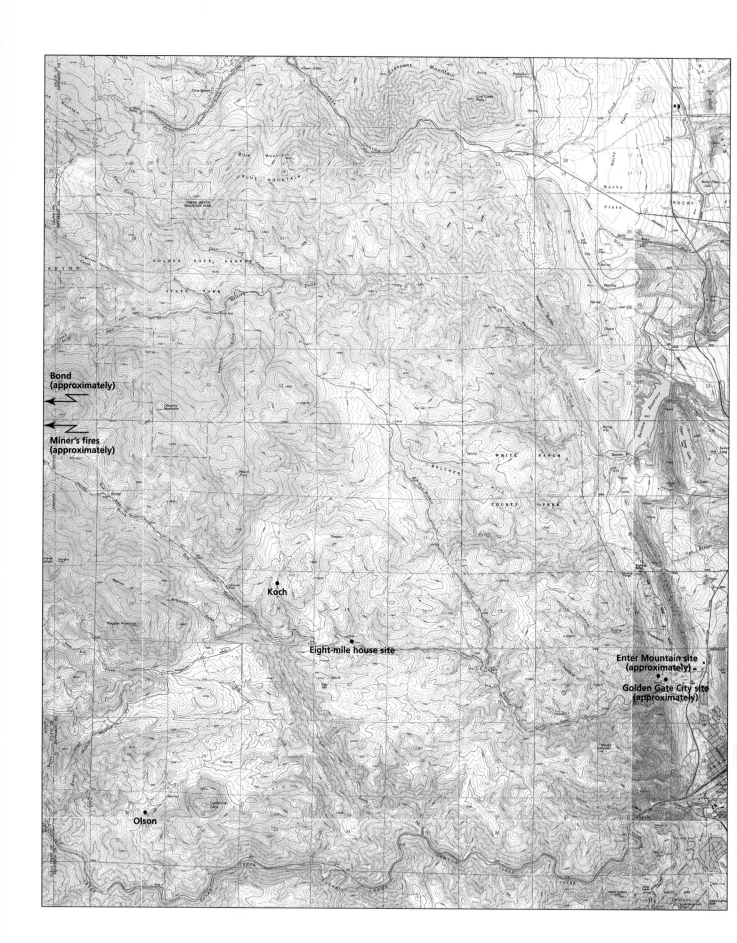

Bond
(approximately)

Miner's fires
(approximately)

Koch

Eight-mile house site

Enter Mountain site
(approximately) –

Golden Gate City site
(approximately)

Olson

Burial Sites

Bond

S/b Black Hawk Quad.

"In the summer of 1865 the [James Bond] family…took the trail through Golden and up the very difficult Tucker Gulch to the big camp of Blackhawk. Here they met their first real tragedy.

They had traversed the worst of the Gulch road and were out in the high and more level piney woods south of Dorey Hill. On July 12, my uncle, James Wesley, was seven years and one month old. He was sitting on the side of the wagon ahead of the rear wheels when they struck a deep chuck hole. He fell from the wagon and under the rear wheel, which passed over him, killing him instantly.

He was buried there at the side of the road, somewhere in Gilpin county, in a location my father and I have searched for several times, but have never found.

My grandmother was inconsolable. She had traveled a thousand terrible miles to see her first born die."

(Source: Bond, Fred C., 1974, *It happened to me, an American autobiography*: p. 9-10, unpublished. Fred's son, Robert F. Bond, used this paper as the basis for his work published in 1989 entitled *The land persists*.)

"James Bond, grief engulfed, looked down at his wife, Mary, as she knelt at the new grave by the side of the road. She had sprinkled mullein seed over the mound so that it would be marked with golden spikes of flowers and the velvety leaves would offer some cover to her first born, only 7 years old, who lay there. An hour ago he had been a happy boy sitting on the edge of their wagon, watching the oxen pull it from a deep hole in the trail. There was a sudden lurch, he lost his balance and, screaming, fell under the wheels. For Mary, this spot on

Dory Hill, so close to the gold fields of Black Hawk and Central City, marked the end of a long, arduous trip towards California and riches."

(Source: Wiberg, Ruth, 1978, *James Bond, restless pioneer*: Denver Post Empire Mag., Oct. 29, 1978, p. 22.)

The grave was lost and never found again. To this day mullein grows on Dory Hill.

Eight-mile House Site

S entrance to Koch Gulch in Golden Gate Canyon.
S/b Ralston Buttes Quad.
S15, T3S, R71W.
Elv. ab. 7500'.

In 1918, while digging a pit for a silo, George Ramstetter and his nephew, Jim Ramstetter, unearthed the body of a man buried upright. (See Ramstetter, James K., 1996, *Life in the early days*, p. 42-43, for more about the skeleton found standing in the hillside. This book is available at the Golden Feed Mill.)

Empty silo over the ground where in 1918 the skeleton of a man was found buried upright. The bicycle belongs to Mike Ramstetter, a fifth-generation Ramstetter occupying the site of the old Eight-mile stage stop. Photographed 1997.

Enter Mountain Site

An E slope burial beside the original road to Gregory's. Exact site unknown.
S/b Ralston Buttes or Golden Quad.

"[Wednesday, June 8, 1859] New as this rugged road is—it was first traversed five weeks ago to-day [Friday, May 4, 1859]—death had traveled it before me. A young man, shot dead while carelessly drawing a rifle from his wagon, lies buried by the roadside on this mountain."

(Source: Greeley, Horace, 1860, *An overland journey from New York to San Francisco in the summer of 1859*: New York, Saxton, Barker & Co., p. 116.)

"Quite a number of accidents have lately happened—several persons have been shot through awkwardness or carelessness. William Herbert, of Georgia, shot himself when at the base of the mountain near Clear Creek, and died instantly."

(Source: Russell, William, letter written from Gregory Gulch, Kansas, June 17th, 1859, in Spencer, E. D., 1966, *Green Russell and Gold*: Univ. of Texas Press, p. 117.)

EDITORS' NOTE: It's possible that William Herbert is the man who died on Enter Mountain.

Fire Deaths—The Miners' Fires

"The trail [to Gregory's] wound through grassy valleys, among enormous rocks, beside mountains with icy springs gushing from their sides, and up and down rugged hills studded with tall pines and white-stemmed aspens.

These cheerful surroundings were succeeded by a dreary black expanse. Fires had raged for two weeks and were still burning. It was impossible to check them, for the ground was half covered with dead fallen trunks, and thickly carpeted with successive layers of pine needles and pitch, which had accumulated for years and were like tinder to the hungry flames. The unendurable heat and suffocating smoke drove me far out of the road. In one ravine the miners had found three charred, blackened corpses. The victims were evidently running for a place of safety when the changing wind blinded them with smoke, and the fiery death overtook them. Their clothing was consumed; their gun-barrels, a case-knife and a quantity of gold dust were the only articles near them. Even their dog had been unable to escape, and his bones lay beside theirs. Several other corpses were discovered the same day; and the number of deaths from the fires was computed more than twenty."

(Source: Richardson, A. D., 1867, *Beyond the Mississippi:* New York, American
Pub. Co., p. 196-197. Story is accompanied by a pen-and-ink sketch
of the fire scene.)

EDITORS' NOTE: Richardson was making his first journey up the new toll road. A diary written by a man who earlier traveled into the interior on Gregory's original trace relates:

"A sad calamity occurred a day or two ago, in which I was near being involved. A fire broke out in the mountains, which swept over an extensive district, causing much alarm and some destruction of life.

The fire lay in the direction I was pursuing, and had I proceeded I must have been encompassed by it; but I was beaten back by the smoke, and forced to retreat. I made good time before it, and took refuge in a ravine, and it was well I did so, for I should have been baked meat to-day. I regret to add that five other persons were not so fortunate, their charred remains, with those of their pack animals, being found the next day.

…It is wonderful that these fires do not occur more frequently. The ground is thickly strewn with fallen pines, and covered to the depth of several inches with dried leaves. It needs but a spark to light a conflagration that may extend for miles and miles.

It is hoped that the miners may be taught by the late catastrophe to observe greater caution."

(Source: *Diary of a journey to the Pike's Peak gold mines in 1859.* Initials
M.V.H.R.: Colo. Room, Colo. School of Mines Library, Document F,
593, W5, p. 378.)

Since each man reached the intersection of Booten and Guy gulches by a different route coming from the E, it would appear that the loss of life described above occurred W of that junction.

> "Twelve men were burned up in the mountains Sunday, and there are about fifty more missing. They set fire to the pine trees and it spreads very fast and for miles, hardly giving time for persons to escape.
>
> Thomas G. Wildman
Denver City, June 20, 1859"
>
> (Source: Hafen, L. R., and A. W., eds., 1961, *Reports from Colorado—The Wildman letters 1859-1865 with other related letters and newspaper reports, 1859:* Glendale, Calif., Clark Co., p. 40.)

"[Dispatch dated Denver, June 20, 1859] But will disemboweling these mountains in quest of gold *pay?* A very pregnant question. I answer—It will pay some; it will fail to pay others...Within this last week, we have tidings of one young gold-seeker committing suicide, in a fit of insanity, at the foot of the mountains; two more found in a ravine, long dead and partially devoured by wolves; while five others, with their horse and dog, were overtaken, some days since, while on a prospecting tour not far from Gregory's, by one of those terrible fires which, kindled by the culpable recklessness of some camping party, finds ready aliment in the fallen pine leaves, which carpet almost the entire mountain region, and are fanned to fury by the fierce gales which sweep over the hill-tops, and thus were all burned to death, and so found and buried, two or three days since— their homes, their names, and all but their fearful fate, unknown to those who rendered them the last sad offices...

P.S.—A friend just in from the Mountains, who had a narrow escape from the flames, confirms our worst rumors of disaster and death. He says not less than *fifteen** men have fallen victims to the conflagration, which is still raging, and threatens even the dense crowd of tents and cabins at Gregory's.

My friend informs me that the fire began very near where we camped during my first weary night in the Mountains, and would seem to have been purposely set by reckless simpletons curious to see the woods in a blaze!

He thinks the victims were generally, if not uniformly, smothered before the fire reached them—the dense, pitchy smoke at once shrouding the vision and obstructing respiration. He says the flames swept through the pines and above their tops to a height of two hundred feet, with a roar and a rush appalling even to look on. He was obliged to run his mule at her utmost speed for two or three miles, in order to effect his escape.

**Another friend just arrived says certainly *seventeen*.*

If this drouth continues—as it is likely to do for months—the mountains this side of the snowy range will be nearly burned over for at least fifty miles north and south of the Gregory trail, driving out all that is left of game, killing much of the timber, and rendering the country everyway more inhospitable—a most superfluous proceeding.

…Another friend just from Gregory's, says he fears the victims of the fires now raging in that quarter will number *one hundred*."

(Source: Greeley, Horace, 1860, *An overland journey from New York to San Francisco in the summer of 1859:* New York, Saxton Barker & Co., p. 143, 146-148.)

"Mining nomenclature is always curious. Prospectors found three blackened corpses in a district of burnt pines, and named the spot 'Dead Man's Gulch.'"

(Source: Richardson, A. D., 1867, *Beyond the Mississippi:* New York, American Pub. Co., p. 307.)

"Stories of the burning of Mountain Cities are carried back to thousands of homes in the States. It will be a long time, if ever, before a summer trip across the prairies to visit the mines will be thought of as a pleasantry. No one who had not been there can imagine how hard journeying through the mountains is.

Adding to the difficulty is the possibility of encountering smoke from unseen fires. The miners burn the growth around where they wish to examine, with no thought for the direction the flames will take."

(Source: Brown's Gazetteer, 1860.)

"We are yet a goodly distance from Cherry Creek but already the miners' fires are visible. The smoke colors the sunsets and much of the mountains seem to be on fire."

(Source incomplete: Pikes Peak Pioneer, Oct. 1860.)

"The Pine forests on the north-west are on fire, lighting up the whole scene with a grandure perfectly striking. Nearby, it looks as if the mountains were lit up by great watchfires, while in the distance they look like beacons jetting out from the rugged sides.

– Newton Pettis, Mount Vernon, Colorado Territory, July 10, 1861."

(Source: Pettis, S. N., 1861, journal entry, in *Letters of S. Newton Pettis:* Colo. Mag., v. 15, no. 1, Jan. 1938.)

In 1864 a law was passed by the territorial government prohibiting miners' fires and expressing the hope that offenders would be hung.

Golden Gate City Site

"In the early 1920's, the only evidence of [Golden Gate's] location was a grave marker for Henry W. Frink, who died October 12, 1860, at the age of twenty-seven."

(Source: Brown, Georgina, 1976, *The shining mountains:* Gunnison, Colo., B&B Printers, p. 101-102.)

Frink's remains were later moved to the old Cemetery hill on the north edge of Golden where, "...on a fallen tombstone, one can read the name of Henry W. Frink... His fallen tombstone is the only one in the old Golden cemetery on which the inscription is still legible."

(Compiled from: Broad, Richard, Jr., *When Golden was the capital:* Colo. School of Mines Library, typed manuscript, Document 33792.)

Cemetery hill, a.k.a. Graveyard hill, fell into disuse. Erosion and ground frost took their toll, and children living on the lower slopes on the steep hill took to hauling old bones home in their wagons. In 1952-53 the graveyard on Cemetery hill was destroyed by Mr. Dennis of Golden in order to build his subdivision. A few of the caskets were moved to other cemeteries, including the Golden Cemetery on Ulysses. Some bones, bereft of caskets, were placed in a common grave in the pioneer section of the Golden Cemetery. But most of the grave sites on Cemetery hill, caskets and all, were simply bulldozed over.

Henry W. Frink did not make it to the Golden Cemetery. Perhaps he went home in a little boy's wagon.

It is now against county regulations to destroy a grave site prior to thorough archaeological investigation.

The Hanging Tree

Once upon a time a long time ago, when the forest was decimated by fires and cutting, a large pine tree that had escaped these fates was used as a hanging tree. The man hung there was buried on the spot with his gun and his boots. The pine, which overlooks the GGC road from the N some distance below the Crawford Gulch junction, was referred to afterward as the hanging tree. Oldtimers told that more than one man was hung there. The forest has since grown up around the tree. The exact location is known only to a few natives.

Hinckley

"A man named D. W. Hinckley was killed near the seven mile house on the road to Mounain City on Wednesday last, by falling under the wheel of a loaded wagon, which passed over his breast, inflicting injuries from which he died in about an hour. From papers in his possession he was supposed to come from Elyria, Lorain Co., Ohio. In his pocket was $10.01, also some receipts but nothing else of value. He was buried near where he died."

(Source: Rocky Mountain News, June 16, 1860.)

(See Ralston Creek Toll Road <u>in</u> Historical Routes for possible location of *7 mile house*.)

Pioneer Site—Koch

The first children born to August and Isabella Koch on their homestead between Mt. Tom and Guy Hill—a son, Basil, followed by a daughter, Claire—died in infancy and were buried in apple crates in an aspen grove above the house.

Pioneer Site—Olson

"Vague information has reached us of the death by a stroke of lightning, on Friday night last, of Mrs. A. Olson, mother-in-law of John Gullickson, living near the Gilpin county line, but we have been unable to have it verified."

(Source: Colo. Transcript, August 26, 1896.)

Mrs. Olson is buried on the John Gulliksen homestead, which was located in a drainage W of Sheep Mountain.

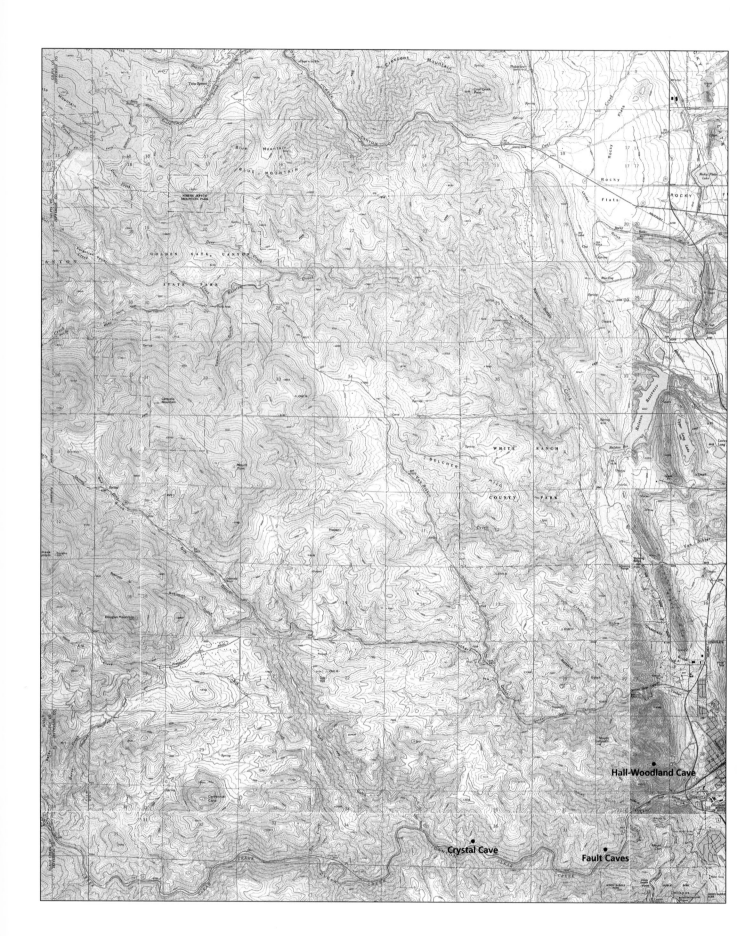

Hall-Woodland Cave

Crystal Cave

Fault Caves

Caves

Crystal Cave

Overlooking the entrance to the Huntsman near the top of the gaping hole known as the Goltra Quarry. (See Goltra Quarry in Mines.)

S/b Evergreen Quad.
S36, T3S, R71W.
Elv. ab. 6200'.

In May of 1988 a fissure opened ahead of a road being built on private ground in Clear Creek Canyon for O. R. Goltra, Chicago businessman, by the Jefferson County Commissioners. County road crews attempted to close the fissure with dynamite, but instead opened a "spectacular 100-foot-high cavern filled with stalagmites, stalactites, and very rare helicitite crystals."

(Compiled from: Rocky Mountain News, May 16, 1988.)

The strangely beautiful cave began immediately to die. Made unsafe by dynamiting, the crystal cavern that took millenia to bloom was ordered destroyed by Jeffco Commissioners, giving geologists little time to study the exquisite landscape.

"Geologists say the cavern is unusual in one aspect: the crystals formed in granite.

Caves usually are formed by water carving out sections of limestone. This cavern was formed by a shift in a fault line about 20 million years ago.

Water droplets ran over rocks, picked up minerals and then seeped into the cavern. When the water evaporated, traces of minerals were left. Over thousands of years, the deposits turned into stalagmites and stalactites."

(Source: Renate Robey, Denver Post, May 22, 1988.)

"This is one of nature's Rembrandts."

(Source: Virginia Mast, Curator, Colorado School of Mines Geology Museum.)

A recreation of a small area of the cave, including pieces of crystal, is on display in the Colorado School of Mines Museum. But the long, breathtakingly exquisite crystal plumes that sprouted from ceiling and wall are no more.

(For an interesting juxtaposition, see Centennial Cone <u>in</u> Heights.)

It is now against county regulations to destroy unusual geologic formations unearthed by new construction, prior to thorough archaeological investigation.

Fault Caves

N slope, Clear Creek Canyon, 0.4 mile above Tunnel No.1.
> *S/b Evergreen Quad.*
> *S32, T3S, R70W.*
> *Elv. ab. 6000'.*

{Var. names: **Fissure Caves, Golden Caverns.**}
The largest cave is ab. 325 yards N up the gully.
These are the largest known granite fault caves in the state.

> The caves were formed by a shifting in the mountains which resulted in a series of cracks or faults extending considerable depth. A Compass and Tape Survey was performed by the Colorado School of Mines Grotto, National Speleological Society.

> (Compiled from: *The ghost's gold*, Denver Post, v. 60, April 13, 1952, p. 35.)

(Also see: *Strange Caves*, Denver Times, v. 15, Dec. 4, 1893, p. 4, col. 2.)

Hall-Woodland Cave

N side of Indian Gulch (pioneer designation) ab. 30 feet up the slope. The center of Golden can be seen from the cave entrance.
> *S/b Golden Quad.*
> *See 1906 BQ for correct map designation of Indian Gulch.*
> *SE 1/4 of S29, T3S, R70W.*

The small cave was investigated by the Colorado Archaeological Society. The cave accommodated an aboriginal occupation that dates from Woodland times.

GORDON RAMSTETTER

"In December, 1965, the owner of the site, Mr. Warren D. Hall, granted permission to excavate the site. In expression of our gratitude to Mr. Hall for his cooperation and for recognizing the significance of the site, we have named it Hall-Woodland Cave after the landowner and the culture found there...

During the months of December and January, the sun hangs low in the southern sky, thus allowing its rays of light to beam back approximately 11 feet into the cave...Most of the animal bones were split until they were in a very fragmentary condition...the inhabitants went to some pains to extract all of the marrow possible...This may suggest that game was not plentiful in the area at the time of occupation, or that conditions were not favorable for hunting. The bone fragments indicate that every edible part of the animal was devoured."

(Source: Nelson, C. H., 1967, *The archaeology of Hall-Woodland cave*, <u>in</u> Southwestern Lore: Colo. Archaeological Soc., v. 33, June 1967, no. 1, p. 1-13.)

The site and surrounding countryside, along with artifacts, chips, and bone fragments, are described in detail in the above bulletin. The stone wall pictured at the mouth of the cave was built after 1967.

Magpie Gulch Cave

S/b Golden Quad.
S30 or 31, T3S, R70W.
Elev. ab. 7000'.

Beautiful, desolate, forbiddingly steep Magpie Gulch—now mapped by the U.S. Geological Survey as Indian Gulch—also boasts a cave. A cave high on the slope facing the sun. Deeper than the length of a 50-foot lariat and darker than a dungeon. Protected by rattlesnakes and long forgotten.

The view from the entrance of the cave in Magpie Gulch. Photographed 1979.

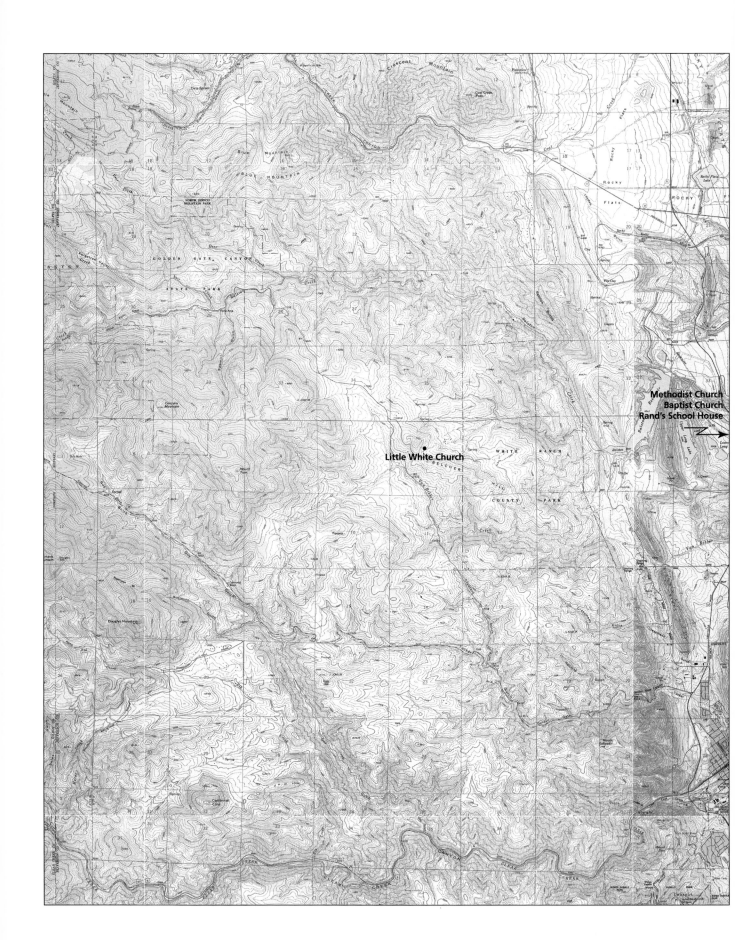

Methodist Church
Baptist Church
Rand's School House

Little White Church

Churches

THE CHURCHES MENTIONED BELOW are not mapped. They are, however, located on the drainages studied here. The opportunity to sift these tiny news releases from the early papers proved too great to pass by.

"Our thrifty neighbors in Ralston Precinct are showing a commendable public spirit. They have nearly completed a Methodist Church building, which will be shortly ready for dedication. It is located a short distance south of the Cheyenne crossing of Ralston Creek, and is a fine building 24 × 36 feet, and will be finished off in plain style, but neat and comfortable. Due notice of the dedication will be given through our columns, when we hope to see a goodly number present from this locality."

(Source: Colo. Transcript, June 30, 1869.)

"The 4th of July will be celebrated on Ralston Creek by a grand Sunday School Concert in the new church. We are promised full particulars for our next. The church will not be entirely completed at that time, but arrangements will be made to have it in a pleasant and comfortable condition."

(Source: *Ibid.*)

"On Sunday evening, after the sermon, the [Methodist] Bishop delivered a telling address to the people and preachers on the relation of Methodism to the Apostolic Commission, and then read the following: Appointments:…Ralston and Clear Creek, Jesse Smith…"

(Source: *Ibid.*)

"Rev. J. Casto [Baptist Church] will preach…every alternate Sabbath at 3 o'clock, p.m., at Rand's School House, on Ralston Creek."

(Source: *Ibid.*)

"RALSTON. This is a farming region, about six miles north of Golden City. A neat little frame church was built here under the pastorate of Rev. Jesse Smith, costing about $1,800. This is the first strictly rural church ever built in Colorado. The pastors of this circuit have been W. M. Smith, D. W. Scott, Jesse Smith, and G. W. Swift, the present pastor."

(Source: *The Rocky Mountain Directory and Colorado Gazetteer for 1871:* S. W. Wallihan & Company, Compilers and Publishers, Denver, p. 138.)

The solitary church shown on the map was on the hillside across from the White Ranch Road in the upper middle of S2, T35, R71W. This was a one-room, nondenominational church painted white. No known photograph.

EDITORS' NOTE: Remember also that mountain schools, sentinels on their solitary outposts, served as churches.

Robinson Hill School, the white building in the center, also served as a church.

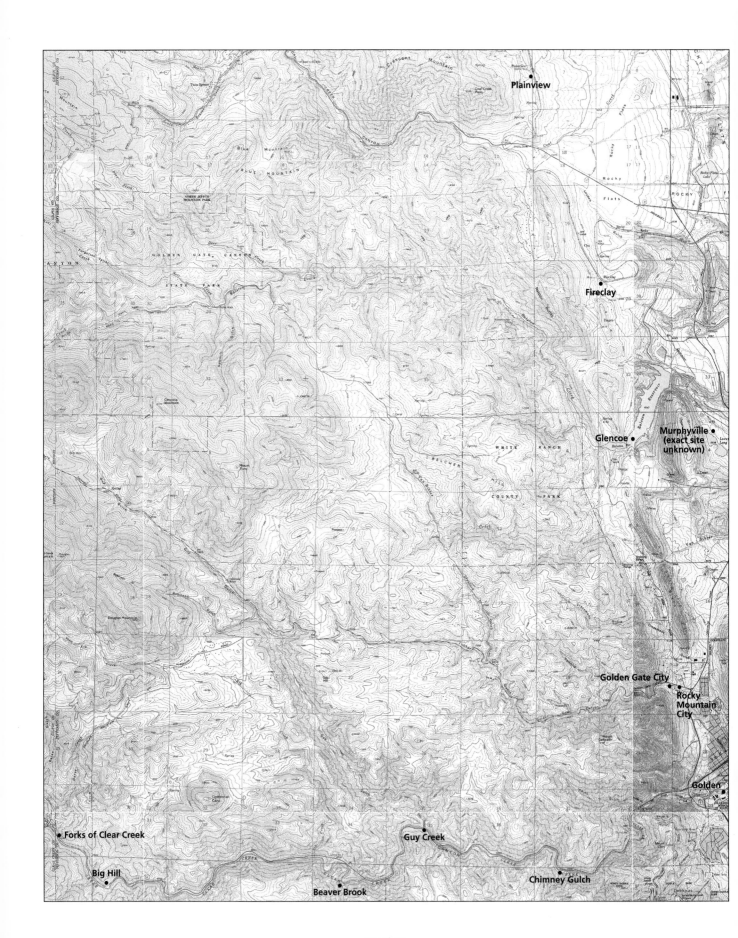

Plainview

Fireclay

Glencoe

Murphyville •
(exact site
unknown)

Golden Gate City
Rocky
Mountain
City

Golden

Forks of Clear Creek

Guy Creek

Big Hill

Chimney Gulch

Beaver Brook

Cities

Clear Creek Canyon

"The lesser towns and settlements of Jefferson are…Beaver Brook…Big Hill…Chimney Gulch…Forks of Clear Creek…Guy Creek…"

(Source: *The Works of Hubert Howe Bancroft: History of Nevada, Colorado and Wyoming, 1540-1888:* San Francisco, 1890, The History Co., v. 25, p. 621.)

Fireclay

S of Arena Siding on the Denver and Salt Lake Railroad.
1942 Ralston Buttes Quad.
S29, T2S, R70W.
Elv. ab. 6400'.

Takes its name from the red clay mined in the area. The mines are no longer worked. The clay mined here was sold to Golden Fire Clay and others. The 1948 RBQ shows two houses. Earlier quads show three. These were frame houses occupied by the railroad section foreman and his helper.

Peterson was one of the foremen who lived here. The houses were burned in the late 1940s or early 1950s to get them off the tax rolls.

Fireclay does not appear on the 1906 Blackhawk Quad.

Glencoe

At the W end of Ralston Reservoir. Site inundated in 1938.

S/b Golden or Ralston Buttes Quad.
S5, T3S, R70W.
Elv. ab. 6000'.

"Later Virg and Gent Bennett of Mount Vernon and the Churches boys gathered their cattle at Glencoe and drove the herds to Denver to be sold at the Union Stockyards."

(Source: Colo. Transcript, January 16, 1901.)

...In 1884, a quarry was established and the settlement christened Glencoe. A branch of the Denver and Middle Park Railroad was run up from the junction at Ralston four and a half miles east in 1884. For a time, the quarry and the little community flourished. The next year, the railroad was extended another mile. However, the site soon languished, probably because equally good quarries were available closer to Golden. In 1911, the railroad track was taken up, a likely indication that the site had been abandoned.

WIKSTROM COLLECTION

Allen Boarding House, Glencoe. Christina Wikstrom is the tall woman third from the right. The Allens are believed to be the tall man third from the left in the back row, and the blonde woman to his right. The dapper gentleman on the far right may be that consummate party animal, Sam Bowser.

...Lela [White] remembers a visit to 'Glencoe Meadow' when she was very young. The family had driven down the hill in a wagon, probably on a picnic. Looking out of a second-story window in one of the abandoned buildings of the ghost town was a bewildered steer. He had climbed the stairs but couldn't manage to go back down. Lela remembers her father leading the animal back down the stairs and out of the building.

(Compiled from: Bond, R. F., 1989, *The land persists:* Jeffco Hist. Com. contest entry.)

One of the buildings abandoned to the reservoir was the Allen Boarding House, a handsome, two-story structure. Timber cutters boarded in the house, which was fashioned from large, white cut stone.

Golden

Golden Quad

{Var. name: **the Lowell of Colorado.** This name stems from the 1880s when Golden's railroad, smelter, and coal-mining activities established it as a manufacturing center.}

"TUESDAY, JUNE 14. Have been jogging all day up hill and down dale, along Clear creek, in search of a pass into the mountains, and toward sunset entered one of the most beautiful valleys my eyes ever rested on. A magnificent natural meadow, skirted by timber, beautifully supplied with clear, running streams, and clothed luxuriantly with a coating of rich and delicate grass. A little paradise in its own way... This valley has been appropriated by Vandeventer & Co., of Sturgis, Michigan, who already have commenced some improvements, and are completing preparations for reducing it to cultivation."

(Source: *Diary of a journey to the Pike's Peak gold mines in 1859:* Colorado Room, Colorado School of Mines campus, F-593-W5, p. 376-377.)

"[After riding until well after dark to reach this place] A peep out doors after breakfast revealed to me, to my great astonishment, an apparently thriving town, consisting of some fifty log and frame buildings of rather respectable appearance. But a few months ago, not a solitary human being dwelled in the beautiful fertile valley that intervenes between the first table and second range of mountains. The discovery of the Gregory Diggings, however, soon brought thousands that were endeavoring to walk in the foot prints of the pioneer Gregory and his companions, to it, with their innumerable herds of all kinds of stock."

(Source: Hafen, L. R., and A. W., eds., 1961, *Reports from Colorado—The Wildman letters 1859-1865 with other related letters and newspaper reports, 1859:* Glendale, Calif., Clark Co., p. 158-159.)

"...passed over an undulating prairie, splendid road; 15 miles to Clear Creek...at which they are laying out 'Golden City,' being half a mile from where you commence the ascent of the mountains to Gregory's and other diggings. enclosed in three sides with mountains, it is one of the most romantic sights for a town in any country… this is the point where all emigration stops and at this time there are a thousand wagons and two thousand persons in this city."

(Source: *Ibid.,* p. 109)

"In the fall of [1858] three men [Tom Golden, James Saunders and Geo. A. Jackson] established their headquarters camp on the site of the present city of Golden and near the entrance of Chimney Canyon…Golden as a town was established about the middle of June, 1859, and took its name from one of the three men above named—Tom Golden."

(Source: *Golden,* in The Golden Globe, Industrial Edition, May 20, 1893, p. 2.)

"A large crowd of Utes that have been camped in our valley for a couple of days left, 'bag and baggage,' on Monday morning. We believe that they are enroute for their reservation on White river. They were very peaceable and quiet during their stay here; we hear of only instance of misbehavior on their part. On Sunday evening one of the 'bucks' visited the house of one of our citizens, and seeing only a little girl, demanded food; upon being refused he pointed a pistol at her, but withdrew quietly upon the approach of the lady of the house. We presume everybody in Colorado will rejoice when they are finally settled upon their reservations."

(Source: Colo. Transcript, July 28, 1869.)

"Our valley and town make a pretty picture of a dark night when lighted up as they were on Monday evening last by the flames issuing from Bell's pottery kiln. At times when the flames from the chimney were the highest the whole valley was illuminated, rendering trees, rocks and cattle visible upon the sides of the adjacent mountains, while the houses of the town were brought out in bold relief, making a beautiful foreground for the picture."

(Source: *Ibid.*)

"…Golden City by daylight showed its meanness and belied its name. It is ungraded, with here and there a piece of wooden sidewalk supported on posts, up to which you ascent by planks. Brick, pine, and log house are huddled together, every other house is a saloon, and hardly a woman is to be seen. My landlady apologized for the very exquisite little bedroom which she gave me by say, it was not quite as she would like it, but she had never had a lady in her house before…
Golden City rang with oaths and curses, especially at the depot."

(Source: Isabella Bird on a visit to Golden, Nov. 13, 1873.)

"Golden has long held the name of 'the Lowell of the west.' The water-power that could be made available at the mouth of the canon, and elsewhere along up the gulch, has never been estimated, but if necessity compelled it would take but a short time to prove that one of the greatest water-powers on earth is here.

Golden is not content with having the name of 'Lowell,' without the great addition of Lowell's manufacturing power and her wealth of manufacturing interests. Maybe someday this will be realized."

(Source: *Colorado,* in The Golden Globe, Industrial Edition, May 20, 1893, p. 6.)

"...within sixty rods of the Miner's Hotel, from which I write, is an abrupt elevation of rock six hundred feet high. The last two hundred feet front in the hotel is almost perpendicular. On the north of the elevation and separated by a gulch, may be seen a brother monster, but with less regularity of proportions. I am told that on top of this is a pond of water, covering some three or four acres of ground. I am not prepared to believe this until I see it..."

(Source: Pettis, S. N., journal entry, Golden City, June 29, 1861, in *Letters of S. Newton Pettis:* Colo. Mag., v. 15, no. 1, Jan. 1938, p. 12.)

Golden Gate City

E entrance, Golden Gate Canyon, both sides of creek.
S/b Golden Quad.
S20, T3S, R70W.
Elv. 6226'.*

*(Source: Hollister, Ovando, 1867, *The mines of Colorado:* Springfield, Mass., Samuel Bowles & Co., p. 29)

{Var name: **Baled Hay City,** for the large amount of baled hay sold here.

Var. name: **Gate City,** for two tall rock formations N of the canyon entrance. One formation held a flat rock hat-like fashion. The lower bases of the formations are still visible. The upper portions were destroyed when dynamite was used to move the road out of the creekbed and up the N side of the mountain.

> (Source: Dan Thatcher, who lived at the entrance to the canyon and reported that Golden Gate Canyon residents wanted iron rods driven into the ground through and beside the formations, and the formations and rods then wrapped with wire, to save them. But, according to Mr. Thatcher, no attempt was made to prevent the formations from tumbling down.)}

Incorporated as Golden Gate Town Company, Dec. 7, 1859. One of only three cities (Golden, Golden Gate and Mt. Vernon) to incorporate in the Territory of Jefferson in 1859. Tom Golden, town promoter, gave his name to this city, to the nearby canyon, and to Golden City.

"GOLDEN GATE. It is a row or two of log houses about one mile North of Golden City, on the old road to the Gregory mines, and at the mouth of the first gulch through which it winds. Several stores and liquor shops are kept here."

(Source: Villard, Henry, 1860, *The past and present of the Pike's Peak Gold Regions:* Princeton, Univ. Press. p. 138.)

Map legend, town of Golden Gate, comprising some forty odd blocks at the entrance to the canyon north of Golden:

"Golden Gate, Arapahoe County, Kansas Territory. Is situated at the base of the Rocky Mountains at the mouth of the canon which is the only practicable pass to Gregorys' Russels' Spanish, Jacksons' and Clear Creek diggins, which are the best diggins yet discovered. A fine stream of water runs through the town and there is plenty of pine timber near, and is surrounded by a fine farming country."

(Source: *Jefferson County Records, Book A.* Opened January 6, 1860. Eli Carter, Recorder, p. 13.)

"*Golden Gate*, Jefferson County, of which no trace now remains, was founded in 1859 by the Golden Gate Town Company, which donated free lots during the winter months to all who would improve them. The town was named for Tom Golden, who first laid out the site. It was located at the mouth of Golden Gate Canyon (Eight Mile Canyon)."

(Source: *Place names in Colorado (G)*, in Colo. Mag., which credits Smiley, Jerome C., *Semi-centennial history of the State of Colorado*, p. 64.)

"…soon reached Golden City, did not stop but went on and soon came to Golden Gate (everything has the name of gold but I have not seen any yet) where we had to pay toll on the road."

(Source: *H. J. Hawley's Diary, Russell Gulch in 1860*, ed. by Lynn I. Perrigo: Colo. Mag., vol. (?), p. 133.)

"The *Rocky Mountain Herald* noted that by May 23, 1860, Golden Gate City boasted several firms, hotels, stores and shops. Records do not show the City ever had a mayor or any type of city government. Yet it contained a respectable number of people, who were also socially inclined. Opening of the Gate City Hotel at Golden Gate City was occasion for a gala inauguration ball Friday evening, April 6, 1860. The affair was given by Captain W. G. Preston and his brother. A large number of ladies were present, the *Mountaineer* reported. 'Supper was quite a surprising array of delicacies no one expected to see. There was dancing until early dawn.' The city had come to be better known as 'Bailed Hay City' due to the fact that every house advertised bailed hay for sale.

The Golden Gate town company was advertising lots for sale or donation during 1859-60. However that spelled trouble. Alfred Tucker had settled in Golden Gate City. He warned all and sundry not to buy lots from the Golden Gate town company, as the land was 'embraced in his farming and ranching claim.' Tucker hailed from Illinois. Besides the land, Tucker was also laying claim to the road up Golden Gate Canyon, which McCleery had put in shape by spending his own money. A bitter feud developed, and assault charges with intent to kill were filed against McCleery by an August Ingleman, who along with Tucker and others, was disputing not only lot sales but road ownership.

Golden Gate City at the entrance of Golden Gate Canyon. "A fine stream of water runs through the town." – Eli Carter, 1860. This is a lantern slide painted in oil, from a photograph taken in 1859, possibly by J. H. Young, a photographer from New York.

FRANCIS RIZZARI COLLECTION

When a jury could not agree, McCleery was cleared of charges. However, this did not end the feud.

Tucker was determined to have the road and carried the matter to court then under jurisdiction of Arapahoe court. He emerged with an order giving him possession. This stirred up the wrath of Goldenites. They stood staunchly behind McCleery, who defied the court writ. Golden went even further and resolved to deny jurisdiction of the Arapahoe court. The episode had an unhappy ending for McCleery, as Tucker and his associates did get the road. It was not too long after his defeat that McCleery left. No mention was made as to whether Harriet, his wife, went with him. Some accounts insist it was Tucker's stubbornness that set back the new town's rising tide of prosperity and partially accounted for growth of the nearby rival towns of Golden City, Arapahoe and Mt. Vernon. Whatever the cause, Golden Gate City was completely abandoned when the new roads through Clear Creek and Mt. Vernon Canyons diverted travel. In the early 1920's, the only evidence of the town's location was a grave marker for Henry W. Frink, who died October 12, 1860, at the age of twenty-seven. Tucker left as his monument Tucker Gulch, where disastrous floods frequently rage into Golden.

…Golden earned the singular distinction of being the 'first merchant to advertise prices in the whole region.' He engaged in the commission business at Golden Gate City along with his other enterprises and later built a hotel there. According to the Rocky Mountain Herald, a brick yard was also established at Golden Gate City, operating until recent years."

(Source: Brown, Georgina, 1976, *The shining mountains:* Gunnison, Colo., B&B Printers, p. 101-102.)

"Golden was a farmer, rancher, sometime-miner, politician and, according to family records out of Virginia, he had the first second-hand store east of the Mississippi…

He allegedly sold equipment to the enchanted wannabe-millionaires setting out to the gold fields, their dreams bigger than the mules and pack horses they used to get there. Later, when the enchantment had worn away and nothing was left but dashed hopes and callused hands they sold their equipment back to Golden who sold it to the next gold-seeking souls trekking up the canyon with high hopes for the big strike or of even finding the Mother Lode…

Golden descendents in the east and mid-west said Tom Golden was born Aug. 18, 1811, in Knox County, KY… [and] lived in the area until his death in the 1870s, [but] there is no record of him at the Golden Cemetery."

(Source: Wyhs, Irma, 1994, *Ranch History,* compiled for Red School Ranch, a.k.a., Pearce Ranch.)

"Mr. Treffesen owns a fine tract of forty acres, three miles north of town near Golden Gates, which he use as feeding ground for his stock used in butchering. This piece of ground has two coal veins of fine quality and large capacity running directly across it…On this land are valuable and practically inexhaustible beds of the finest plastic clay…Here is a chance for a brick manufactory on a large scale…"

(Source: *John Treffeisen,* in The Golden Globe, Industrial Edition, May 20, 1893, p. 5.)

"The towns of Arapahoe, Mount Vernon, and Golden Gate were mining camps in the spring of 1859…the latter at the mouth of another canon called the Gate of the Mountains."

(Source: *The Works of Hubert Howe Bancroft: History of Nevada, Colorado and Wyoming, 1540-1888:* San Francisco, 1890, The History Co., v. 25, p. 620.)

The map by John Pierce, Surveyor General's Office, Denver, February 10, 1867, shows the public road N of Tucker Gulch from the edge of the mountains to where the road and the creekbed part company.

As late as 1930, a large, two-story brick building commonly referred to "the boarding house out at the brickyard" existed N of the road in the general vicinity of where the new county shops are now located. This boarding house may well have been one of Golden Gate City's old hotels.

July 1988—Jeffco Commissioners purchased 125 acres at the entrance to Golden Gate Canyon for $858,000 for a new shop site, opening up an industrial corridor at the edge of the Front Range.

October 1988—Jeffco Planning Department notified the Jeffco Commissioners that the proposed shop site was inappropriate for industrial use.

Despite numerous county documents placing the gold-rush cities astraddle the public road, Commission spokespeople ignored a firestorm of public protest to insist that the gold-rush cities had been located on the rise to the S of Tucker Gulch, and refused to allow archeologists to study the pastures in the vicinity of the proposed shop site with ground-penetrating radar to locate subsurface anomalies.

March 1989—Easter weekend. Jeffco, with the help of outside contractors, worked three days' overtime to scrape the surface of the proposed shop site clear of topsoil. All traces of the cities of Golden Gate and Rocky Mountain, including the hotels, the grave sites, and the brick works, were obliterated.

Public hearings were held in April 1989, well after the land was scoured out.

Only known photograph of the city as a whole: Terry Mangan's "Colorado on glass," published by Sundance:

> "It was taken in 1869 by the grandfather of a man named Young, who donated it to the Colorado Historical Society and left no contacting address. It is unquestionably the only photo of Golden Gate City preserved today.
> The picture shows a community consisting of a dozen or more buildings."

(Source: Akal, Dorothy, 1989, Questions about Golden Gate City always will remain: Golden Transcript, Jan. 24, 1989, p. 1, 6.)

Only known photograph of Gate City Hotel, built N of the road: Owned by John Brunel, private collection.

(See Golden Gate City <u>in</u> Items of Interest.)

It is now against county regulations to destroy a historic site prior to thorough archaeological investigation.

Murphyville

E entrance, Ralston Creek Canyon.

S/b Golden Quad.

Estimated to have been in the N½ of S4, T3S, R70W.

"Explorations about the [Golden] vicinity revealed the existence of valuable coal beds, and on Ralston Creek the Murphy mine was opened, from which good and cheap fuel was furnished."

(Source: Hall, Frank, 1889, *History of the State of Colorado:* Chicago, Blakely Printing Co., p. 225.)

Ralston Creek

COAL BANK,

D. M. MURPHEY, Proprietor

———

As the coal from these banks is justly popular with consumers, the proprietor has opened additional mines, and enlarged his facilities for supplying the public, and is now prepared to furnish the

Best Quality of Coal,

In unlimited quantities, delivered either in Golden City, Denver, or at the mines. He has upon the ground

FAIRBNKS' PLATFORM SCALES,

and will weigh all coal *Free of Expense,* and guarantee all weights. Orders solicited. Coal delivered at Golden City at ten dollars per ton.

Address
D. M. Murphey,
41-2tf   Golden City, Colorado.

Colo. Transcript advertisement, June 2, 1869.

Jone Heivner originally found this deposit and in 1865 sold the claim to Murphy, Loveland, and Armor.

"Five miles north of Golden City is the well known Murphy mine, with a bed of coal of the best quality, eighteen feet in thickness."

(Source: Colo. Transcript, July 28, 1869.)

"George W. Parfet was born in Pennsylvania and came to Colorado with his parents in 1875. He lived at Murphyville on Ralston creek two years and in 1877 the family came to Golden... Fourteen years or more ago Mr. Parfet became convinced that the clay beds of Golden contained a product that was capable of becoming the foundation of a good business. He began work and has never ceased."

(Source: *George W. Parfet, his fine clay bed and business—sketch of his history,* in The Golden Globe, Industrial Edition, May 20, 1893, inside cover.)

Plainview

E entrance, Coal Creek Canyon, N of the highway.

1965 Eldorado Springs Quad.

S12, T2S, R71W.

Elv. 6796'.

In 1993 only seven occupied residences remained.

(Compiled from: Brescia, Janice, *Coal Creek Canyon history:* Jeffco 1991 North Mountains Area Community Plan.)

Rocky Mountain City

E entrance, Golden Gate Canyon, both sides of creek E of Golden Gate City.

S/b Golden Quad.
S21, T3S, R70W.
Elv. ab. 6000'.

Sprang up as a supply camp early in June 1859 for miners rushing to the Gregory strike. Laid out so that the road to Gregory's would pass through its center.

> "Rocky Mountain City, July 18th, 1859
>
> …Large numbers emigrated this spring with a speculative idea, bringing with them groceries, provisions, and always whiskey, glutting the market to such an extent with the latter, that it is impossible to sell it at any price by wholesale, and the retail business is so overdone that it is unprofitable. Grocery and provision business is fair. Competition is so great that the profits are comparatively small. The dry good business is exceedingly dull. Articles of that character can be had at very reasonable prices. Several saw mills are already in successful operation in the mining district. Lumber is selling for $50 per 1,000 feet. Two weeks ago it was selling for $200 per 1,000 feet…
>
> K"
>
> (Source: Hafen, L. R., and A. W., eds., 1961, *Reports from Colorado—The Wildman letters 1859-1865 with other related letters and newspaper reports, 1859:* Glendale, Calif., Clark Co., p. 128)

> "…and it was expected that a large trading post would soon be in operation here. It did not grow, however, and by the end of the following August was little more than a place name, with a grocery in a tent and two or three covered wagons to denote a settlement. These were gone in a short time, and Rocky Mountain City was a ghost town by 1860."
>
> (Source: *Place Names in Colorado (R),* in Colorado Magazine, which credits Smiley, Jerome C., *Semi-centennial history of the State of Colorado,* v. 1, p. 266.)

Sent a delegate, Frank DeLaMar, to the Convention to Form a Provisional Government, October 10, 1859, but did not incorporate.

The Rocky Mountain City site was ordered destroyed by Jeffco Commissioners in 1990 prior to archaeological investigation and with no public hearing before the fact. (See Golden Gate City.)

No known photograph.

It is now against county regulations to destroy a historic site prior to thorough archaeological investigation.

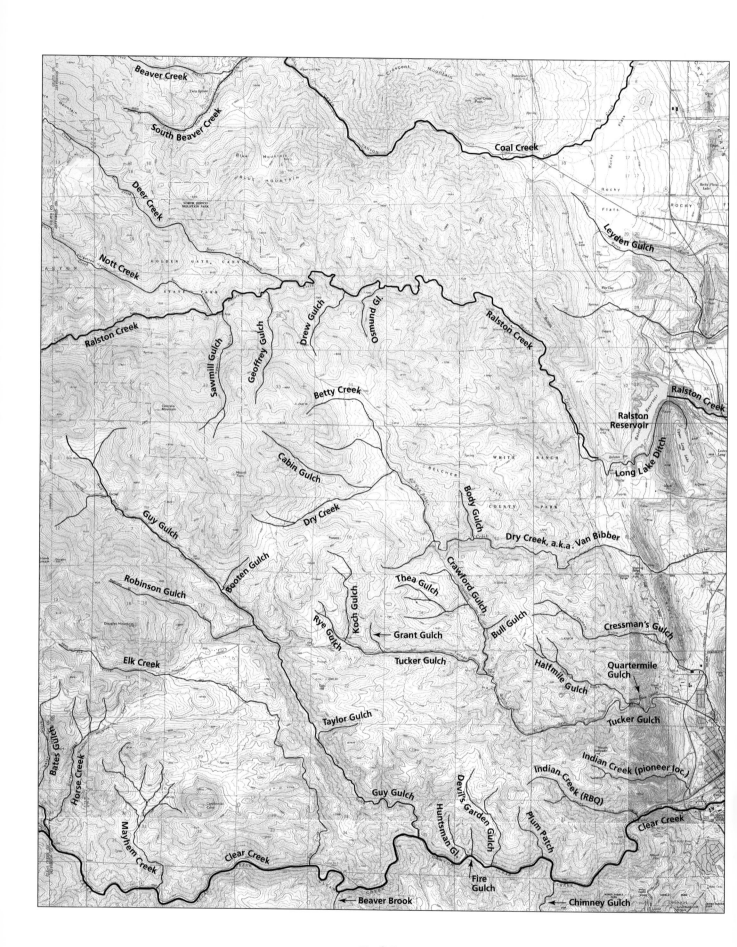

Beaver Creek

South Beaver Creek

Coal Creek

Deer Creek

Nott Creek

Ralston Creek

Leyden Gulch

Sawmill Gulch

Geoffrey Gulch

Drew Gulch

Osmund Gl.

Ralston Creek

Ralston Creek

Betty Creek

Ralston Reservoir

Cabin Gulch

Long Lake Ditch

Guy Gulch

Dry Creek

Body Gulch

Dry Creek, a.k.a. Van Bibber

Booten Gulch

Robinson Gulch

Crawford Gulch

Thea Gulch

Cressman's Gulch

Rye Gulch

Koch Gulch

Grant Gulch

Bull Gulch

Elk Creek

Tucker Gulch

Halfmile Gulch

Quartermile Gulch

Taylor Gulch

Tucker Gulch

Bates Gulch

Horse Creek

Guy Gulch

Devil's Garden Gulch

Indian Creek (pioneer loc.)

Indian Creek (RBQ)

Huntsman Gl.

Plum Patch

Clear Creek

Mayhem Creek

Clear Creek

Fire Gulch

← Beaver Brook

← Chimney Gulch

Drainages

Beaver Brook

Ab. 9 miles long. Opens on Clear Creek from S across from Tunnel No. 2. Stop on Colorado Central Railroad.

1965 Squaw Pass and Evergreen quads.
S9-10-15-14-11-12, T4S, R72W, and S7, T4S, R71W Squaw Pass.
S7-8-5-4-9-3, T4S, R71W Evergreen.

Named tributaries in ascending order: Bear Gulch, Soda Creek, North Beaver Brook, Pat Creek.

Beaver Creek

Ab. 3.5 miles long. Rises on NE slope of Thorodin Mountain. Opens on Coal Creek from S.

1972 Tungsten and Eldorado Springs quads.
S7, T2S, R71W, and S12-1, T2S, R72 Tungsten.
S7-8-9, T2S, R71W Eldorado Springs.

Named tributary: South Beaver Creek.

Betty Creek

Ab. 1.5 miles long. Rises on NE slope of Mt. Tom. Opens on Dry Creek from N.

S/b Ralston Buttes Quad.
S33-34, T2S, R71W, and S3-2, T3S, R71W.

Drains large open meadows which before the turn of the century were home to aspen trees and countless beaver dams. Named after Betty homestead located in SE corner of S34, T2S, R71W. Foundation remnants and rocked wall located E of creek ab. 0.25 mile above Belcher Hill School (second location).

The sunlit summit of Mt. Tom overlooking the S fork of Betty Creek. Photographed 1983.

Body Gulch

Ab. 0.5 mile long. Opens on Dry Creek from the N.
S/b Ralston Buttes Quad.
S1-12, T3S, R71W.

The upper region of this gulch was part of the old Wikstrom homestead. Oscar Dahlberg was the only grandson of homesteaders Lars and Martha Wikstrom. A rancher until his death in 1978 when he was knocked down and trampled while feeding his cows in his corral, Oscar told that the name *Body* refers to a man found dead in the gulch in the late 1800s.

Booten Gulch

Ab. 0.6 mile long. Drains S slope of Mt. Tom, opens on Guy Gulch from the N.
S/b Ralston Buttes Quad.
S9-8-17, T3S, R71W.

Accommodated the original road to Gregory's which descended into Guy Gulch after crossing the pass between Dry Creek and Guy Gulch.

Named for Daniel Booten who built his house at the junction of the original road with the later toll road. (See Centennial Ranch <u>in</u> Stage Stops.)

For early maps of the region see: 1) Burt, S. W., and Berthoud, E. L., 1860, *Quartz mining region of the Rocky Mountains:* Denver City, Rocky Mountain News Printing Co., map insert. And 2) Deane, Cecil A., Surveyor General's Office, Denver, August 1867 map. T. III. S. R. L. XXI. W.

Cabin Gulch

Ab. 2 miles long. Drains SE slope of Mt. Tom, opens on Dry Creek from the NW.
S/b Ralston Buttes Quad.
S4-3, T3S, R71W.

{Var. name: **Deep Gulch.** The family of Joseph Jully, Sr., who homesteaded nearby, refers to the drainage as Deep Gulch.}

The cabin midway up the gulch is known as the Walker cabin.

Dick Walker's cabin.
Photographed 1970s.

Chimney Gulch

Ab. 1.6 miles long, opens on Clear Creek from the S ab. 1.2 mile above Tunnel No. 1.
Stop on Colorado Central Railroad.
S/b Evergreen Quad.
S12-1, T4S, R71W, and S6, T4S, R70W.

> "Dan McCleery…is credited with building the first road through Chimney canon, so called by reason of the long survival of the tall chimney attached to the toll gate house at its mouth."
>
> (Source: Broad, Richard, Jr., *When Golden was the capital:* Colo. Room, Colo. School of Mines Library, typed manuscript, Document 33792.)

The gulch was a rich source of minerals: *Amelia H. Mine,* gold. *Wheeler Mine,* gold. *Champion Mine,* zinc. And other diggings whose names are not known.

Clear Creek

Ab. 80 miles long. Rises in the SW mountains of Clear Creek County, flows E into South Platte River.

Tributaries too numerous to list.

Takes its name from the clear stream of water flowing into the muddy South Platte. {Var. name: **Cannon Ball creek.** "...from the size & form of the stone in its bed."*

*(Source: Bell, J. R., 1820, *The Journal of Captain John R. Bell, Official Journalist for the Stephen H. Long Expedition to the Rocky Mountains, 1820.* Bell, quoting members of his party, represents the creek as "abounding with fish & a beautiful stream of clear water.")

Var. name: **Long's creek.**†

†(Source: Bell, J. R., 1820, *Ibid.*)

Var. name: **Vasquez Fork.** Mountain men Louis Vasquez and Andrew Sublette built an adobe trading post at the creek's confluence with the South Platte in 1835 and called it Fort Vasquez.

Var. name for the south fork from Spanish Bar to the W foot of Floyd Hill: **Cedar Canyon.** Written references are extremely rare.}

"In comparison [with Coal Creek, which collects runoff from a drainage basin of 15 square miles] Clear Creek, which spills from the mountains at Golden, collects runoff from 575 square miles."

(Source: Bisque, Ramon, and Rouse, George, 1996, *Geology of the Blue Mountain Water District and Related History:* Golden, West by Southwest, p. 39.)

What happened to Clear Creek shouldn't happen to a river. The water spruce, living statues 100 feet tall and better with trunks thick as wagon wheels, were cut down. The beaver dams that choked the tributaries were blown up. The willows and aspen clinging to the little islands in the current were blasted away. All because of the gold sparkling in the water. And this was just the beginning.

"July 25, 1885. We learn that the bars along Clear Creek are about to be worked for all there is in them. Mr. J. E. Wannamaker has sold the old Arapahoe bar...to a company which intends to put in patent machinery that has worked well in similar ground...

September 5, 1885. The hydraulic mining scheme to work the bars on Clear Creek is progressing successfully...The excitement regarding placer diggings on Clear Creek has assumed a new phase...the Ohio Placer Mining Co...have ten machines on the way and intend placing them abreast and pushing their way up to the Ford street bridge carrying everything with them.

November 14, 1885. ...Hydraulic appliances have been recently adopted in several localities.

August 6, 1892. Many years ago Clear Creek was as clear as a crystal. Speckled trout found a home in its waters, and the weary traveler quenched his thirst as he journeyed onward. But the march of civilization has changed the aspect of the beauty and added renewed wealth to it, even if it is now discolored by rejected sand and mud."

(Source: Jefferies, Marguerite, *Mineral Mining Activities from 1875—:* typed manuscript stamped "Jefferson County Museum, Old Court House, Golden, Colo.")

Clear Creek Canyon

Evergreen Quad.
The lower 12 miles of the canyon from the edge of the mountains upstream to the forks of the river.
Squaw Pass, Evergreen, Morrison, and Golden quads.

Tributaries too numerous to list.

Takes its name from the creek.

{Var. name: **Toughcuss Canyon.**

"Golden City stands at the mouth of Toughcuss, otherwise Clear Creek Canyon…"

(Source: Bird, Isabella, 1873, *A lady's life in the Rocky Mountains:* New York, G. P. Putnam's Sons, p. 220.)}

First came the miner, pointing his hydraulic hoses at the banks and sandbars, washing them into his sluice boxes. All the little valleys created by the crooks in the river as it roared down through the canyon were obliterated. Huge piles of worked gravel grew everywhere, forcing the streambed this way and that. Next came the railroad builder, nicking at the granite walls, paring off the corners to bend his tracks around. Last came the highwayman, drilling and shooting, blowing and going. Picturesque fellows all. All gone away. And everything gone with them, except the rocky ribs and the waters that still sparkle gold in the sun.

"For several years all was quiet in the Grand Canon of Clear Creek, but now contractors are blasting away for a modern highway. It in turn will carry its millions of passengers and tons of freight, but these passengers will never experience the thrill of a first ride through this canon on a narrow gauge excursion train. Too many tunnels and destroyed scenery. But such is progress."

(Source: Davis, E. O., 1949, *Building Colorado's first mountain railroad:* Colo. Mag., v. 26, no. 4, p. 304.)

About 1918 the Forest Service began to refer to various mountain roads between Estes Park and Manitou as the Peak-to-Peak Highway. In 1935 the Bureau of Public Roads asked Colorado to consider constructing a direct connection between the Peak-to-Peak Highway and Denver.

January 1932, after a survey of several months, state highway engineers announced that Clear Creek Canyon was the only feasible route for a highway to Idaho Springs. In 1940 Colorado's highway program carried out such a project. The railroad had not yet been abandoned, and blasting was a constant problem because of damage to the tracks. The tunnels were the first work to be done, and contracts were let for two tunnels (now known as Tunnels No. 2 and 3). The tunnels were completed in 1941. By 1943, 4.294 miles of road were finished.

July 8, 1941, Colorado Central Railroad sent its last train through the canyon. World War II curtailed road building materials and highway construction was not resumed until 1948.

By July 22, 1952, the 14.9-mile stretch of asphaltic paving was completed and Clear Creek Canyon was ready for traffic.

> (Compiled from: Wiley, Marion C., 1976, *The high road:* Bicentennial project of the Division of Highways, State Department of Highways, State of Colorado, p. 29.)

Coal Creek Canyon

Ab. 7 miles long. Accommodates Coal Creek. Drops off Wondervue Pass and runs S and E to Rocky Flats.
Tungsten and Eldorado Springs quads.

Tributaries too numerous to list.

> "Geo. W. Jackson, the gold discoverer…is supposed to have been the first one to discover coal in this county, or near it, the site of the discovery being in Coal creek, which thus secured a name for itelf. Charles Judkins, it is claimed, hauled the first load of coal into town."

> > (Source: Broad, Richard, Jr., *When Golden was the capital:* Colo. School of Mines Library, typed manuscript, Document 33792, p. 72.)

> "There was an old Irishman by the name of Jimmy O'Brien who owned a place at the mouth of the canyon [August 15, 1876]."

> > (Source: Lake, Carlos, 1936, *The kidnapping of Judge A. W. Stone,* in address given at meeting of Bar Association of First Judicial District, Denver, Sept. 23, 1936: Colo. Mag., v. 17, n. 1, Jan. 1940, p. 19-26.)

> "**Rand's Saw Mills,** / on Coal Creek, Colorado, / **GEORGE & WM. RAND, Prop'rs.** / These mills are situated near a fine body of timber, and we are prepared to supply / **Any Quality of Lumber,** / **and Lath,** / to order. We will deliver Lumber and Lath at Golden City, Denver, in the mountains or in the county, as / *Low as the Lowest* / *Market rates…*"

> > (Source: Colo. Transcript advertisement, June 2, 1869.)

Columbine Gulch

One of the upper forks of Halfmile Gulch. According to Dan Thatcher, who lived at the mouth of Tucker Gulch, Columbine Gulch took its name from being full of columbines.

Cottonwood Gulch

Ab. 3 miles long. Drains S slopes of Ely Hill. Opens on Clear Creek from the N ab. 2 miles above forks.
1942 Black Hawk Quad.
S11, 14, 23, 26, 27, T3S, R72W. (Not mapped in this book.)

Named tributaries in ascending order: Arbuckle Gulch, Lake Fork, Sumner Gulch.

Probably named for large groves of cottonwood as evinced in the large groves that today occupy the lower mile of the gulch.

Crawford Gulch

Ab. 1.5 miles long. Drains the S side of Bowser Hill. Opens on Tucker Gulch from the N.
1942 Ralston Buttes Quad.
S11-14-13-24, T3S, R71W.

Named tributaries in ascending order: Bull Gulch, Thea Gulch.

According to Dan Thatcher, the first house passed on the way up Crawford Gulch in the early 1900s belonged to Harold Crawford. This may have been where the name *Crawford* originated. (For another possibility, see Crawford Peak <u>in</u> Heights.)

In 1867 there was no road through Crawford Gulch.

(Reference: Deane, Cecil A., Surveyor General's Office, Denver, August 1867 map. T. III. S. R. L. XXI. W.)

By 1906 a road approximating the current road had been put through. (See 1906 BQ.) The post office presently designates the 4-mile-long mail delivery route from Golden Gate Canyon to the White Ranch intersection as the *Crawford Gulch Road*. This stretch of road was paved April 1996.

Cressmans Gulch

Ab. 3.5 miles long. Drains the lower foothills region, opens on Tucker Gulch from the N.
1965 Ralston Buttes and Golden quads.
S18-17, T3S, R70W Ralston Buttes.
S17-21, T3S, R70W Golden.

{Var. name: **Crisman Gulch.** The Colo. Transcript, July 28, 1869, refers to "Messrs. Crisman & Fitzpatrick, of the 'Brick mills' in this town..." The Jan. 30, 1878, edition refers to this gulch as Crisman's.}

Beryl, feldspar, mica, and uranium were mined in this gulch.

Deer Creek

Ab. 5.5 miles long. Rises on SE slope of Thorodin Mountain in Gilpin County. Opens on Ralston Creek from the NW ab. 0.25 mile E of the foot of Drew Hill.

1972 Tungsten Quad, 1942 Black Hawk and Ralston Buttes quads.

S11-12-13, T2S, R72W, and S18, T2S, R71W Tungsten.

S18-19, T2S, R71W Black Hawk.

S19-20-21-28, T2S, R71W Ralston Buttes.

Empties into Ralston Creek approximately 0.25 mile E of the foot of Drew Hill in Jefferson County.

(See GGC State Park map for trail in creek vicinity.)

Devil's Garden Gulch

Ab. 1.5 miles long. Opens on Clear Creek from the N ab. 1.6 mile above Tunnel No. 1.

S/b Evergreen and Ralston Buttes quads.

S25-36, T3S, R71W Ralston Buttes.

S36, T3S, R71W Evergreen.

{Var. name: **Rough Gulch** for the rough nature of the gulch.}

The Thomas Harris Shephard and Otto Albert Ramstetter homesteads are located in the upper regions of this drainage. The striking jumble of rocks that give the garden its name make the gulch easy to identify from across Clear Creek Canyon. From the porch of the Mt. Vernon Country Club the rocks can be seen as ab. one-third of the way up the draw.

Homesteader Thomas Shephard fell to his death in the garden around the turn of the century.

Drew Gulch

Ab. 1 mile long. Runs N/NE from the top of Drew Hill into Ralston Creek ab. 1.25 miles E of the foot of Drew Hill.

S/b Ralston Buttes Quad.

S34-28-27, T2S, R71W.

The Carl "Charlie" Nelson homestead is located in the lower region of this drainage.

Dry Creek

Ab. 15 miles long. Rises on E slope of the pass between Guy Gulch and the top of the Dry Creek drainage. Runs E to enter Ralston Creek at North Jeffco Park off W 58th Ave.
1906 Blackhawk Quad.

{Var. name: **Van Bibber.** Source unknown.}

Takes its name from the dry creekbed in the summer. The Crawford Gulch Road crosses Dry Creek 2 miles N of the Crawford Gulch/GGC intersection.

"In April of 1874, some Georgetown miners prospected extensively on Dry Creek, eight miles northwest of Golden, and developed roughly a very large deposit of mica."

(Source: Jefferies, Marguerite, *Mineral mining activities from 1875—:* typed manuscript stamped "Jefferson County Museum, Old Court House, Golden, Colo.")

Colo. Transcript advertisement for the Dry Creek Sawmill, June 2, 1869.

Elk Creek

Ab. 6.5 miles long. Drains S slope of Black Hawk Mountain. Opens on Clear Creek from the N ab. 0.2 mile above Tunnel No. 3.
Stop on Colorado Central Railroad.
1965 Black Hawk, Ralston Buttes, Evergreen quads.
S24, T3S, R72W, and S19, T3S, R71W Black Hawk.
S19-20-21-28-27-34, T3S, R71W Ralston Buttes.
S34, T3S, R71W Evergreen.

Named for the large number of elk which occupied the drainage.

Elk Creek Falls.

CROWELL COLLECTION

July 26, 1996, Samuel Galin Nankervis was killed when thrown off a bulldozer while building a road E of Centennial Cone on the W side of the Elk Creek drainage. Sam was a Golden native. He retired from Jefferson County as Director of Road and Bridge. His family ranched extensively throughout the Golden Gate Canyon region.

Fire Gulch

Ab. 0.4 mile long. Opens on Clear Creek from the N ab. 2.6 miles above Tunnel No. 1. Entrance is ab. 0.1 mile to the E of the Huntsman.

1965 Evergreen Quad.
S36, T3S, R71W.

History unknown.

Fourmile Gulch

Ab. 4 miles long. Accommodates Dory Hill Road. Opens on Clear Creek below Black Hawk.

1942 Black Hawk Quad.
S31, T2S, R72W, and S6-7, T3S, R72W. (Not mapped in this book.)

Four-mile house was located at the top of this gulch. (See Burt and Berthoud map. Note that the 1860 road down the gulch began W of the westernmost fork. Later the road was moved parallel to the E fork.)

Remnants of the latter road may be seen on the right-hand side of the E fork. Approximately 0.3 of a mile from the top are the shattered rock walls of an old stage station.

Geoffrey Gulch

Ab. 1.5 miles long. Drains N slope of Mt. Tom. Runs parallel to Sawmill Gulch located ab. 0.5 mile to the W. Opens on Drew Hill Road ab. 0.25 mile above Ralston Creek.

S/B Ralston Buttes Quad.
S33-28, T2S, R71W.

The only building in the gulch is the Buzz Hunt cabin, ab. 0.25 mile above Drew Hill Road. This cabin, which does not show on the 1906 BQ, can be located high in the SW¼ of S28 on later quads.

> "My father bought his land from William Dorsey. Originally, Buzz bought 320 acres but he immediately sold 40 to John and Hertha Benjamin (who had loaned him the money to buy the property.) The Benjamins owned what is now the Vigil property…
> Although one room was there when my father bought the property, he built the rest himself (after building a sawmill, powered by an old truck engine.)"
>
> (Source: Robinson, Joan, personal correspondence dated Sept. 2, 1996.)

Burrowes "Buzz" Hunt, who graduated from Princeton in 1938, did part of the teaching at the Ralston Creek Ranch, a tutoring ranch for dudes. (See Ralston Creek Ranch <u>in</u> Stage Stops.)

Golden Gate Canyon

The canyon takes its name from the 1859 gold-rush supply town at the E entrance to the canyon. The phrase *Golden Gate Canyon* has evolved to represent that region of the Front Range bounded on the N by Golden Gate Canyon State Park and the Ralston Creek drainages, on the S by Clear Creek, on the W by State Highway 119, and on the E by the prairie.

This region is roughly 130 square miles and occupies portions of Black Hawk, Eldorado Springs, Evergreen, Golden, Ralston Buttes, Squaw Pass, and Tungsten quads.

Tributaries too numerous to list.

Even by arid Colorado standards, the lower elevations of Golden Gate Canyon are unusually dry. Parched washes and gulllies crease the hillsides, brown with brittle grasses. Everywhere pine and spruce trees, stressed by lack of water and fed on by beetle and budworm, wait like old ghosts for fire and wind to bring them down.

Oldtimers built their houses and barns in the lee of the hills, leaving the high knobs and ridges to the wind. Today's better building materials have made those high summits with their sweeping views of the snow-covered back range and the eastward prairies the ultimate in ambiance.

Attempts to save the past for the future

In January 1972, the Colorado Legislature passed Senate Bill 35. Under SB35 a landowner can not apply for more than one well permit on less than 70 acres. SB35 also gives counties the authority to regulate subdivision development.

As a result, in August 1972 Jefferson County revised its subdivision regulations to recognize SB35 by requiring "adequate evidence of sufficient water supply in quality, quantity and dependability" for all new subdivisions. However, the water does not have to be on site. Water can be purchased at lower elevations for wells drilled at higher elevations as long as the wells are on a drainage that opens on the basin from whence the water was procured. These are called augmented, or paper water rights. The decision as to who gets what paper water is made by the Greeley Water Court.

Unfortunately Greeley and the Colorado State Water Engineer do not always agree on what constitutes adequate evidence of sufficient water supply. A case in point is Window Rock, a 1996 subdivision on 10+ acre parcels overlooking White Ranch Park.

Window Rock was platted with paper water drawn on the Laramie-Fox Hills Aquifer of the Denver Basin. Both the Colorado Water Engineer and the Assistant Water Engineer expressed concern over quantity and dependability of water at Window Rock. As a result, the subdivider was required by Jeffco to incorporate a shared-well agreement into the sale contracts.

October 1996, worried about the cumulative effects of paper-water trafficking on water supplies, wildlife, and existing roadways, Golden Gate residents began a grassroots effort to downzone thousands of acres in the heart of the most undeveloped land in Jefferson County. The downzoning increased the minimum lot size for new divisions of land from 1-, 5-, and 10-acre plots, to 35 acres. And resulted in a new county zoning designation, A-35.

The size and shape of the region rezoned A-35 is based on its geological configurations—Ralston Creek to the north, Tucker Gulch to the south—and on the existence of two major parks to the east and west, Golden Gate and White Ranch.

A-35 reflects both the long-range goals of the North Mountains Community Plan and the water concerns of Senate Bill 35. It also reflects countless long hours and hard work spent by Jeffco Planning and Zoning staff in traveling about the area, preparing information for and notifying land owners of community meetings, responding to community concerns, drawing up charts and compiling landowner response, mapping and writing the new zoning designation—and all the other myriad details demanded by a downzoning of this size.

On July 2, 1997, Jefferson County Commissioners Patricia Holloway, Michelle Lawrence, and John P. Stone, by unanimous vote, and after exempting those landowners who asked to be exempted, created A-35 and applied it to over 9,200 acres in Golden Gate Canyon. In so doing, commissioners and residents alike gave an extraordinary gift to the metro Denver region and, by their example, to the State of Colorado as a whole.

Grant Gulch

Ab. 0.25 mile long. Opens on Tucker Gulch from the N.
> *S/b Ralston Buttes Quad.*
> *S15, T3S, R71W.*

Takes its name from the old Grant Ranch, a.k.a. the Buckman Ranch, at the mouth of the gulch.

Guy Gulch

Ab. 8 miles long. Opens on Clear Creek from the N ab. 0.8 mile above Goltra Quarry. Stop on Colorado Central Railroad.
> *1965 Black Hawk, Ralston Buttes, Evergreen quads.*
> *S6-7, T3S, R71W Black Hawk.*
> *S7-8-17-16-21-28-27-34-35, T3S, R71W Ralston Buttes.*
> *S35, T3S, R71W Evergreen.*

{Var. name: **Guy Creek.**}

Named tributaries in ascending order: Taylor Gulch, Robinson Gulch, Booten Gulch.

Guy Gulch is the deepest canyon opening on Clear Creek Canyon between Golden and the forks of the creek. The inauspicious entrance gives no hint of the settlement and railroad depot that once occupied this part of the world. As for Loveland's wagon road up though the gulch to the Gregory Road, faint indentations may still be found here and there alongside the gulch walls.

Prior to settlement the upper regions of the gulch were full of beaver dams.

Named for John Guy, the first settler to homestead in the gulch in 1859. The Guy House, on the Gregory Toll Road in the gulch below the junction of Robinson Hill and Guy Gulch roads, is the only house shown on the Deane map of 1867.

> (Reference: Deane, Cecil A., Surveyor General's Office, Denver, August 1867 map. T. III.
> S. R. L. XXI. W.)

"Fair diggings were reported to have been found in Guy Gulch."

(Source: Hall, Frank, 1889, *History of the State of Colorado:* Chicago, Blakely
Printing Co., p. 225.)

Guy Gulch. The floor of the gulch can be seen in the lower lefthand corner. From here the gulch swings in to the right and opens again immediately over the top of the dead pine. Douglas Mountain is in the background. Photographed 1981.

"A road company composed of W. A. H. Loveland, 'Uncle' Smith, etc., built a wagon road in 1862-63 up Clear Creek and thence up Guy Gulch. The first coach came over the road August 30, 1863. But the gulch portion of the route did not prove practicable and was soon abandoned."

(Source: Denver Commonwealth, Sept. 3, 1863.)

But hope persisted:

"MINERS REGISTER. FEB. 9, 1864. The road down Guy Gulch and Clear Creek was in prime order. A little rough in places but free from dust and sand; believe it will take all travel this coming spring and summer."

(Source: Ramstetter, James K., 1996, *Life in the early days:* p. 7.)

"COLORADO TRANSCRIPT, MARCH 6, 1867. We took a ride over the new road up Clear Creek as far as the mouth of Guy Gulch and were glad to find it in most excellent condition. It is now completed for its whole length to the old road at Guy's House. There are three bridges between Golden and Guy Gulch. It will be necessary to raise the road before the high waters of spring come. A toll house is now being built."

(Source: Ramstetter, James K., 1996, *Life in the early days:* p. 8.)

The funnel-like shape of the gulch as it opens on Clear Creek results in heavy flood runoffs. The Deane map of 1867 shows the wagon road already abandoned and ending ab. 0.5 mile up the gulch from Clear Creek. Foot traffic then used the game trail which climbs over the pass between Guy and Huntsman gulches (see 1924 Denver Mountain Parks Map) to reach Clear Creek. This steep, narrow path does not appear to have been a wagon road. The upper regions of Guy Gulch presently accommodate ab. 3 miles of the Golden Gate Canyon highway.

In 1965 a 3-mile road named the Guy Gulch Road was proposed by Jefferson County to connect U.S. 6 in Clear Creek Canyon to Golden Gate State Park. The new road would have cut the existing route by 8 miles and opened up several thousand acres of private land for residential development. The shortcut has not yet materialized.

Halfmile Gulch

Ab. 1.75 miles long, opens on Tucker Gulch from the N.
 1965 Ralston Buttes Quad.
 S18-19-20, T3S, R70W.

{Var. names: **Kerosene Gulch** and **Coal Oil Gulch** for the oil seep in the gulch. Coal oil ran out of a fissure, but early-day attempts to commercialize the site failed.}

Takes its name from being 0.5 mile above Golden Gate City on the Gregory Toll Road.

Huntsman Gulch

Ab. 0.6 mile long. Opens on Clear Creek from the N at the Goltra Quarry.
Stop on Colorado Central Railroad.
S/b Evergreen Quad.
S35-36, T3S, R71W.

Named for the ranch at the mouth of the gulch.

The W ridge accommodates a once well-traveled pass between the Huntsman and the lower reaches of Guy Gulch.

After the depot at the entrance to Guy Gulch was abandoned, the train stopped at the Huntsman Ranch. This stop may have originated earlier, as the trains were very accommodating.

(For destruction of the gulch entrance see Goltra Quarry <u>in</u> Mines.)

ABOVE *Looking NW into Clear Creek Canyon and beyond. In the middle ground is the pass over the Huntsman. On this side of the saddle is Huntsman Gulch, which opens on the highway glimpsed to the lower left. On the far side of the saddle is Guy Gulch. Above the high fluted edges of Guy Gulch are the upper pastures of the Elk Creek meadows. The pass over the Huntsman was used by residents living in the lower regions of Guy Gulch to travel horseback and by shank's mare to and from Clear Creek. Photographed 1980, before Goltra Quarry was opened.*

BELOW *The white speck in the lower left background is the Huntsman Ranch. This is the only known picture of the ranch that named the drainage and the railroad bridge and stop in the bottom of Clear Creek Canyon. Note the bridgework to the left.*

COLORADO RAILROAD MUSEUM

Indian Gulch—Pioneer Location

Ab. 1.25 miles long. Drains the lower foothills region, opens on the prairie from the W ab. 0.25 mile N of Clear Creek.

S/b Ralston Buttes and Golden quads.
S30-29, T3S, R70W Ralston Buttes.
S29-28, T3S, R70W Golden.

{Var. name: **Arapahoe travois trail.** (See Historical Routes.)}

Site of Hall-Woodland Cave. (See Prehistoric Sites.)

Takes its name from the Indian traffic the gulch accommodated. The old Gorman homestead is located at the E entrance to Indian Gulch.

This gulch is correctly labeled on the 1906 BQ, but not on the later RBQ.

Indian Gulch (pioneer designation) as seen from Graveyard Hill. The Arapahoe Travois Trail climbed through this gulch, angled to the left above the fourth hump, and mounted the distant summit following the snowline. Photographed 1981.

Indian Gulch (pioneer designation). The Arapahoe Travois Trail reached the river through this gulch. The old Gorman homestead occupied the entrance. The gulch itself is now owned by Jeffco Open Space. The once peaceful entrance has given way to humpty-dumpty trophy homes. Photographed 1985.

Indian Gulch—Ralston Buttes Quad

Ab. 1.75 miles long. Drains the lower foothills region, opens on Clear Creek Canyon from the N ab. 0.5 mile inside the E entrance.

1948 Ralston Buttes and Golden quads.
S30-31-32, T3S, R70W Ralston Buttes.
S32, T3S, R70W Golden.

{Var. name: **Magpie Gulch** for the large numbers of magpies roosting here in the winter.}

Extremely rugged hillsides and numerous rock outcroppings. In many places the watercourse is too rough to accommodate the trail, which passes above on the hillside.

Early settlers named this gulch Magpie Gulch. When the Ralston Buttes Quad was created out of portions of the Blackhawk Quad, the name *Indian Gulch* was mistakenly applied to this, the Magpie Gulch.

Koch Gulch

Ab. 1 mile long. Drains the higher foothills region, opens on Tucker Gulch from the N at the site of Eight-mile House.

S/b Ralston Buttes Quad.
S10-15, T3S, R71W.

ISABELLA (BENGSON) KOCH COLLECTION

Homesteaders Ernest and Elizabeth Koch, for whom Koch Gulch is named.

Named for Ernest S. Koch, Sr., who homesteaded at the top of the gulch in 1862. The original buildings are in ruins. A large red brick house c. 1890 is still standing and was recently reroofed. Mica was mined in this gulch.

(See S15, T3S, R71W <u>in</u> Settlement for more about Koch.)

The road through Koch Gulch linked the original road to Gregory's, as it crossed the pass between Dry Creek and Guy Gulch, with the later toll road up Eight-mile Gulch.

(Reference: Burt, S. W., and Berthoud, E. L., 1860, *Quartz mining region of the Rocky Mountains:* Denver City, Rocky Mountain News Printing Co., map insert.)

Remains of Ernest Koch, Sr., barn. The barn blew down in 1985. Photographed 1978.

ISABELLA (BENGSON) KOCH COLLECTION

Homestead of Ernest Koch, Sr., at the head of Koch Gulch, c. 1920.

Lake Eva

On the Burt and Berthoud map, Lake Eva appears approximately midway down the extreme right-hand side of the map. The lake, as depicted in a figure-eight shape, is roughly midway between Ralston and Coal creeks.

> (Reference: Burt, S. W., and Berthoud, E. L., 1860, *Quartz mining region of the Rocky Mountains:* Denver City, Rocky Mountain News Printing Co., map insert.)

{Possible var. name: **Kenneer's Lake.**

Carlos W. Lake, in an address given in Denver, Sept. 23, 1936, speaks of a Kenneer's Lake as "about half way between Denver and Boulder" and goes on to say:

> "…We left Golden about two o'clock in the morning, rode out to Kenneer's Lake, and lay around there in the brush and kept out of sight…Pretty soon the train whistled, coming through a deep cut on the east of the lake…The carriage drove down and we loaded the judge into the carriage and struck out for Coal Creek Canyon. That was about four miles…"

> (Source: Lake, Carlos, 1936, *The kidnapping of Judge A. W. Stone,* <u>in</u> address given at meeting of Bar Association of First Judicial District, Denver, Sept. 23, 1936: Colo. Mag., v. 17, n. 1, Jan. 1940, p. 21-22.)}

Lake Eva is listed here on the RBQ to fix it against the Ralston and Coal Creek information. Correctly located, the lake would appear on the GQ. But exactly where, no one knows anymore.

Leyden Gulch

Ab. 5 miles long. Empties into Leyden Lake.
1965 Ralston Buttes and Golden quads.
S18-19-20, T2S, R70W Ralston Buttes.
S20-21-28-27-26-25, T2S, R70W Golden.

Opens between Rocky Flats and the Ralston Dike and passes S of Arena Siding. Named for the Leyden Coal Mine.

EDITORS' NOTE: Somewhere along the way Martin picked up an extra *e* in his last name. But what's an *e* more or less when you've named a gulch, a lake and a city?

In 1911 the mine was destroyed in a terrible fire that killed ten miners. Mattie D. Merrick, whose husband, Frank Merrick, died in the fire, brought suit against Leyden Coal Company but lost. Later that year the company announced plans for a concrete shaft. For a fascinating insight on the lives of miners and their families in general read Maria Rogers' *In other words: Oral histories of the Colorado frontier:* Fulcrum Publishing.

LYDEN'S
CoalMine.

DEALERS and the public are notified that my coal mines are

Now Opened,

and I am prepared to deliver

A Superior Quality of Coal,

in quantities to suit. These mines are situated on Lyden Creek, one mile north of Ralston,

13 miles from Denver and 6 from Golden City,

over good roads. I have

Fairbanks Scales

on the ground where coal is weighed free, and all weights guaranteed. Coal delivered at the mines at $3.50 per ton, including weighing.
44-3 tf   MARTIN LYDEN.

Colo. Transcript advertisement, March 16, 1870.

Long Lake Ditch

Ab. 2 miles long. Dug in conjunction with Ralston Reservoir. The ditch, seen clearly in the 1948 RBQ, parallels Ralston Creek from near the center of S31, T2S, R70W, RBQ to the W end of the reservoir where it passes around to the S and empties into Upper Long Lake in S4, T3S, R70W, GQ, immediately E of the reservoir.

Macy Gulch

Ab. 1.25 miles long. Rises high on the SW face of Ely Hill. Flows W and S into Smith Creek.
S/b Black Hawk Quad.
S11-10, T3S, R72W. (Not mapped in this book.)

Believed to have been named for a man living on Ely Hill. Just below the entrance to Macy Gulch, E of the Smith Hill Road, is the original site of the Bay State School. The old foundation is still visible. The school itself was moved to a site high on the Smith Hill Road in the Enterprise Mining District but retained its original Bay State name.

Magpie Gulch

(See Indian Gulch—Ralston Buttes Quad.)

Mayhem Creek

Ab. 1.5 miles long. Tributaries drain the large basin to the W of Sheep Mountain. The Mayhem opens on Clear Creek at Roscoe, *i.e.*, that place in Clear Creek Canyon 3 miles above Tunnel No. 3 where the Roscoe Depot was located.

> *Ralston Buttes, Evergreen, Squaw Pass quads.*
> *S29-32-31, T3S, R71W Ralston Buttes.*
> *S31, T3S, R71W Squaw Pass.*
> *S31-32, T3S, and S5-6, T4S, R71W Evergreen.*

Named for homesteader Mayhem.

CROWELL COLLECTION

Miller Gulch

Ab. 2 miles long. Divides in S26 to drain the E slope of Guy Hill and the N slope of Saulsbury Peak. Opens on Tucker Gulch from the S ab. 0.5 mile below Crawford Gulch/GGC junction.

> *S/b Ralston Buttes Quad.*
> *S22-23-24, T3S, R71W.*

{Var. name: **Four-mile Gulch** for the distance above Golden Gate City on the Gregory Road.}

Named for Miller who homesteaded here. The flat ground at the gulch entrance was a favorite stopping place for wagons. The house here was called Four-mile House. (Do not confuse this house and gulch with the house and gulch on Dory Hill.) The John H. Nare homestead was on this drainage. At the top of the drainage are the large meadows crossed by the Arapahoe Travois Trail.

Entrance to Miller Gulch, a.k.a. Four-mile Gulch. Photographed 1975.

Nott Creek

Ab. 3 miles long. Rises on the SE slopes of Thorodin Mountain in Gilpin Co. Flows SE into Ralston Creek above Deer Creek.

> *1965 Black Hawk and Ralston Buttes quads.*
> *S24, T2S, R72W, and S19-30, T2S, R71W Black Hawk.*
> *S30-29, T2S, R71W Ralston Buttes.*

{Var. Name: **Nut Creek.** (Source: 1906 BQ.)}

Named for homesteader Sylvester G. Nott who proved up in 1869.

> (Compiled from: Stevenson, Malcolm, 1996, GGC State Park Historian, misc. papers.)

(See the GGC State Park map for trails in the vicinity of the creek. The 1906 BQ shows a road all the way through Nott Creek to the Gap Road, as does the 1948 RBQ.)

Nott homestead remains, on Nott Creek, now part of Golden Gate Canyon State Park. Photographed 1996.

Osmund Gulch

Ab. 0.75 mile long. Runs N/NE from half-way down the ridge N of Drew Hill into Ralston Creek.

> *S27, T2S, R71W, Ralston Buttes.*

Possibly named for a settler. The remains of a cabin are in the lower region of this drainage.

Plum Creek

Ab. 1 mile long. Drains S slope of Crawford Peak. Opens on Clear Creek from the N ab. 1.6 mile above Tunnel No. 1.

1965 Ralston Buttes, Evergreen quads.
S36, T3S, R71W Ralston Buttes.
S36, T3S, R71W, and S31, T3S, R70W Evergreen.

{Var. name: **Plum Patch.**}

Named for a large grove of wild plum trees located in the higher regions of the gulch.

Quartermile Gulch

Ab. 0.25 mile long. Opens on Tucker Gulch N of highway.

S/b Ralston Buttes quad.
S20, T3S, R70W.

A steep, shallow draw above the remains of the old toll station. Takes its name from being 0.25 mile above Golden Gate City.

Ralston Creek

Ab. 25 miles long. Rises in the mountains of NE Gilpin Co. Flows E into Adams County to join Clear Creek immediately E of Sheridan Blvd. and N of W 55th Pl.

Black Hawk, Ralston Buttes, Golden, Arvada quads.

Tributaries too numerous to list.

At one time the creek was full of beaver dams.

> Originally called Ralston's creek for a goldseeker by that name who discovered gold near the mouth of the creek, c. 1850. The goldseeker's given name has not been determined.
>
> (Compiled from: Hafen, L. R., ed., 1941, *Pike's Peak gold rush guidebooks of 1859*: Clark Co.p. 36, ft. no. 34.)

> "That summer [1857] Green looked into another matter besides land farming, one having to do with gold. Seven years before a party of Cherokees headed by Lewis Ralston had found a small showing of gold [on Ralston Creek] in the Rocky Mountain region on their way west to California. It was said that they made a map of its location."
>
> (Source: Spencer, E. D., 1966, Green Russell and Gold: Univ. of Texas Press, p. 40.)

Green Russell contacted the Cherokees and made his plans. In 1858 he reached Ralston Creek with a party of 104 men made of relatives and family acquaintances and Cherokees. The gold findings on Ralston Creek were discouragingly meager and the party quickly disintegrated. By the time the Cherry Creek discovery was made, as the party worked its way south, only thirteen men remained. These thirteen men rode the crest of the wave that was the Pike's Peak gold rush. For a good, well-documented description of Green Russell's adventures in this region read E. D. Spencer's *Green Russell and Gold*.

According to a yellowed scrap of newspaper found in an old album, Jone Heivner discovered coal near Ralston Creek in 1865. He sold this claim to M.L.A. This is the earliest known discovery of coal.

> "January 8, 1881. Nicholls & Hoagland mined 11,000 tons of coal during 1880, and are preparing to mine double that amount the present year, as the demand in the mountains is rapidly increasing. This firm will have a railroad track laid to their Ralston Springs mines as soon as the weather will permit of work thereon."
>
> (Source: Jefferies, Marguerite, *Mineral mining activities from 1875—*: typed manuscript stamped "Jefferson County Museum, Old Court House, Golden, Colo.")

> "Magnetic iron ores are found in large deposits on Ralston, Bear, Turkey and Elk creeks. The bed near Ralston creek gives in plain view a forty-foot vein of magnetic iron, carrying forty-nine per cent of pure iron without sulfur or phosphorus. This will be in time of great value."
>
> (Source: *Jefferson County*, in The Golden Globe, Industrial Edition, May 20, 1893, p. 3.)

> "The Jefferson Ranch, by Ro[?] McDonald and Geo. S. Akin, situated on Rallston Creek about three miles below the crossing of the old Gregory Road, about ten miles from Central City, and about the same distance from Gold Dirt, is one of the best mountain ranches in the country. These responsible gentlemen keep faithful herdsmen and do guarantee the faithful delivery of all stock entrusted to their care when called for, in fine condition and at reasonable charges. Their ranch has an abundance of excellent feed and pure water, good picket corrals and shelter from the winds. Stock received at their ranch, also at Young's hay yard, Gregory's, and at the yards of Morton & Co., and M. C. Daly, Gold Dirt."
>
> (Source: Colo. Transcript, day missing.)

The RBQ labels this junction at the confluence of Nott and Ralston creeks, S29, T2S, R71W, as the *Ralston Creek Ranch*.

The first recorded gold strike in Colorado was made on Ralston Creek (near what is now called Van Bibber Park) in 1850 by a group of prospectors on their way to California.

GGC State Park literature is a good source of creek highlights. (See Ralston Toll Gate in Toll Gates for additional details. Also see Ralston Creek Wagon Road in Historical Routes.)

Ralston Reservoir

Ralston Buttes and Golden quads.

Takes its name from Ralston Creek.

> "About seven miles north easterly from Golden and fifteen miles north west of Denver, entirely in the valley, along the eastern base of the foot hills, is the widely known stock and dairy ranch of Mr. Henry Wagner…There is a fine site for a reservoir and it is the intention of Mr. Wagner at some time in the future to have as fine a body of water for all purposes of irrigation as are needed to cultivate the land…The Arapahoe Ditch Company have surveyed for a reservoir…"

> (Source: *Henry Wagner's Ranch*, <u>in</u> The Golden Globe, Industrial Edition, May 20, 1893, p. 15.)

> "In 1936, the great block of the Ralston Dike was put to use to help water Denver's lawns. An earth-filled dam was thrown across Ralston Creek at the north end of the dike to impound western slope water for the Denver Municipal Water System. Water from the Fraser River and Jim Creek on the Western Slope of the Continental Divide was siphoned through the Moffat Water Tunnel, conveyed by South Boulder Creek and by canals and conduit to Ralston Creek. The dam is 1175 feet long, 945 feet wide and 180 feet high. It holds two million cubic feet of earth, weighing four million tons. As the fifteen thousand acre feet of water began to fill the reservoir in early 1938, the site of the town of Glencoe was buried forever."

> (Source: Bond, R. F., 1989, *The land persists:* Jeffco Hist. Com. contest entry.)

Robinson Gulch

Ab. 1.5 miles long. Drains the region N of Douglas Mountain to open on Guy Gulch. Accommodates Robinson Hill Road for lower 0.6 mile.

1965 Black Hawk and Ralston Buttes quads.

S18, T3S, R71W Black Hawk.

S18-17-16, T3S, R71W Ralston Buttes.

Named for homesteader Robinson who settled W of the gulch on the flats overlooking the Elk Creek drainage.

Chrysoberyl and black tourmaline (poor quality) were mined in lower regions of the gulch.

Rye Gulch

Ab. 1 mile long. Drains higher foothills region. The S fork of Tucker Gulch.

S/b Ralston Buttes Quad.

S15, T3S, R71W.

Takes its name from the large field of rye planted at the head of the gulch. Chrysoberyl, along with other minerals of poorer quality, was mined in the lower regions of the gulch.

The 1867 Deane map shows a road through the Rye Gulch.

This road splits from the main road at the junction of the Rye and Koch gulches and ascends the Rye Gulch to cross the flat to the W where it crosses a steep water course and loops out on the further shoulder to drop into Guy Gulch. In the 1906 BQ the Rye Gulch Road is gone.

The existence of the Rye Gulch Road, in addition to the Koch Gulch Road, created an important junction on the Gregory Toll Road. The Deane map shows a saw mill at this junction, one of two sawmills on the map. All this activity led to the construction of what would be called the Eight-mile House. (See Stage Stops.)

Sawmill Gulch

Ab. 2 miles long. Drains the N slope of the ridge between Centralia Mountain and Mt. Tom. Enters Ralston Creek from the N immediately below Nott Creek.

1965 Ralston Buttes Quad.

S5, T3S, R71W, and S32-29, T2S, R71W. (Not mapped in this book.)

Named for the sawmill which operated midway up the gulch in the SE¼, S32. This was a fair-sized settlement. Railroad ties were made here. Remnants of the mill remain, along with rock work and depressions that indicate numerous cabin foundations.

Smith Hill Gulch

Ab. 2.25 miles long. Accommodates Smith Hill Road. Drains W slopes of Ely Hill.

1942 Black Hawk Quad.

S10-9-16-21, T3S, R72W. (Not mapped in this book.)

Named tributaries in ascending order: Mesa Gulch, Macy Gulch.

{Var name: **Smith Creek.**}

The gulch flattens out at the top of an unnamed pass, elv. 8752', between Ely Hill on the E and a smaller unnamed peak on the W. Smith Hill Road divides here.

The main road up the draw and the offshoot turning sharply to the SE to the Robinson Hill Road, approximate the old Arapahoe Indian travois trail on its route between Golden and the north fork of Clear Creek. (See Arapahoe Travois Trail in Historical Routes.) The offshoot to the NE comes out on the Golden Gate Canyon road at the site of the old Junction Ranch.

The Smith Hill Road and its divisions, as well as the Junction Ranch, appear on the 1906 BQ. (See Smith Hill in Heights for more about the road.)

Smith Hill Station, a railroad depot and water tank at the confluence of the gulch and North Clear Creek, is listed in Crofutt's *Grip-Sack Guide* as 32 miles W from Denver. Fare $2.60.

South Beaver Creek

Ab. 2 miles long. Rises on the E slope of Miramonte Mountain and runs E, SE and N to open on Beaver Creek.

1972 Tungsten and Eldorado quads.
S7, T2S, R71W Tungsten.
S7-18-17-8-9-4, T2S, R71W Eldorado.

Not to be confused with the much larger and better known South Beaver Creek that rises on the N side of Fairburn Mountain, crosses Highway 119, and flows N/NE into South Boulder Creek ab. 6 miles from its source.

Alas, so many beaver creeks and so few beaver.

Taylor Gulch

Ab. 0.5 mile long.

S/b Ralston Buttes Quad.
S27, T3S, R71W.

Runs NE to SW down N side of Taylor Peak into Guy Gulch. Accommodates an old wagon road. Originally accommodated the Arapahoe Travois Trail which descended the west-facing slopes into Guy Gulch.

On W side of Guy Gulch the same configuration—the old wagon road overlying the travois trail—can be seen angling NW uphill out of the gulch headed for the Elk Creek flats.

(See Arapahoe Travois Trail <u>in</u> Historical Routes.)

Thea Gulch

Ab. 1 mile long. The longest canyon opening on Crawford Gulch from the W between the top of Bowser Hill and GGC. Divides after ab. 0.25 mile into two evenly defined forks.

S/b Ralston Buttes Quad.
S14-13, T3S, R71W.

Named for Theodore Koch who homesteaded in S14 of the gulch—the same Theodore Koch who, with his wife Bessie, later purchased Centennial House.

Tucker Gulch

Ab. 8 miles long. Major E/W watershed opening on prairie approximately 1 mile N of and parallel to Clear Creek Canyon. Empties into Clear Creek at Vanover Park, Ford Street bridge.

1965 Ralston Buttes and Golden quads.
S15-22-23-24-25, T3S, R71W, and S30-19-20, T3S, R70W Ralston Buttes.
S20-21-28-27, T3S R71W Golden.

{Var. names: **Golden Gate Canyon, Gate Canyon, Eight-mile Canyon/Gulch, Tucker Canyon.**}

Named tributaries in ascending order: Quartermile Gulch, Halfmile Gulch, Miller Gulch, Crawford Gulch, Koch Gulch, Rye Gulch.

Named for Alfred Tucker who operated the toll gate inside the canyon entrance at the foot of Quartermile Gulch, 1860-1871.

(Compiled from: *Arvada, Just between you and me, 1904-1941:* Arvada Hist. Soc., 1985, p. 5.)

(See Golden Gate City <u>in</u> Cities for more about Alfred Tucker.)

"June 21, 1884. The old Golden Gate copper mine now being worked…is looking finely. A tunnel is now being driven to strike the vein at a depth of 75 feet from the surface. …[a test gave] the astonishing run of $185 to the ton."

(Source: Jefferies, Marguerite, *Mineral mining activities from 1875—:* typed manuscript stamped "Jefferson County Museum, Old Court House, Golden, Colo.")

"July 5, 1884. The Imperial Mine formerly known as the General Thomas… is proving up fine. …Recent assays of the ore struck run as follows: Gold, $1/12$ ounces—$22.50. Silver, 1 oz—$124.33. Copper, 24 per cent—$38.40.

…Ore from the old workings of this mine, shipped to Swanea, Wales, some years ago, paid to the owners $150 per ton…

The mine is only about two miles from Golden, an all down-hill road to the smelters, giving it an additional advantage."

(Source: Jefferies, Marguerite, *Mineral mining activities from 1875—:* typed manuscript stamped "Jefferson County Museum, Old Court House, Golden, Colo.")

Road construction in Tucker Gulch as seen looking W from Hartzell Hill, spring 1972. Note old Hartzell Hill road to the left.

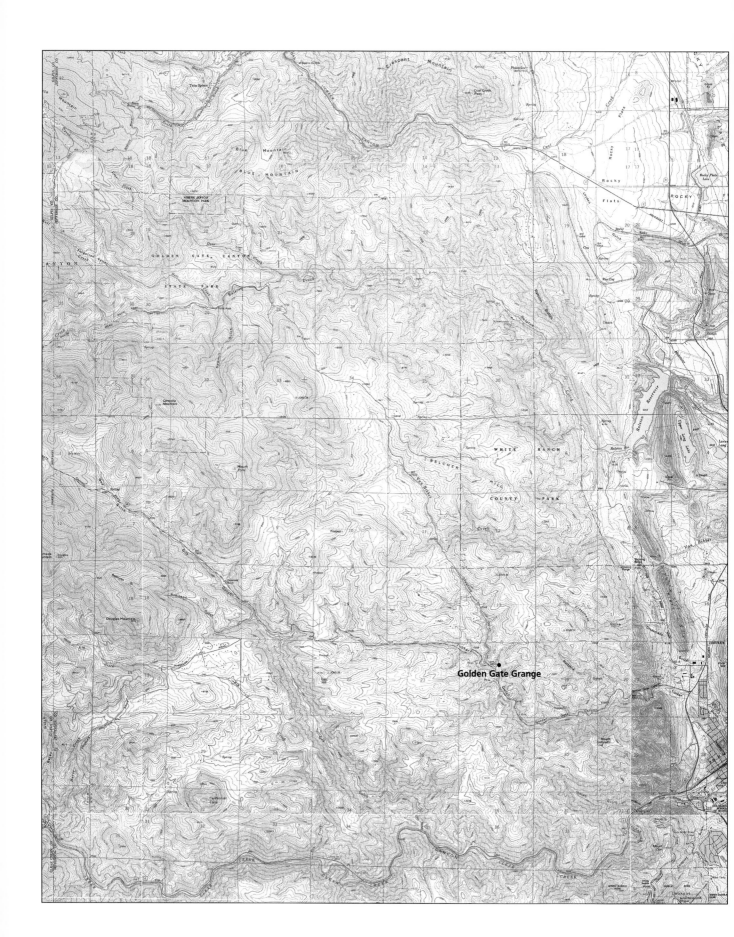

Golden Gate Grange

Grange

Golden Gate Grange No. 451

Golden Gate Canyon, 0.1 mile E of Crawford Gulch entrance.

1965 Ralston Buttes Quad.
S24, T3S, R71W.
Elv. ab. 6900'.

Organized the 25th day of July 1940. George Koch was Master at the time. Met monthly in Belcher Hill School until 1953 when rancher Bessie Nare donated land to the community for a road maintenance shop and a community center. Under the able guidance of Clarence "Bud" Nicholls, then Master, the grange organized labor and donations to build the center and took over the management. Mary Jane Nare, Bessie's daughter, later donated an additional acre to the community center to increase the parking area. Duane Nelson is the newly elected Master.

    The bronze plaque attached to the front door by the grange reads

IN MEMORY OF
BESSIE AND MARY JANE NARE
GOLDEN GATE PIONEERS
WHO DONATED THIS PROPERTY
TO THE GOLDEN GATE GRANGE
FOR THE
BENEFIT OF THE COMMUNITY

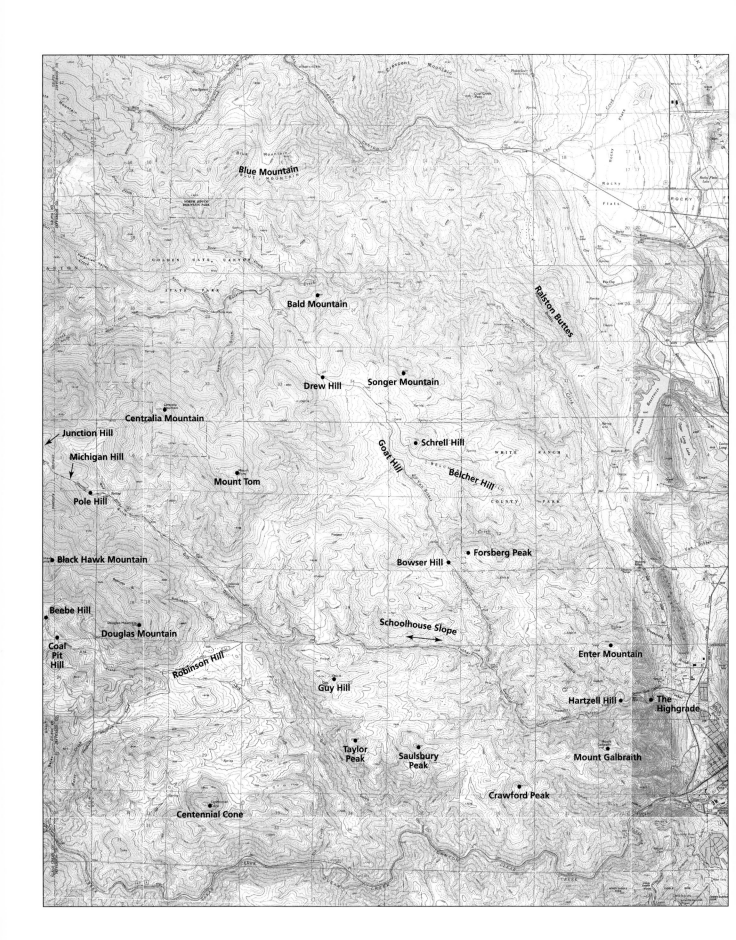

Blue Mountain

Bald Mountain

Drew Hill   Songer Mountain

Centralia Mountain

Junction Hill

Michigan Hill

Pole Hill

Mount Tom

Schrell Hill

Goat Hill

Belcher Hill

Forsberg Peak

Bowser Hill

Black Hawk Mountain

Beebe Hill

Douglas Mountain

Schoolhouse Slope

Coal Pit Hill

Robinson Hill

Enter Mountain

Guy Hill

Hartzell Hill   The Highgrade

Taylor Peak

Saulsbury Peak

Mount Galbraith

Crawford Peak

Centennial Cone

Ralston Buttes

Heights

Bald Mountain

S of Ralston Creek, extreme left margin of section.

S/b Ralston Buttes Quad.
S27, T2S, R71W.
Elv. 7900' (1965 RBQ).

Takes its name from the open pastures that run SE from the summit down into Drew Gulch.

Beebe Hill

Summit is crossed by Smith Hill Road 2.4 miles NW of the road's junction with Douglas Mountain Road.

S/b Black Hawk Quad.
S13, T3S, R72W.
Elv. ab. 8750'.

The Beebe ranch named the hill.

The name may have some connection with early Golden surveyor F. W. Beebe:

> "[Golden town founders in 1859] selected 1,280 acres on both sides of Clear creek and laid out a town. F. W. Beebe surveyed 3.9 acres that season, but the survey was completed in 1860 by Berthoud."
>
> (Source: *The Works of Hubert Howe Bancroft: History of Nevada, Colorado and Wyoming, 1540-1888:* San Francisco, 1890, The History Co., v. 25, p. 620.)

No house appears in this vicinity on the 1906 BQ.

Belcher Hill

Forms N shoulder of Van Bibber Creek. A large portion of the ground, including the old Belcher Hill Road, has been incorporated in the White Ranch Park.

1965 Ralston Buttes Quad.
S1-2-11-12, T3S, R71W.
Elv. ab. 8150'.

"We went down the Belcher Hill road to the Belcher ranch, got there about ten o'clock; got some fresh milk and loafed there for a while. And, by the way, this Belcher ranch, the proprietor was there, Gill Belcher, who was one of the County Commissioners and one of the members of the board of directors of the railroad."

(Source: Lake, Carlos, 1936, *The kidnapping of Judge A. W. Stone,* in address given at meeting of Bar Association of First Judicial District, Denver, Sept. 23, 1936: Colo. Mag., v. 17, n. 1, Jan. 1940, p. 24.)

"History records a sheriff in Jefferson County named Gilbert A. Belcher; also an early Golden business directory lists a G. N. Belcher as owner of an establishment called the Elkhorn House. The Tom Belcher family of upper Golden Gate Canyon, whose descendants still live there, is not related to the earlier Belcher family."

(Source: Wyhs, Irma, 1994, *Ranch History,* compiled for the Red School Ranch.)

"On April 5, 1866, the Rocky Mountain News reported that a man had frozen to death on the ranch of G. N. Belcher, three miles from Golden City. The unfortunate man was E. K. Bickford, 65. He had apparently walked to Golden City for food for his wife and child and been caught by one of the ferocious spring blizzards common to the Front Range. The News ended the story with a plea for donations for the destitute widow."

(Source: Bond, R. F., 1989, *The land persists:* Jeffco Hist. Com. contest entry, p. 6-7.)

In the first half of the 20th century Belcher Hill and Robinson Hill were alternating sites for the Golden Gate Community Annual 4th of July picnic. People came from near and far, afoot, horseback and automobile.

Games for young and old included foot races, balloon blowing, three-legged race, bean race, slipper kicking, hitting a scarecrow dummy with a rolling pin, clothes pin tossing, high jump, potato broad jump, weight lifting, nail driving, and log sawing. The most popular entertainment was the horse events. These included fast races, a costume race, slow race, musical chairs, needle threading, bareback wrestling, a stake race, and consolation races.

The fast races drew the most attention. A great deal of money exchanged hands at the fast races. These were quarter-mile and half-mile races and were easily viewed by the picnic-goers.

Fourth of July horse race on Robinson Hill.

The courses were along the ridgeline of Belcher Hill, and over the high pastures of Robinson Hill. Both sites were N of the public road. Occasionally longer races were run to the S of the picnic areas.

The picnic was followed by a dance. These dances could last until dawn.

> "The fourth of July picnic went off with a big 'bang.' Besides the familiar Colorado eleven and sixty license numbers there was a Pennsylvania and a California license tag. Jim Noble, in his Piper Cub, flew over the crowd, entertaining it with a few stunts. The day was topped off with a dance at Frees. Golden people were in the majority."
>
> (Source: Ladies Columbine Club Notes, July 1941.)

EDITORS' NOTE: See Ferree's Mountain Park <u>in</u> Parks for location of Peter Ferree's dancehall.

Black Hawk Mountain

Rises equidistant between the summits of Douglas Mountain and Ely Hill.

1942 Black Hawk Quad.
S12, T3S, R72W.
Elv. 9998'.

Takes its name from the town of Black Hawk. And where did the town get its name?

- From Black Hawk, an Arapahoe Indian chief?
- From the early mining machinery bearing the trademark Blackhawk in memory of a famous chief of an Eastern tribe?
- From Jim Sanders, the squaw man and early trapper nicknamed Black Hawk, who ran around with George Jackson and Tom Golden?
- From Black Hawk the white man who was hung in Golden City for stealing horses?
- Or from someone whose name never crossed the printed page?

No one knows anymore.

This was Arapahoe country. Their travois trail crossed the open trees directly ahead, entered the black belt of timber angling uphill to the right, and crossed the lower shoulder of the Saulsbury to reach the big, open meadows behind Guy Hill (the bare knob to the right middle in the picture). Douglas Mountain is in the center background. Black Hawk Mountain sprawls in the distance behind Douglas. Photographed 1991.

Blue Mountain

Rises between Ralston Creek and Coal Creek canyons.

1948 Ralston Buttes Quad.
S17-16, T2S, R71W.
Elv. 9322'.
The southern slopes are in T2S, R71W of the RBQ. The summit is in the ESQ.

Takes its name from the light, gunmetal blue color, as seen from the distance, of the rock out-croppings which predominate on the mountain.

Bowser Hill

Pass over high ground between Crawford Gulch and Van Bibber Creek drainages. Accommodates Crawford Gulch Road.

S/b Ralston Buttes Quad.
S11, T3S, R71W.
Highest elv. ab. 7480'.

Named for Samuel S. Bowser who homesteaded 80 acres (N½ of SE¼ of S11, T3S, R71W) in the Dry Creek drainage in 1912. His house was located at the N foot of Bowser Hill W of the road.

That area of the Bowser homestead E of the county road, through which Dry Creek flows, was known as Sam Bowser's park. Numerous old pictures show this park with the rock formations as the backdrop. Sam himself must have been a convivial fellow—he appears at family gatherings throughout the region.

WIKSTROM COLLECTION

Sam Bowser and team on his homestead at the N foot of Bowser Hill.

Centennial Cone

Overlooks Clear Creek Canyon from the N. Located W of Elk Creek.

1965 Ralston Buttes Quad.
S32, T3S, R71W.
Elv. 8679'.

{Var. name: **Sheep Mountain.** Seen from a distance, the heavily timbered mountain resembles a sheep, head down, ready to charge. Sheep Mountain is the more common name locally.

This is the only mountain indicated on the 1867 Deane map. It is not named.

The large flat directly E of the summit at one time yielded numerous Indian artifacts.

In 1988, testifying at a Jeffco hearing regarding the Sheep Mountain Quarry, Carla Swan Coleman told of stories handed down by her mother about Indian activities on Sheep Mountain. These activities included sunrise ceremonies on the mountain, and an after-dark farewell ceremony with torches. She also told of a jewelled cave, described by the Indians as a huge, domed cave underground extending the distance of several city blocks, and which the Indians said they sealed.

(Compiled from: Scott, Jacque, *Fiery goodbye to Indians' sacred hill:* Golden Transcript, date unknown.)

Sheep Mountain, a.k.a. Centennial Cone. Photographed 1990.

(For more about the crystal cave discovered in the immediate vicinity of Sheep Mountain see Crystal Cave <u>in</u> Caves. For more about the Sheep Mountain Quarry see Goltra Quarry <u>in</u> Mines.)

Centralia Mountain

NW of Mt. Tom. Three distinct points. Connects with Mt. Tom by a 9400' ridge.

1965 Ralston Buttes Quad.
S31, T2S, R71W and S6, T3S, R71W.
Elv. 9795'.

Origin of name unknown.

Portions of the top and N slopes have been incorporated in the Golden Gate State Park.

Coal Pit Hill

The hill where Smith Hill Road crosses the Gilpin County line.

S/b Black Hawk Quad.
S24, T3S, R72W.
Elv. ab. 8700.

{Var. name: **County Line Hill.**}

At the bottom of the hill to the E, thence up the draw to the N, was a large charcoal-making operation.

A large, lone pine tree stands at the bottom of the hill on the E side of the road. At one time a second large pine stood across the road. According to Oliver Kolin, area rancher, these two pines were used as landmarks.

> "There were lots of charcoal pits on the Green Ranch. They would dig a big hole and light a big fire in the hole. When it got very hot in the hole, green lodge pole would be cut to the hole's length and piled in the hole. Then they would shovel the dirt back to cover the timber. Later they would dig it up and find charcoal. The reason for the charcoal would be to sharpen the drills before the railroad brought the coal in. These pits were in the thick lodge pole forests and showed as a mound."

> (Source: Ken and Lela Green.)

Crawford Peak

Between Tucker Gulch and Clear Creek Canyon.
1965 Ralston Buttes Quad.
S25, T3S, R71W.
Elv. 7703'.

{Var. name: **Eldridge,** possibly for early Arapahoe City settlers, Stephen and/or L. Eldridge. This old name continues in common use by local ranchers.}

Crawford Gulch appears on the quads as early as 1906. The name *Crawford Peak* does not appear on the quads until after 1948.

The activities of D. C. Crawford, County Clerk in Golden City in 1869, may have had something to do with the naming of Crawford Gulch and Crawford Peak. D. C. Crawford advertised as a notary public and conveyancer and as the local agent for The Pacific Insurance Company of San Francisco.

Douglas Mountain

A high, steep-sided mountain with two distinct points approximately midway between Mt. Tom and Centennial Cone, one section to the W.
1942 Black Hawk Quad.
S18, T3S, R71W.
Elv. 9665'.
The lower eastern slopes of this mountain appear in S18, T3S, R71W, of the RBQ.

Douglas Mountain is one of two mountains, the other being Mt. Tom to the N, that form the backdrop for the region as seen from the eastward prairies.

Believed to have been named for unsuccessful presidential candidate Stephen A. Douglas, whose strong stand against secession won him the admiration, if not the vote, of Lincoln supporters in the 1860 election.

Douglas Mountain looking W from the highway over Guy Hill. Photographed 1989.

Douglas Mountain to the left and Mt. Tom to the right, looking N from the top of Sheep Mountain (a.k.a. Centennial Cone) c. 1915. The old Claude Ballinger Ranch, later known as the Bingham Ranch, can be seen in the open basin directly over the tops of the trees.

CROWELL COLLECTION

Drew Hill

High mountain pass between Betty Creek and Ralston Creek drainages. Accommodates Drew Hill Road.

S/b Ralston Buttes Quad.
S34, T2S, R71W.
Elv. ab. 8200'.

Named for Drew Ranch. (See Stage Stops.)

Chrysoberyl was mined on Drew Hill, along with muscovite and black tourmaline (poor quality).

Ely Hill

A mountain overlooking Bay State School.

1942 Black Hawk Quad.
S11, T3S, R72W.
Elv. 10058'.

Summit is 0.5 mile due N of Bay State School.

History unknown.

Enter Mountain

A high, bald-faced mountain overlooking the E entrance of Golden Gate Canyon from the N.

S/b Ralston Buttes Quad.
S20, T3S, R70W.
Elv. ab. 7150'.

{Var name: **Big Hill.**

EDITORS' NOTE: Guy Hill was also called Big Hill, but this came later, after Enter Mountain had been abandoned for the toll road through Tucker Gulch.}

During the winter of 1858-59 the Pike's Peak gold rush lured an estimated 50,000 people to Cherry Creek to search for float gold in the streams that spilled out of the mountains. The easy pickings were soon gone, but lack of experience as to how to search for gold at its source kept would-be gold miners from following the streams into the mountains. In spring 1859 an experienced Georgia gold miner by the name of John Gregory, searching the mountains, found a promising lead—pieces of burnt-orange quartz shot through with gold. As he hiked back to the prairie, he blazed a wagon road through to the edge of the mountains.

On May 4, 1859, he returned to the interior with a party of goldseekers from Indiana. His trace led straight up the face of this mountain.

John Gregory's subsequent discovery of lode gold, when he washed four dollars worth of gold out of a pan of dirt, forever put an end to charges that the Pike's Peak gold fields were a hoax.

The original road to Gregory's was lost until recently. As a result, quotes lamenting the difficulties of the climb are often assigned other routes by contemporary historians.

(Compiled from: Koch, Mary, 1978, *The lost highway:* Golden Transcript, Dec. 1, 1978.)

A careful study of the mountaintop against the sky from the N side of Golden reveals a niche much like that of a gunsight. The niche is formed by rocks thrown aside to accommodate a road. Closer inspection of the site reveals a tumble of rocks below and to either side of a solid rock ledge approximately two feet high and eight feet wide. The loose rocks may have served as a crude ramp. If so, teams would have been unhitched from the wagons and driven around the rocky lip. Once above it, and rehitched to the end of the wagon tongue with long chains, they were then able to pull the wagon up the loose rock and over the ledge.

(For more about the road up the face of this mountain see original road to Gregory's <u>in</u> Historical Routes. Also see Enter Mountain Site <u>in</u> Burial Sites—Historic.)

Enter Mountain as seen from the top of Washington Hill in Golden. This particular angle of Golden against the rural backdrop of the Front Range was a favorite of advertising media before the arrival of the county shops, and later the Coors subdivision known as Mountain Ridge. Photographed 1979.

Forsberg Peak

Overlooks Bowser Hill from the E.

S/b Ralston Buttes Quad.
S12, T3S, R71W.
Elv. 7829' (1948 RBQ).

Named for homesteader George(?) Forsberg. On January 29, 1902, one Mary J. Forsberg signed the autograph book of Christina Wikstrom, a neighbor. Hilda Forsberg signed the book on February 19, 1902.

Galbraith Mountain

A prominent peak NW of Golden.
1994 Ralston Buttes Quad.
S29, T3S, R70W.
Elv. 7169'.

Named for Den Galbraith, Colorado School of Mines Professor and Golden area historian, 1918-1974.

Every October at Golden's "greatest social event," a wine and cheese tasting party held in memory of Galbraith, a $3,000 scholarship to the Colorado School of Mines is presented to a Golden High School student.

Galbraith wrote 23 articles for the Golden Transcript which ran for over 20 weeks in 1973. The Jefferson County Library Foundation is currently raising funds to print a one-book compilation of these articles entitled "The Galbraith Chronicles."

Galbraith Mountain, center right, as seen from the First Presbyterian Church. Mt. Tom is in the distant background to the right. Photographed 1991.

Goat Hill

Located on Crawford Gulch Road ab. 3 miles from the Crawford Gulch/GGC junction.
S/b 1942 Ralston Buttes Quad.
S2-3, T3S, R71W.

The 1942 RBQ shows a steep road climb out of the bottom of Dry Creek near the Wikstrom homestead and up the mountain to the E. This was Goat Hill. The road was very narrow. Later relocations of the road, together with subsequent widening and reductions in the grade, have smoothed out the conditions that gave Goat Hill its name.

For the road's location prior to Goat Hill, see the 1906 BQ.

WIKSTROM COLLECTION

The Wikstrom surrey with the fringe on top, c. 1905. Taken on the public road beside Dry Creek, looking E. The backdrop is Goat Hill. It accommodates today's highway. The original Goat Hill climb began out of sight to the left. Wikstrom ranch buildings are in the background.

The man holding the horse is John Wikstrom. The boy in the front seat is John's nephew, Oscar Dahlberg. The women are unidentified. On the ground is Oscar's father, Nels Dahlberg.

Guy Hill

Directly E of Guy Gulch.

1965 Ralston Buttes Quad.
S22, T3S, R71W.
Elv. 8104'.

{Var. name: **Big Hill,** a name commonly applied to heights which accommodated roads.

Var. name: **Flag Hill.** In early aircraft days, large flags were flown on top of the hill to signal its height to pilots.}

Named for John Guy, homesteader, 1859. John Guy gave his name to this mountain, to the gulch to the W, and to the stage stop in the bottom of the gulch.

> "Guy Hill can now boast of a newspaper—*Sickle and Sheaf*—which made its first appearance three weeks ago. Its general make-up would indicate that it is pub-

lished in the interest of Guy Hill and East Denver. The local editor wears hay-seed in his hair and makes it uphill work for us to collect original items."

(Source: Colo. Transcript, Sept. 12, 1896.)

Fred Buckman, who bought the GGC toll station from James Bond, named his son Guy Hill Buckman. Guy Hill, who was born in the toll station, became a prominent rancher in the region and in later years owned a coal and feed yard in Golden.

Looking N up empty, eerie Guy Gulch. The summit of Guy Hill is in the distance. Photographed 1981.

Hartzell Hill

A short, steep hill over a small saddle S of the creek in Tucker Gulch. The old road over Hartzell Hill is directly S of the 2-mile marker.

> *S/b 1906 Blackhawk Quad.*
> *S20, T3S, R70W (SW quarter of section).*
> *Elv. ab. 6400'.*

Accommodated early GGC wagon road. Road remnants can still be seen from the highway which now follows the creek around the base of the hill.

Origin of name and correct spelling unknown. On July 1, 1868, one Frank A. Hartzell dissolved his co-partnership under the firm name of Hartzell, Brown & Co., (Colo. Transcript, Jan. 6, 1869). There may be a connection between this hill and Frank Hartzell.

The old pass over Hartzell Hill is directly ahead (see arrow). Photographed 1994.

The Highgrade

Denotes that portion of the road which is the greatest distance between the creekbed and the Tucker Gulch road.

S/b Ralston Buttes Quad.

S20, T3S, R70W. (See 0.5-mile section of road in SW corner of section).

The name came into use as an appellation of that piece of new road built uphill out of the creekbed in the 1930s.

The Highgrade begins at Logan's sandpit and ends at the E foot of Hartzell Hill. The top curve of the Highgrade, near Hartzell Hill, was recently widened.

The mountain ground S of the Highgrade has recently been purchased by Jeffco Open Space.

Junction Hill

S/b Black Hawk Quad.

S1, T3S, R72W.

Elv. approx. 8740'.

The W side of Michigan Hill is called Junction Hill.

The name Junction comes from the Junction Ranch which was named for its location at the junction of the Gregory Toll Road with the Enterprise Toll Road. One of the buildings, an old barn, is still standing W of the road.

TRIPP COLLECTION

Junction Ranch from the top of Junction Hill, a.k.a. Michigan Hill. Bear Mountain, a.k.a. Tremont, with its granite spires is directly ahead. In more recent times this is known as the Lee place. The barn, center left, is still standing and has recently received a new roof.

Michigan Hill

This hill is the N shoulder of Black Hawk Mountain. The hill accommodates the GGC Road over the high ground between the Guy Gulch and Ralston Creek drainages. The N/S Gilpin-Jefferson county line is crossed on the summit of this pass. The E side of the hill is called Michigan Hill. The W side of the hill is called Junction Hill for the old Junction Ranch which was located approximately halfway up the hill.

> *S/b Black Hawk Quad.*
> *S1, T3S, R72W.*
> *Elv. approx. 8740'.*

Origin of the name *Michigan* unknown. It may be that a company from Michigan gave Michigan Hill its name.

Or the name may have originated with goldseekers from Michigan City, Indiana.

The Mine

A mountain overlooking Bay State School.

> *S/b Black Hawk Quad.*
> *S15, T3S, R72W.*
> *Elv. 9563' (1942 BQ).*

Summit is 0.5 mile SW of the Bay State School.

Named for the sulphur mine located on the mountain.

Mt. Tom

1965 Ralston Buttes Quad.
S5, T3S, R71W.
Elv. 9735'.

{Var. name: **Golden Peak** in 1906 Blackhawk Quad and Nell's 1910 Map of Colorado.

Var. name: **Lady Bug Peak** for the great numbers of lady bugs which congregate in late August and September on the top of the peak. Lady bugs gather in this fashion on high points throughout the mountains to prepare for hibernation. When the temperatures drop, the lady bugs crawl into crevices and under leaves for the winter.}

Named for Tom Golden, founder of Golden Gate City at E entrance to Golden Gate Canyon. Tom Golden is also credited with naming Golden (see Cities).

The peak is the site of the crash of a B-25 bomber on Tuesday, April 8, 1952. Ten airmen and one civilian were killed while flying from Leavenworth, Kansas, to Denver. For two days bad weather obscured the crash site. Thursday, April 10, the morning dawned clear and cold.

"This is the tragic scene on Golden Peak, 25 miles northwest of Denver, where a B-25 bomber crashed Tuesday, killing its 11 occupants. The camera is looking east toward Denver. It shows the path of human and mechanical destruction left as the big plane crashed a short distance below this scene and smashed its way up the mountainside. The bomber roared in at 200 miles per hour just over the hills in the background. All 11 persons aboard died instantly. The wrecked plane was found yesterday."

(Source: Rocky Mountain News, April 11, 1952, caption, front page photo by Morris A. Engle.)

"Rancher Hiked Up Peak to Crash Site Alone. William Koch, a 22-year-old-bachelor-rancher, was the first to reach the wreckage of the B-25 which crashed near the summit of Golden peak northwest of Golden. This is his account of his findings.

By William Koch

I was the first to reach the wreckage, I guess.

It was the most horrible sight I've ever looked upon. I don't think I'll ever forget it. I didn't know what to do. They were all dead. And there was just nothing I could do for them.

I was doing some chores on my ranch when I first saw the black hole in the timber near the top of the peak. The peak is about three miles away. But I knew something had happened, because I'd never seen that black hole before.

I told some friends in Golden about it. Then I started the long hike up the mountains. There was a lot of snow and that slowed me down. But I got there about 10:30.

Mt. Tom. Notice the scar from the B-25 bomber crash site near the summit. The old Tom Pearce, Sr., homestead is in the foreground. Photographed 1990.

There it was. Bodies were all around. The plane was a mass of twisted metal. I found eleven men. I was looking for survivors, of course. But there weren't any.

One place I found a man's jaw and part of a face. I wanted to run away. But I knew I should stay. There was nothing I could do, but I knew I should stay.

One man had been burned pretty badly. Another man, his head decapitated, hung from a tree. And all over there were things—instruments from the plane, and other things. I saw half a leg with the shoe still on the foot jutting out of the snow. It was awful.

Parachutes were hanging in the trees as if the men had tried to bail out. But I guess that isn't so. I guess they didn't see the mountain till the last seconds. The fog was awfully thick last Tuesday. You could hardly see your hand in front of your face.

I didn't touch anything. I knew the Air Force would want to see things just as they were. But I did look for the men. I knew there couldn't be any survivors, but still I thought there was a chance there might be and I might be able to do something.

I'll never forget how quiet it was up there before the rescue parties arrived. There was all that wreckage and all those bodies. I was glad to see you fellows come."

(Source: The Denver Post, Friday, April 11, 1952, interview with rancher William Koch, p. 15.)

Capt. Hilton B. Wilcox, Jr., Decatur, Illinois, was 26 years old when he died in the crash of the B-25 on Mt. Tom. Today, 46 years later, much of the record regarding the crash is still sealed.

U.S. AIR FORCE

"Clouds rolled back from the mountain areas west of Denver yesterday and disclosed the tragic fate of 11 airmen missing on a B-25 bomber since Tuesday morning.

On the southeastern summit of Golden Peak, locally known as Tom's Peak, 10½ miles northwest of Golden, the blackened, twisted remains of the once sleek twin-engine aircraft were scattered through a 75-yard swath of broken lodge pole pine trees.

Low-hanging clouds which have shrouded the area for the past three days caused the crash of the silver bomber, after it lost its way while making a land approach to Lowry Air Force Base.

The plane was last heard from at 10:44 a.m., Tuesday, when it radioed the control tower at Lowry Air Base and reported it was 45 miles out, flying at an altitude of 9000 feet and was approaching the field on instruments.

Crash site of B-25 bomber on Mt. Tom, Tuesday, April 8, 1952.

The bomber was apparently flying at the same elevation when it crashed head-on into the side of 10,003-Golden Peak, striking the almost perpendicular side of the peak about 400 feet from the summit.

It struck the boulder-strewn mountain side on an almost straight east-west lie, 25 air miles from Denver. All 11 passengers and crewmen were killed instantly when the plane exploded against the mountain side, and burned briefly afterward.

Scores of Civil Air Patrol, Lowry Air Base and Fourth Rescue Squadron aircraft searched Tuesday and Wednesday for the missing bomber, but were prevented from making a thorough search of the mountain and foothill areas west of the city by the persistently low-clinging clouds. When the weather lifted yesterday, search planes again took to the air to hunt the wooded and rock-strewn hills and mountains… William Koch, a rancher living west of Golden was one of the first to arrive at the crash scene at 10:30 a.m. He was soon joined by other search parties, who battled their way over high boulders, fallen trees and hip-deep snow drifts up the steep slopes.

Exhausted searchers reaching the scene were struck speechless by the devastation which met their eyes. A funeral-like atmosphere settled over the area as searchers went about, speaking in hushed tones as they collected bodies, bits of clothing and other personal possessions of the dead…

The largest part of the airplane found was the tail section. It was found near the bottom of the 75-by-30-yard swath. Another twisted piece—possibly the nose section and part of the fuselage—was found near the top of the blackened cut…"

(Source: The Denver Post, Friday, April 11, 1952, report by Al Nukkula captioned: *11 Die in B-25 on Golden Peak*, p. 5.)

"The official air force investigation of the crash of the ill-fated B-25 bomber may never reveal why the pilots of the plane failed to detect the change in instrument signals when they passed over Lowry air force base in a heavy fog last Tuesday.

The plane, on a routine flight, was following Lowry's radio beam on instruments from the first point of contact forty-five miles east of Denver.

When the plane passed the field, the radio beam signal automatically changes. But the plane continued on its east-to-west path, and crashed a few minutes later into the face of Golden peak twenty-five air miles from Denver."

(Source: The Denver Post, Friday, April 11, 1952, report by Thor Severson captioned: *Wreckage Fails to Show Why B-25 Passed Lowry*, p. 15.)

"Weary rescue parties began the grim task Friday of packing the bodies of eleven men down from the steep and heavily timbered slopes of Golden Peak...

An air of solemnity hung over the seared peak as pack-horse patrols began picking their way through waist-deep snow down the hillside with their grisly burden to waiting hearses below.

Low-hanging clouds and heavy fog hampered the rescue efforts, but volunteer civilian parties and air force patrols went ahead, nevertheless, with their grim work."

(Source: The Denver Post, Friday, April 11, 1952, report by Thor Severson captioned: *Rescue Parties Take Out Bodies by Pack Horse*, p. 15.)

Before the site was abandoned, those portions of the plane still intact were blown up, scattering pieces of metal the length of the scar and into the trees on either side. This was done to prevent the possibility of the bomber's being mistaken for other downed planes.

The scar, now overgrown with aspen trees and raspberry bushes, is clearly visible on the E face.

Pole Hill

A segment of the wagon road up the E side of Michigan Hill.
S/b Black Hawk Quad.
S1, T3S, R72W.
Elv. ab. 8600'.

A hill on the larger climb up Michigan Hill out of the Guy Gulch drainage. Took its name from the large number of poles laid in the marshy ground to provide a solid base for wagon wheels.

Ralston Buttes

1965 Ralston Buttes Quad.
S30, T2S, R70W.
Elv. 7788'.

{Var. names: **Ralston Peak, Red Hill, Storm Peak, Beartooth Mountain, Indian Head Mountain.**}

An outcropping on the Ralston Dike. The dike takes its name from Ralston Creek. These are the buttes that name the Ralston Buttes Quad.

The dike was caused by a volcanic eruption which occurred about 64 million years ago. The eruption burst through what is called the Golden Fault to produce the Ralston Dike, North Table Mountain and South Table Mountain.

(Compiled from: Bond, R. F., 1989, *The land persists:* Jeffco Hist. Com. contest entry.)

The E face of the Ralston Buttes above Ralston Dam. The white scar in the middle ground is an old clay pit. Photographed 1997.

The W face of the Ralston Buttes as seen from Belcher Hill Road. Photographed 1997.

Robinson Hill

The S shoulder of Douglas Mountain as intersected by Robinson Hill Road.
1965 Ralston Buttes Quad
S19-20-17, T3S, R71W.

Named for homesteader George Robinson.

George Robinson homesteaded on what were called the Elk Creek flats S of the present-day road. (See Belcher Hill for information on the Robinson Hill picnics.)

The Robinson Hill road across the flats was paved in April 1997.

June Crowell on Robinson Hill Road. June later lost her life in an automobile accident on this same stretch of road.

Saulsbury Peak

Due E of Taylor Peak between Tucker Gulch and Clear Creek Canyon.
S/b Ralston Buttes Quad.
S26, T3S, R71W.
Elv. 7853' (1942 RBQ).

Named for homesteader A.(?) Saulsbury. Remnants of the house and potato cellar can be found on the S slope of the drainage immediately to the W of the peak.

Ruins of Saulsbury homestead below Saulsbury Peak. Photographed 1981.

Saulsbury potato cellar ruins. The potato cellar is located by walking W from the homestead buildings to the drainage coming down from the N and following up this drainage ab. 0.5 mile. Photographed 1981.

Schrell Hill

Overlooks Jack Pearce Ranch and White Ranch Park.

N of White Ranch Road.
S/b Ralston Buttes Quad.
S2, T3S, R71W.
Elv. ab. 8200'.

Named for homesteader Schrell.

Schoolhouse Slope

S/b Ralston Buttes Quad.
S15-14-13, T3S, R71W.
Elv. ab. 7700'.

The high slope behind the original location of the Guy Hill School is commonly referred to as the schoolhouse slope. This slope rises on the extreme E side of S15 and falls off on the W side of S13.

Smith Hill

Smith Hill is not a singular peak but the ridge at the top of the gulch that bears its name. At 8752', the steep gulch walls give way abruptly to open meadows. One-half mile higher, at 8940', travelers outbound from Clear Creek leave the meadows and enter thick timber. This high ridge is the W shoulder of Ely Hill. Water falling on the gulch side of the ridge heads for Clear Creek, water falling in the timber heads for Ralston Creek.

1942 Black Hawk Quad.
S10, T3S, R72W.

Takes its name from the wagon track hewed through the gulch by road builders Ensign B. and N. K. Smith in 1860 in building their Enterprise Toll Road.

In naming Smith Hill, the Smith boys also gave their name to Smith Creek and the Smith Hill Ranch. The ranch made its headquarters at the top of the hill where the road divides one way to Junction Ranch and the other to Robinson Hill. Not apparent from the main road is another road ab. 0.8 mile above the junction. This road, not as old as the Enterprise Road, wanders off to the NW, eventually climbing through an unnamed tributary of Mesa Gulch to reach the top of Fourmile Gulch, or Dory Hill Road. This trace is not a public thoroughfare.

Stage coach drivers were the best liked, most honored people in the country through which they traveled. Their saleries averaged $300/month, in addition to the perks, which were considerable. Passengers riding on the seat with the driver treated him to drinks and cigars on the road. Drinks were also free at the stations. However, drivers seldom drank on the road and many not at all, owing to their being temperence men.

Their dress was the finest, their clothing made to order, boots and hats of the best designs. They were not tipped with mere coins but with silk handkerchiefs, good cigars, silver-mounted cigar cases, gloves, boots, hats, etc. Autocrats of the road at all times, their orders were expected to obeyed with the greatest celerity.

KEN AND LELA (WHITE) GREEN COLLECTION

The water tank at the bottom of Smith Hill looking E.

...when the mountain road to Central was the terror of the West.

Among those who handled the reins in and out of Denver, the chief was Bill Opdyke, who drove the mountain line to Central City. That was a route required the maximum of skill and endurance, and Bill drove it for years. He was a man of powerful form, with an arm like a piece of steel, bluff, hearty, good-natured, daring, and unexcelled in the management of a coach-and-six.

One of the long descents on the Central City route…was known as Smith's Hill. Down this Bill was accustomed to drive at a furious gallop, and sometimes on a dead run…

The Dutchman's ranch was a few miles this side of Blackhawk, to which camp [the Dutchman] made a daily trip with milk. Returning home late in the afternoon, he would be ascending Smith's Hill with his old horse and cart just about the time the coach came along. The milk peddler frequently got in the way of the coach, and Bill used to curse him roundly… The old Dutchman paid no attention to the warning, so one day Bill calculated his distance and took a wheel off the cart as neat and clean as if cut with an axe, without even checking the speed of the coach, and leaving the milk man a picture of consternation and despair.

For several days the Dutchman disappeared from the hill. He was having his cart repaired. The day he drove it home I was sitting on the box with Jake Hawk, whose run it was that day, and as we started down the Smith's Hill grade, Jake called my attention to the old fellow, near the foot of the hill, beating his horse in a frantic attempt to make a turnout ahead of the coach. He got there in safety, and as the coach swept by at its usual speed, the Dutchman looked up and, seeing Jake Hawk on the box, exclaimed with a tone of relief: "Mine Got! I dot it var de Opdyken!"

(Compiled from: William R. Thomas, "Lectures on History," in Davidson, L. J., and Blake, F., eds., 1947, *Rocky Mountain tales:* Norman, Univ. of Okla. Press., p. 104-105.)

Songer Mountain

S of Ralston Creek and E of Drew Hill Road.
S/b Ralston Buttes Quad.
S35, T2S, R71W.
Elv. 8333' (1948 RBQ).

Named for homesteader Frederick Songer.

Old foundation still in existence. (For more about the Songer family, read Bond, R. F., 1989, *The land persists:* Jeffco Hist. Com. contest entry.)

Taylor Peak

Overlooks Guy Gulch from the E. Rises in a nearly direct line between Guy Gulch to the W and Saulsbury Peak to the E.
S/b Ralston Buttes Quad.
S27, T3S, R71W.
Elv. 7838' (1965 RBQ).

Named for homesteader Taylor.

{Var. name: **Nankervis Hill.** Dedicated September 1996 in memory of Sam Galin Nankervis, Golden Gate native, killed in a bulldozer accident in Elk Creek. (see Elk Creek <u>in</u> Drainages.) A flat cement stone, approximately 3' by 2', has been laid under a lone pine tree at the top of the hill. A bronze plaque in the center of the stone reads *Nankervis Hill.*}

Sam Nankervis, for whom Nankervis Hill, a.k.a. Taylor Peak, is named.

Jeffco's Road and Bridge Central Shops at the entrance to Golden Gate Canyon are also named after Sam.

PEG NANKERVIS COLLECTION

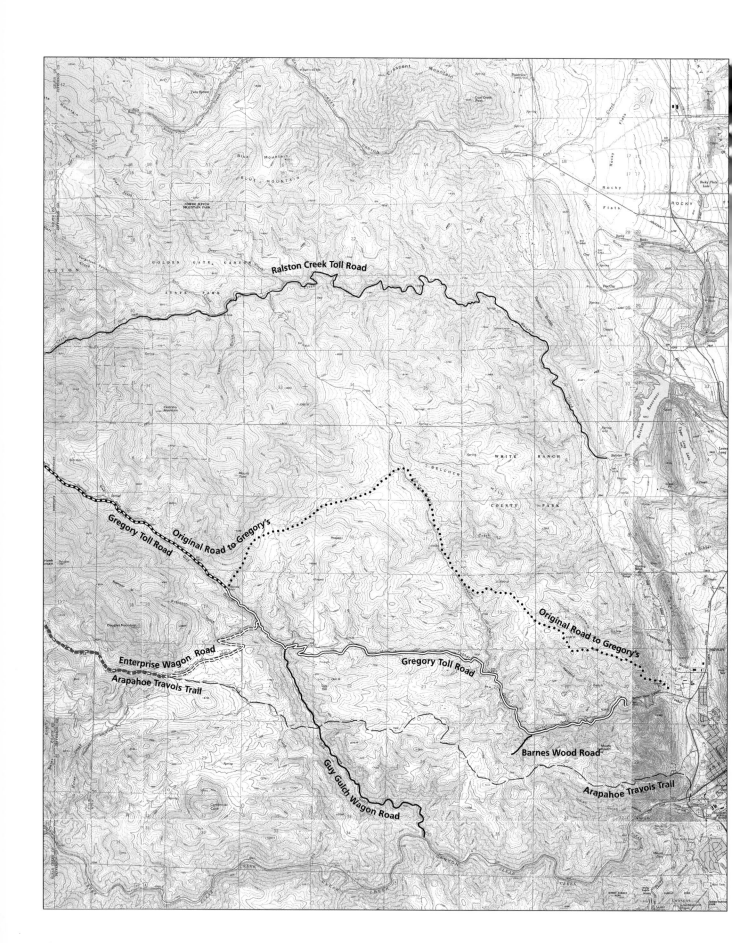

Ralston Creek Toll Road

Gregory Toll Road

Original Road to Gregory's

Original Road to Gregory's

Gregory Toll Road

Enterprise Wagon Road

Arapahoe Travois Trail

Guy Gulch Wagon Road

Barnes Wood Road

Arapahoe Travois Trail

Historical Routes

Arapahoe Travois Trail

S/b Golden, Ralston Buttes and Black Hawk quads.

Left the prairie at S28, T3S, R70W, GQ. Traveled W through Indian Gulch (pioneer designation), arriving on top of the mountains at S30, T3S, R70W, RBQ.

Proceeded due W, descending Taylor Gulch to cross Guy Gulch at S27, T3S, R71W, reaching Elk Creek at S21, T3S, R71W. Thence approximated contemporary Smith Hill Road up Elk Creek and around the W side of Douglas Mountain and down to the N fork of Clear Creek in S21, T3S, R72W, BQ.

Ab. 16 miles long. This good trail leaving the valley N of Clear Creek is the Arapahoe counterpart, albeit much shorter, of the famous Ute trail which climbed onto the backs of the mountains S of Clear Creek. The Ute used their trail to travel all the way through the mountains to the western slope. The Arapahoe probably traveled no further than the headwaters of the N fork of Clear Creek, as the big parks on the western slope were under the control of unfriendly nations, including the Ute.

> "In just about 50 years, from 1840 to 1890, the plains Indian civilization reached its apogee and then plunged to the verge of extinction. In his 1885 painting *Caught in the Act*, Charles Russell, the 'cowboy artist,' depicted a starving Indian family reduced to stealing ranchers' cattle. By this time the plains tribes had suffered the ravages of the white man's diseases, the debasing effects of his whiskey, the harassment of his army, and the grim hardship resulting from his senseless slaughter of the buffalo. Having smashed the Indian's way of life beyond repair, the American government confined him to the reservation."
>
> (Source: Garraty, John, 1966, *The American Nation, a history of the United States:* New York, Harper & Row, p. 470-471.)

By 1875 reservations for the plains Indians had been established, but the process of confining the Indian proved long and painful. Settlers throughout the region were visited by Indians both begging and bartering until well after the turn of the century.

The Arapahoe Travois Trail crossed these meadows at the top of Devil's Garden Gulch. To follow the trail coming from the E, start at the notch in the center of the skyline. From here the trail is out of sight as it rounds the nearer shoulder of mountain. Now it is coming into sight to the SE above the remains of the Otto Ramstetter homestead. Passing the homestead buildings the trail enters the trees to the left, heading for a pass over the lower E shoulder of the Saulsbury into the big basins at the head of Miller Gulch. Photographed 1981.

View from the Arapahoe Travois Trail (later followed by a wagon road) as it crosses the E shoulder of the Saulsbury. Douglas Mountain is in the distance. The nearer bald summit is Guy Hill. Directly ahead are the high meadows that drain into Miller Gulch. Photographed 1982.

The only known historical reference to the Arapahoe Travois Trail was made by Horace Greeley writing from Mountain City, Gregory Diggings, June 1859:

> "I hear that the Arapahoes say that a good "lodge-pole trail"—that is, one which a pony may traverse with one end of the lodge-poles on his back, the other trailing behind him—exists from this point to the open prairie where Clear Creek debouches from the mountains, a trail which doubtless winds along the steep sides of the ravines and avoids the rugged heights necessarily traversed by the miner's wagon-road."
>
> (Source: Greeley, Horace, 1860, *An overland journey from New York to San Francisco in the summer of 1859:* New York, Saxton, Barker and Co., p. 121.)

Horace Greeley, American journalist and political leader, visited this region in 1859. His eye for detail and his lucid prose afford the most complete description known of the original road to Gregory's. The conclusion he draws with regard to the Arapahoe avoiding the rugged heights, however, is incorrect.

The travois trail journeyed along the backs of the mountains. As such, it put the enormous mountain parks SE of Guy Hill less than a hour's ride from the prairie up through Indian Gulch. Gus Koch, pioneer rancher and a friend of the Indians, told of how it amused the Indians to see the white man push his animals through the dust of the narrow, crooked canyons when the backs of the mountains were so broad. Another story Gus told was of how the Indian boys liked to have him put iron shoes on their ponies.

Only known contemporary reference: Koch, Mary, 1979, *The first wagon to the Gregory diggings:* Standley Lake Collection, Colo. Hist. Soc. Centennial Essay Contest Entry, p. 12.

ISABELLA (BENGSON) KOCH COLLECTION

Gus Koch breaking a horse. Ernest Koch, Jr., is leaning against the corral. The man on foot inside the corral is unidentified. In the background is the residence of homesteaders Ernest S., Sr., and Elizabeth Koch.

Barnes Wood Road

Length indeterminate.

S/B Ralston Buttes Quad.
S25, T3S, R71W.

Old wood road. Plainly visible when the snow is deep enough to fill the ruts but not deep enough to cover the adjoining grasses.

There may be a connection between this wood road and the David Barnes who came to Golden in 1864 and built the town's first flour mill. Barnes' Premium Flouring Mills offered custom grinding and flour and feed. The site is now occupied by the Golden Mill. The elegant old mansion owned by Roberta and Bill Law on 622 Water Street was built by David Barnes.

Convict Highway

That portion of the GGC road located in Tucker Gulch.

By the turn of the century the road at the canyon's E entrance had been moved from its original location beside the creek* to run past the Brunel ranch buildings.

> (*For the road's original location see the John Pierce map, Surveyor
> General's Office, Denver, February 10, 1867.)

As the mountains began to fill with farms early in the 20th century, farmers increasingly complained of being unable to get to town to sell their produce because of road washouts due to the road's repeated crossing of the creek.

In the early 1900s chain gangs from the state prison labored to move the entire length of the Tucker Gulch road out of the creekbed and onto the N side of the creek.

Hence the name "the Convict Highway."

> **"CONVICTS START WORK ON ROADS**
> *Prisoners Prefer Hard Outdoor Labor to Gloomy Walls of Bastille*
> Secretary Clarence E. Hagar of the state board of charities and corrections returned yesterday from a trip to Canon City, where he inspected the state penitentiary and conferred with Warden John Cleghorn relative to certain new measures passed by the recent legislature. Two of the bills relate to work upon the public roads, and the warden is now preparing to send out regularly equipped gangs of convicts to carry out some of the important work laid out."

> (Source: *Daily Pickings:* Golden, Colorado, State Industrial School newspaper,
> April 26, 1907, v. 2, no. 102.)

It was during this time that the rock columns that named Golden Gate City were toppled by dynamite work going on beneath the columns. (See Golden Gates <u>in</u> Potpourri. Also see Golden Gate City <u>in</u> Cities.)

Enterprise Wagon Road

Ascended Smith Hill. Divided at the top, running NE to Junction Ranch and SE to Robinson Hill. Named for the Enterprise Mining District where it originated.

S/b Black Hawk and Ralston Buttes quads.

The Enterprise Wagon Road Company received authorization October 3, 1861:

> "An act to incorporate the Enterprise Wagon Road Company by Nelson K. Smith, Clinton M. Tyler and others; a road known as Smith Road commences at or near the Michigan House in Cold Springs Valley to the B. F. Dalton Mill near Black Hawk in the Gregory Diggings, Colo. Territory. Also includes the Kehler & Phleger Road. Tolls as follows: Wagons drawn by one span of horses, mules or oxen or carriage by any animal, 15 cents each. Horsemen 10 cents each. Livestock 5 cents head."

> (Source: Acts of the Territorial Legislature, <u>in</u> Ramstetter, James K., 1996, *Life in the early days,* p. 13.)

> "The Enterprise road was built by N. K. and E. B. Smith from Golden Gate to Black Hawk... Later, N. K. Smith became a prominent citizen of Boulder and built a fine home at the corner of 13th and Hill streets (now the site of the Christian Science church.)"

> (Source: Boulder Camera, 1945, *Toll roads in Boulder County and the pioneers who constructed them:* April 3, 1945.)

According to the Western Mountaineer of June 28, 1860, the road up from Clear Creek connected with the Gregory Toll Road at the foot of Robinson Hill. This nails down the Guy Gulch leg of the toll road.

The Rocky Mountain News of August 2, 1860, reports the new road opened by Smith as reaching the toll road 3 miles above Guy's. Three miles above Guy's is the old Junction Ranch on the W side of Michigan Hill, a.k.a. Junction Hill. The legend on the 1866 Map of Gilpin County (see Donald C. Kemp's *Colorado's Little Kingdom*) reads JUNCTION HOUSE, J. BOUTWELL. The map also carries the notation JUNCTION BRANCH.

However, Junction Ranch was not the commencement point for the Enterprise Toll Road. That honor, as outlined in the 1861 Act, goes to "the Michigan House in Cold Springs Valley," which was upstream from Junction Hill on Ralston Creek.

Some very fine remnants of rock walls on the old toll road may be seen to the E of today's road a short ways above Colorado 119 in Smith Creek. This is a steep road. While it served as a handy shortcut between the Gregory Toll Road and the N fork of Clear Creek, it is possible that heavily loaded freighters outbound from the N fork favored Dory Hill.

EDITORS' NOTE: See Ramstetter, James K., 1996, *Life in the early days,* for staging problems on the Smith Hill Road. This book is available at the Golden Feed Mill.

Golden Gate Canyon Road

Between 1933 and 1943 the Works Progress Administration (WPA) made considerable improvements to the road. These improvements included widening the road and constructing large concrete water ducts and rock reinforced walls. Henry Ramstetter, Sr., and his brothers-in-law August and Theodore Koch contracted for the dirt work on the road. Ernest Koch, Jr., another brother-in-law, supervised the building of the rock embankment walls.

(See Convict Highway for earlier road work.)

Work on paving the road through Tucker Gulch and Guy Gulch began in 1972 and was completed in 1975.

Today's highway follows the Gregory Toll Road as far as the top of Dory Hill. On Dory Hill the old and the new separate. Today's highway continues W to Colorado 119, whereas the toll road turned S down Fourmile Gulch to the N fork of Clear Creek.

COLO. HIST. SOC.

Buggy on the Golden Gate Canyon Road.

BESSIE (BROWN) NARE COLLECTION

Construction of the still-extant bridge at the entrance to Crawford Gulch, c. 1930. Note that portion of road in the creek bottom being abandoned.

TROY SCOTT PARKER

Golden Gate Canyon Road bridge over Crawford Gulch, 1996.

Original road to Gregory's

Ab. 22 miles long. The first wagon road into the mountains N of Clear Creek Canyon. Engineered in 1859 by John H. Gregory who led a party of Indiana gold seekers from Arapahoe City through the wilderness to the north fork of Clear Creek where Black Hawk is now located. It was Gregory's discovery of lode gold deep in the interior that put an end to charges that the Pike's Peak gold fields were a hoax.

S/b Golden, Ralston Buttes and Black Hawk quads.

Using fire wheels (wagons with the back axle removed) to accommodate their supplies, John Gregory led the goldseekers up Enter Mountain (the mountain directly N of the entrance to Golden Gate Canyon) on May 4, 1859. On May 6, 1859, he discovered gold high on the N fork of Clear Creek and immediately sent his family in Georgia $5,000.*

*"My wife will be a lady and my children will be educated."

(Source: Byers, W. N., 1901, *Encyclopedia of biography of Colorado:* Chicago, Century Pub. Co., v. 1, p. 36.)

The face of Enter Mountain as seen by Horace Greeley when he wrote, "I never before saw teams forced up such a precipice..." The original road to Gregory's entered the draw in the lower center beneath the sunlit slope, angled uphill to the middle ridge as outlined in the sun, and turned sharply W, climbing to the summit along the line of shadow. Once on top the road swung slightly to the left around the true point of summit and followed the top ridge line as it disappears to the left behind the nearer mountain. Photographed 1979.

The angle of ascent of the steep grade up Enter Mountain (the original road to the Gregory diggings) can be clearly seen against the skyline as viewed from Golden Gate Canyon. Photographed 1980.

The original road to Gregory's followed the ridge line W from the top of Enter Mountain. Just out of sight to the left in the creek was Logan's sandpit. Photographed 1991.

Gregory left the prairie immediately N of the entrance to GGC (S20, T3S, R70W, GQ). Climbed 7120' Enter Mountain and proceeded W/NW along the backs of the mountains. Crossed over the pass (Bowser Hill) between Crawford Gulch and Dry Creek, descended into Dry Creek and followed up that creek to where it forks, and thence up the W fork. Crossed over the pass between Dry Creek and Guy Gulch and descended into Guy Gulch through Booten Gulch (S17, T3S, R71W, RBQ). From Centennial House in Guy Gulch his route approximated the contemporary Golden Gate Canyon Road as far as Dory Hill.

On Dory Hill at the top of the W fork of Fourmile Gulch* (NW¼ of S6, T3S, R72W), he swung S down the W side of the W fork of Fourmile Gulch to Clear Creek.

(*Not to be confused with the Four-mile Gulch that empties into Tucker Gulch. The Fourmile Gulch mentioned here is the Dory Hill Road.)

It should also be mentioned that the 1860 Burt and Berthoud map does not assign a name to what is now called Dory Hill. The 1866 Map of Gilpin County (in Donald C. Kemp's *Colorado's Little Kingdom*) calls it Blackhawk Hill.

Like moths to a flame goldseekers from the Cherry Creek diggings followed Gregory's trace into the interior.

"Auraria, June 8, 1859

...Men are perfectly wild and crazy...No man believes another, but goes to see for himself."

T."

(Source: Hafen, L. R., and A. W., 1961, *Reports from Colorado—The Wildman letters 1859-1865 with other related letters and newspaper reports*, 1859: Glendale, California, Clark Co. Letter sent from Denver City, p. 36.)

"June 14, 1859

Dear Mother...We are in a great hurry to get into the mines as every moment a great many are coming in and we want to get the start of them.

Thomas G. Wildman
Denver City"

(Source: *Ibid.*, p. 92-93.)

"The hill on which we were to make our first essay in climbing, rose to a height of one thousand six hundred feet in a little more than a mile—the ascent for most of the distance being more than one foot in three. I never before saw teams forced up such a precipice; yet there were wagons with ten or twelve hundred weight of mining tools, bedding, provisions, etc., being dragged by four to eight yoke of oxen up that giddy precipice, with four or five men lifting at the wheels of each. The average time consumed in the ascent is some two hours. Our mules, unused to such work, were visibly appalled..."

(Source: Greeley, Horace, 1860, *An overland journey from New York to San Francisco in the summer of 1859*: New York, Saxton Barker & Co., p. 116.)

Horace was injured on his journey across the prairies when his wagon went over,

"hitting the ground a most spiteful blow...I had a slight cut on my left cheek and a deep gouge from the sharp corner of a seat in my left leg below the knee..."

As a result of this injury the newspaperman was forced to ride his mule to the top of Enter Mountain.

"My companions all walked, but I was lame and had to ride, much to my mule's intense disgust. He was stubborn, but strong, and in time bore me safely to the summit...

We traveled some two miles along the crest of this mountain, then descended by a pitch equally sharp with the ascent, but shorter, to a ravine, in which we rested our weary animals and dined. That dinner—of cold ham, bread and cheese—was one of the best relished of any I ever shared."

(Source: *Ibid.*)

EDITORS' NOTE: Greeley and his party dined in the immediate vicinity of Sam Bowser's park at the N foot of Bowser Hill.

"The road was swarming with travelers. In the distance they were clambering right up a hill as abrupt as the roof of a cottage. It seemed incredible that any animal less agile than a mountain goat could reach the summit; yet this road, only five weeks old, was beaten like a turnpike; and far above us toiled men, mules and cattle, pigmies upon the alps. Wagons carrying less than half a ton were drawn up by twenty oxen, while those descending dragged huge trees in full branch and leaf behind them as brakes…"

We all dismounted to ascent except Mr. Greeley, still so lame that his over-taxed mule was compelled to carry him. The astonished brute yielded to destiny and climbed vigorously…

In an hour and a half we reached the summit. Far below, on the top of Table Mountain gleamed a little lake. At the foot of the long hill were the pigmies again; and beyond, the valley of the Platte with its dark timber and shining water. Before us mountain lay piled upon mountain; some grassy, others gaunt and bare. From most rose the pine, spruce and hemlock in perfect cones, interspersed with quivering aspens; while brilliant flowers clothed the desolate rocks with beauty.

…Up and down the steep mountain sides, across swift-running, ice-cold streams, over jagged rocks and through deep canyons overshadowed by sullen walls, we wound our toilsome way. An eager crowd kept pace with us; some walking, others with ox-wagons pack-horses or mules, and all pressing toward the mines."

(Source: Richardson, A. D., 1867, *Beyond the Mississippi:* New York, American Pub. Co., p. 180.-181)

One of the argonauts who shouldered his pack and trudged up Enter Mountain was H.A.W. Tabor. And the faithful companion left alone at the foot of the mountains to guard the wagons? None other than Augusta herself, who cared for their 21-month-old son and the livestock from July 1 until Tabor's return on July 26, 1859. For an entertaining and well-researched account of Augusta, read Betty Moynihan's *Augusta Tabor, a pioneering woman.*

"Arrapahoe, K.T., July 6, 1859

Messrs Editors…The road was exceeding steep and difficult to ascend. On arriving at the summit, I was astonished beyond measure at the scenery. Instead of barren and desolate mountains, we were greeted with beautiful garden plots, abounding with gooseberry and currant bushes, and orchards of wild plum and cherry. Parks of various dimensions and shapes, dotted with pine trees, and fringed with grassy openings; all planned and planted in nature's own beautiful order. The air was very cool and bracing. We seated ourselves beside a beautiful brook, clear as crystal, and so cold that one would imagine that it came from the heart of an iceberg. Leaving this magic scenery, we passed along through pine

The original road to Gregory's as seen from the Crawford Gulch Road is visible as a faint indentation running W through the Jully homestead meadows (see arrow). Douglas Mountain is in the background. The old Wikstrom homestead pastures occupy the slopes in the foreground. Photographed 1996.

groves and grassy openings, over gentle rolling land, when to our surprise we were compelled, in order to follow the road, to descend a mountain so steep that it might almost be called perpendicular…" [W. H. Kidd's letter to his editors from the gold mines. Published in the Missouri Democrat, July 20, 1859.]

(Source: Hafen, L. R., and A. W., 1961, *Reports from Colorado—The Wildman letters 1859-1865 with other related letters and newspaper reports, 1859*: Glendale, Calif., Clark Co., p. 111.)

EDITORS' NOTE: Following Gregory's trace the Kidd party descended a S shoulder of the Forsberg to the pass between the Crawford and Dry Creek drainages (Bowser Hill). Thence down the N side of Bowser Hill.

The easternmost portion of the original road to Gregory's (from the prairie up over Enter Mountain to the bottom of Guy Gulch) was abandoned two months later, July 1859, in favor of the toll road through Eight-mile Canyon (Tucker Gulch). The abandoned thoroughfare, however, except for the face of Enter Mountain itself, continued to be used by homesteaders and local commerce—sawmills, mines, etc.

Only known diary that deals with Gregory's engineering of the road: Albert Dean diary as excerpted in The Denver Post, 1927. (See Items of Interest. Also see Enter Mountain in Heights.)

Only known sketch of the original road to Gregory's: Richardson, A. D., 1867, *Beyond the Mississippi*: New York, American Pub. Co., p. 180.

Only known map: Burt, S. W., and Berthoud, E. L., 1860, *Quartz mining region of the Rocky Mountains*: Denver City, Rocky Mountain News Printing Co., insert.

Most comprehensive description known: Greeley, Horace, 1860, *An overland journey from New York to San Francisco in the summer of 1859*: New York, Saxton Barker & Co., p. 116-119.

Only known contemporary references: 1) Koch, Mary, 1979, *The first wagon to the Gregory diggings*: Standley Lake Library, Colo. Hist. Soc. Centennial Essay Contest Entry, p. 20. And 2) 1978, *The lost highway*: Golden Transcript, Dec. 1, 1978, p. 9 and 12.

Gregory Toll Road

July 1859, using black powder and teams (dynamite was not invented until 1866), Dan McCleery and Tom Golden wedged a wagon road upstream through the rocks and timber that choked the bottom of the gulch above Gate City.

Reaching the headwaters of the gulch, the narrow, crooked road climbed the hill and slithered and bumped down through rocks and thick timber into the bottom of a deeper waterway. A mile up this waterway (where Centennial House now stands) the new road reached the original road.

From Centennial House in Guy Gulch (S17, T3S, R71W, RBQ) to Dory Hill and thence down to the N fork of Clear Creek the Gregory Toll Road overlay the original road to Gregory's.

"July 18, 1859

...A new road has been discovered to the base of the mountains, which, when opened out properly, will prove a great advantage to the entire gold region; the old road being one of the most dangerous character, crossing mountains so steep that to ascend or descend them with cattle would appear almost impossible.

K
Rocky Mountain City"

(Source: Hafen, L. R., and A. W., 1961, *Reports from Colorado—The Wildman letters 1859-1865 with other related letters and newspaper reports, 1859:* Glendale, California, Clark Co., p. 127.)

"After [Greeley] left me Denver grew monotonous and I again started for the mountains. At Clear creek under the vast shadow of Table Mountain I found a new town springing up called Golden City... A few miles further, a few rudimentary log huts were named Golden Gate. The hill-road [up Enter Mountain]...was already abandoned. I entered the mountains by a newly-cut thoroughfare, threading the easy canyon of a tumbling, foamy brook, enclosed by gloomy walls more than a thousand feet in height.

The narrow pathway resounded with the tread of many feet, some slow and inelastic from weariness and disappointment; others keeping step to the jubilant song, 'I'm bound for the land of gold.' Horses oxen and mules struggled on, heavily loaded with shovels, sacks of flour sugar and meat. Many exhausted animals lay dead or dying along the way.

The trail wound through grassy valleys, among enormous rocks, beside mountains with icy springs gushing from their sides, and up and down rugged hills studded with tall pines and white-stemmed aspens."

(Source: Richardson, A. D., 1867, *Beyond the Mississippi:* New York, American Pub. Co., p. 196.)

Richardson left Denver for the mountains the first time with Horace Greeley on June 8, 1859. The journey described above was made early in July.

"Golden City, Clear Creek, Aug. 25, '59

...The old road which was travelled for over two months after Gregory had made his lucky strike, was so rugged that but few wagons ventured upon it; most of them were left behind at the foot of the second range, by parties that proposed to prospect the mountains, with one or two persons for protection."

Unsigned. Appeared in the *Missouri Republican*, September 5, 1859.

(Source: Hafen, L. R., and A. W., eds., 1961, *Reports from Colorado—The Wildman letters 1859-1865 with other related letters and newspaper reports, 1859:* Glendale, Calif., Clark Co., p. 159.)

"Saturday, April 21st [1860].—Fine morning. Started rather late, and took right hand road up a pleasant valley 2 miles to Golden Gate, a village of 26 buildings in all stages of completion. Entered mountains here, thru a toll gate, paying 75 cents per wagon. Traveled up gulch, crossing a brook very often with muddy and steep banks. At 24th crossing, 2 houses; woman washing. Above 33, stopped for dinner, at 5 mile house from gate? Snow on the hills all day, and down beside the road in P. M. Hauling very severe. At 37th crossing White broke single tree. At 8 mile house, head of gulch, and 50th crossing of stream, camped for night. I slept in tent with White's party. Enoch in house, others in wagon. A little snow fell in eve.

Sunday, 22nd.—Fair most of day; a few spits of snow. Left camp rather late, and doubled teams up ridge. Descent quite long and steep."

(Source: *Diary of a Pike's Peak gold seeker in 1860:* Colo. Mag., v. 14, no. 6, Nov. 1937, p. 213-214.)

Overnight the Gregory Toll Road became the established route to the gold mines.

First trip between Denver and Central City by stage coach, June 1860. Billy Updike drove. Two relays of horses, Golden and Guy House.

(Compiled from: Georgetown Courier, Oct. 7, 1913.)

The old Gregory Toll Road on the W side of Guy Hill. Photographed 1991.

"[The stage drivers] first appeared on the scene in 1860. A breed unto themselves they were aptly described by an early writer as: 'brave as a lion and as tender-hearted as a woman. The recklessness and profanity of a driver were equaled only by his skill as a reinsman and his kindness and liberality as a man.' Such was Billy Updike who stood head and shoulders above all his associates and had their universal respect. A native of New York, Updike spent most of his life in the box of a stage coach. In the spring of 1860, he was driving for the Western Stage Company in and out of Denver and to Central. In 1866, he drove the fast line between Denver and Georgetown for Wells Fargo and Company with Jake Hawk…

His favorite team was known as the Mountain Maids—five were handsome bays with Mollie, the leader, and Old Joe, the nigh leader. Six finer animals never went into harness. They were fleet, strong, spirited, well trained…

COLO. HIST. SOC.

Billy Updike at the reins in Guy Gulch. The team was called the Mountain Maids.

A story was classic among stage drivers of how Updike in 1868 drove Generals Grant, Sherman and Dent from the summit of Guy Hill in Golden Gate Canyon to Golden—a distance of nine miles in thirty-six minutes. Comments by the three passengers weren't related. They were probably speechless."

(Source: Brown, Georgina, 1976, *The shining mountains:* Gunnison, Colo., B&B Printers, p. 61.)

By March 1860 the California Overland and Pike's Peak Express was running two stage lines tri-weekly from Denver City through Golden Gate City and up the Gregory Toll Road to Mountain City. In Golden Gate City, Thomas Golden was operating a storage, commission, ranching and forwarding business.

By April 1860 the Express was running a daily line (dubbed the Rocky Mountain Express) up the toll road. Time between Golden Gate City and Mountain City, with a stop for dinner and to change horses, four to five hours.

"The wheels of the coach were heavy, with wide thick tires. Its strong body, built of white oak, was braced with iron bands and slung upon stout leather thorough-braces. There were adjustable leather curtains designed to keep out wind, rain, snow, and dust, but from early accounts of stage passengers it would seem that these were never completely efficient. The box holding treasure and express was placed beneath the driver's seat, while the passengers' baggage was carried in the boot. Passengers were allowed twenty-five pounds of baggage free of charge, with excess at one dollar a pound. Mail sacks were also carried in the boot, except when there was an overflow, and then they were thrown upon the floor of the coach to slide about, much to the discomfiture of the passengers.

Despite its drawbacks, the overland coach, with its brilliant red body striped with black and its straw-colored chassis, was an impressive sight as it pulled into the stage station drawn by its lively animals and accompanied by much fanfare.

…Seventeen hundred mules and horses were in use on the Holladay line. Holladay instructed his stock buyers to select only the best of livestock and insisted that they be well cared for. The animals varied in weight. On the six-horse strings, the team nearest the coach, called wheel-horses or wheel-mules on the plains, was the heaviest, weighing usually from one thousand to twelve hundred pounds. In the mountains the wheel-horses were called tongue-horses or tongue-mules…Teams were matched in color, the bay and brown animals predominating, although Holladay had some gray and white teams. On the Georgetown division in Colorado territory six snow-white horses hauled the brilliant coach. Although this was considered the most beautiful team on the line, the Benham mules which worked from Denver were reported to be the fastest. It had a rival in the 'catfish' group of dapple grays. This team established a record of fifteen miles in fifty-five minutes on the road from Denver to Golden…"

(Source: Frederick, J. V., 1940, *Ben Holladay, the stagecoach king:* Calif., Arthur H. Clark, p. 82-83.)

"WESTERN MOUNTAINEER. June 28, 1860. The road from this city (Golden City) to Gregory's via Golden Gate has been graded throughout and the heaviest wagons pass over it daily without difficulty. Over 40 Quartz Mills with their ponderous boilers have gone into and over the mountains and we have not learned of a single accident worthy of note."

(Source: Ramstetter, James K., 1996, *Life in the early days:* p. 2.)

Sometime early in 1862 the Express came under the ownership of Ben Holladay's Overland Stage Line. Ben Holladay operated the line into the 1870s when Wells, Fargo & Co. took it over.

(Compiled from: *History of Gilpin County in History of Clear Creek and Boulder Valleys:* Chicago, Baskin, 1880, p. 258.)

"A daily express stage ran between Denver and Black Hawk in 1863, leaving Black Hawk at seven-thirty in the morning and arriving at Denver at ten in the evening. Large quantities of express and treasure were hauled on the branch line. Some of the buyers shipped three hundred ounces of gold at a time, while Clark and company, bankers, shipped four hundred and thirty-four ounces of clear retort."

(Source: Frederick, J. V., 1940, *Ben Holladay, the stagecoach king:* Calif., Arthur
H. Clark, p. 136-137.)

Freight wagon descending Dory Hill.

COLO. HIST. SOC.

"Distances from Denver City to Gregory Mines, by Golden City

MINERS' HOTEL.—Golden City 15
GOLDEN GATE 2
EIGHT MILE HOUSE.—Robinson and Baker. Good water
Ranche. From here you ascend a steep canon, until you reach
the top of a very steep mountain; great care will have to be
taken to properly block your wagon. This mountain is
half-a-mile from the top to the bottom. Half-a-mile from the
foot of the hill is. 6
GUY'S HOTEL 2
GREGORY MINES . . . . .12"

(Source: Burt, S. W., and Berthoud, E. L., 1860, *Quartz mining region of the
Rocky Mountains:* Denver City, Rocky Mountain News Printing Co.,
p. 65.)

"October 3, 1861, the legislature of the Territory of Colorado authorized the 'Enterprise Wagon Road Company' from Michigan House in Cold Spring Valley to Dalton's Quartz Mill in Gregory Diggings.

August 15, 1862, the legislature authorized the 'Golden Gate and Gregory Road Company' from Golden Gate via Tucker's Canon or nearest and best route to Michigan House in Cold Springs Valley."

(Source: Ridgeway, Arthur, 1932, *The mission of Colorado toll roads:* Colo. Mag., v. 9, no. 5., p. 164-165.)

As of 1862 two tolls were taken on the Gregory Road, the first at the entrance to Golden Gate Canyon and the second at Michigan House. Wagons leaving Black Hawk for Golden or Boulder City paid their first toll at the Dory Hill or Smith Hill toll gates.

"[The road] pierces the first range of the Rocky Mountains by the canon of a small stream, at the mouth whereof are four or five log-houses, styled Gate *City!* [The writer is bemoaning the 'vulgar, snobbish custom of attaching *City* to every place of more than three houses.'] The defile is very narrow, abrupt, and with such sudden turns that for a space the road seems every moment to come to a sudden termination. Huge masses of dark red and purple rock topple on either side; there is little timber to be seen but a profusion of wild gooseberries and cur-rants, and a bush resembling the boom. The bed of the brook is crowded with young cotton-woods and box-elders, in the shade of which new varieties of wild flowers grow luxuriantly. I hailed the Alpine harebell as an old friend, and inhaled the delicious perfume blown from clumps of mountain roses. The wild hop-vine was very abundant, spreading its arms over the rock, in lieu of other supports.

After two or three miles the pass became broader and straighter, and we could look up to the crest of the mountains. It was dismal to see how much of the pine forests, with which the steeps were clothed, have been wantonly carelessly destroyed by fire. The rock now appeared to be a kind of gneiss, gray, with pale orange oxydations, which gave the scenery something of the character of the Apennines. I did not find, as I expected, much vegetation. The dry soil, the bare masses of rock, the dusty road, and the hot, cloudless sky overhead, all suggested Southern Europe, rather than Switzerland or our mountain regions of the East.

We followed this canon for some eight or ten miles, occasionally passing a saw-mill, or tavern-ranche, patronized by the freighters. Then we reached Guy's Hill, where the road crosses the divide, and we were requested by the driver to climb to the summit on foot. It was but half a mile of rather breathless walking in the thin air, and we stood upon a narrow crest, overlooking a deep-pine-clad valley in the heart of the mountains."

(Source: Taylor, Bayard, 1867, *Colorado, a summer trip:* New York, G. P. Putnam & Son, p. 52.)

The dust in the canyon was so bad that difficulty in breathing experienced by the laboring teams, particularly the yoked cattle, toiling along head down, made quick work of them:

> "The road from Golden Gate to Central City has been made much more pleasant to travel than it was a month or two ago, by the removal and burning of the dead cattle that were so frequent along it. But few now remain that are offensive, and the road proprietors are rapidly lessening the number. Recent changes in the road, by making side cuts around the bends of the stream, have considerably reduced the number of the crossings on the 'Eight Mile gulch;' but the roadway is still in many places too narrow, and teams are obliged to lose much time in waiting at the turn-outs for others to pass."

> (Source: Daily Evening News edition of the Rocky Mountain News, May 13, 1861.)

> "Those who remember the old road over the hill north of Golden Gate up which it took seventeen yokes of oxen to haul one sack of flour, will after traveling over this one, acknowledge the march of improvement."

> (Source: Denver Commonwealth, Sept. 3, 1863.)

A heavily loaded coach and six on the Gregory Road. Seven up top and more inside. Note the man riding shotgun on the front seat. The man in back appears to be holding a rifle and wearing his powder pouch over his shoulder.

COLO. HIST. SOC.

In the free-fall of events that followed Gregory's discovery, the climb up Enter Mountain was quickly forgotten.

But that portion of the road W from the summit of Enter Mountain continued to be used. This route along the backs of the mountains was better than the toll road in several respects: 1) there were no heavy flood run-offs to contend with, and 2) the Booten Gulch descent into Guy Gulch was gentler than the Guy Hill descent.

Just as Enter Mountain had been the scourge of the first road to Gregory's, so did the infamous Guy Hill become the curse of the new toll road:

> "It was a long pull to the top of Guy Hill and then down the old zig, zag road to Guy Gulch. Traces of this road can still be seen on the south side of the gulch. You may have noticed the sharp curves on this old stretch of road where it was necessary in coming up the hill from the west with a long bull team to unhitch the leading bulls and let the wheelers pull the wagon around the sharp curves."
>
> (Source: Hanington, C. H. 1942, *Early Days of Central City:* Colo. Mag., v. 19, no. 1, Jan. 1942, p. 4.)

> "Tomorrow my sister Charlotte and I start for a visit to the friends in the mountains. …the road in places is perfectly terrific, especially the big hill, as they call it, where the road is dug down the side of a mountain almost perpendicularly, and on the lower side of which is a deep gulch into which many a luckless wagon has found its way and been crushed to a thousand pieces."
>
> (Source: Morrison, S. B. 1860, in a letter written Sept. 16, 1860, to his brother, in *Letters from Colorado, 1860-63:* Colo. Mag., v. 16, no. 3, May 1939, p. 92.)

Heavily loaded wagons could be raised mechanically. In 1859 a whim was built on the W side of the pass over Guy Hill to hoist wagons several hundred feet up the steepest part of the mountainside. (See Ramstetter, James K., 1996, *Life in the early days,* p. 25-26, for a description of the whim and of the wagon road. This book is available at the Golden Feed Mill.)

Wagons could also be lowered mechanically:

> "It was a perfect spring day. My partner and I had secured seats on the top with the driver, and every minute and foot of the journey was a pure delight. At Guy hill the descent at one place was so steep, and the road so bad, that the stage people had installed a block and tackle at the high point, by the aid of which the rocking coach was safely lowered down the most dangerous place."
>
> (Source: Van Wagenen, T. F., 1871(?), Colorado: Colorado School of Mines Master's Thesis, Colorado Room Document M36-683.)

In 1860 Alfred Tucker laid claim to the road and attempted to collect tolls. He applied to the Kansas Probate Court of Arapahoe County for an injunction to restrain McCleery. Golden Gate

City and Golden City held public meetings and passed resolutions opposing Tucker and supporting McCleery:

> **"The Gregory Toll Road.** We do not design entering as extensively into a 'toll road' discussion as has our contemporary, the *Mountaineer,* of this city, but we deem it an act of justice to refer briefly to a recent decision of the people in regard to the road, built by our old friend D. McCleery, leading into the mountains from Golden Gate.
>
> It is well known to all who have traveled over the route that Mr. McCleery has spent a great deal of money in its improvement, for which he collects toll from teams passing over it.
>
> A Mr. Tucker, has also laid claim to a portion of the same road, and has attempted the collection of toll thereon.
>
> Recently he applied to the Kansas Probate Court of Arapahoe county for an injunction to restrain McCleery, which he obtained, when the people stepped in, and held meetings strongly endorsing, and pledging their support and assistance to Mr. McCleery.
>
> The following resolution was adopted by the people of Golden Gate at a meeting held at that place on the 17 inst. *Resolved.* That we (the citizens of Golden Gate, uphold the said McCleery in the possession of the road against said parties, the decision of the Kansas Courts notwithstanding, and further that we will not recognize any decision of the Kansas Courts as having any jurisdiction of this country.
>
> Other resolutions of the same tenor were adopted at the same time, and subsequently similar ones were passed by a people's meeting, held at Golden City.
>
> One of them is as follows:
>
>> **Resolved.** That we as citizens, will support and uphold the said Daniel McCleery in the possession of his road, and all rights which he may have in and by virtue of it. And that we will repudiate and discountenance any effort or action which any party or parties may make by, through, or under the authority of this Kansas Court, in anywise to rob or wrest the possession of this said road from Daniel McCleery, the rightful owner thereof...
>>
>> ...Mr. McCleery is the owner of the road."
>
> (Source: Colo. Transcript, Oct. 20, 1860.)

Alfred Tucker got his injunction and took control of the road.

A road to evade the toll station was soon opened through Cressmans Gulch to the top of the pass between Crawford and Cressmans gulches, and hence down a steep draw to the junction of Crawford Gulch with Tucker Gulch. The Cressman grades were not good for heavy loads, nevertheless the by-pass succeeded in hastening the demise of the Gregory Toll Road.

This breathtaking, full-page illustration by Theodore R. Davis appeared on page 88 of Harper's Weekly, February 8, 1868. Close examination of the newspaper reveals lines on the illustration where it was folded into a packet for dispatch to New York.

The years hurried by, the traffic hurried by. The old trace up the gulch behind the Centennial House became just another road to another ranch. That it was the original road to Gregory's, the road up and down which thousands trudged, was forgotten.

The heavy wagons and large droves that followed the toll road destroyed the fragile vegetation that grew along the creek beds. Floods tore the exposed dirt free of the creek banks. The bottoms of the crooked, narrow canyons grew wider and wider, the roads sidestepping this way and that to avoid washouts. Side cuts were made to increase the turnouts. Climbing the passes, the roads were moved again and again, away from the deep washes caused by water following the wheel-ruts. Pieces of old road are everywhere pressed into the earth, wending through the trees, clinging above the creek banks. A fine piece of old road-cut may be seen over the bank below the highway in Tucker Gulch 1.6 miles above the GGC/SH 93 junction. Another fine piece of the old road descends the W side of Guy Hill, leaving ruts in the rocks.

The red wrecked car seen far below the highway on the W side of Guy Gulch has come to rest on a piece of old wagon road.

The only known drawing of the bridge in the bottom of Guy Gulch appears in Harper's Weekly, February 8, 1868. The caption on the pen-and-ink sketch reads,

> "OVERLAND MAIL-COACH CROSSING THE ROCKY MOUNTAINS—SCENE IN GUY'S GULCH.—Sketched by Theodore R. Davis.—[See Page. 87.]"

Page 87 reads:

> "THE OVERLAND MAIL-COACH. Although the 'passage of the plains' and the 'ascent of the Sierra Nevada Mountains' by the Pacific Railroad has somewhat contracted the hitherto long route of the Overland Pony Express and Mail-Coaches, these primitive institutions, ever seen in the van-guard of the army of civilization, continue to cross the Rocky Mountains and carry mails and passengers between the termini of the two roads.
>
> …on the next page we give a fine engraving, showing one of the many difficulties which the overland coach has to encounter in making the toilsome and dangerous ascent of the Rocky Mountains. The road pursued by the coaches is necessarily very narrow, as it is made on the side of the steep mountains, and usually overlooking some deep gorge. In winter portions of the road are found to be sheets of ice, and the streams which dash down the sides of the mountains are bordered by huge icicles, or rather glaciers of great size and magnificence. The coach in our engraving is represented in the midst of one of the heavy windstorms which prevail in the ravines or gulches of the Rocky Mountains; and the air is filled with the snow-flakes which have been disturbed in their rest on the side of the mountain.
>
> The sketch which we thus reproduce was made by our artist in 'Guy's Gulch,' a ravine on the eastern slope of the Rocky Mountains, about thirty miles west of Denver City, Colorado."
>
> (Source: Harper's Weekly, February 8, 1868, p. 87-88.)

The sweeping view from the old stage road on the W side of Guy Hill overlooking Guy Gulch. Douglas Mountain is in the background. Photographed 1991.

The Davis sketch was made ab. 0.25 mile S of the intersection of Guy Gulch with the Robinson Hill Road.

Only known illustration of the Tucker Gulch portion of the toll road: Richardson, A. D., 1867, *Beyond the Mississippi:* New York, American Pub. Co., p. 196.

Earliest known map of the entire toll road: Burt, S. W., and Berthoud, E. L., 1860. *Quartz mining region of the Rocky Mountains:* Denver City, Rocky Mountains News Printing Co., insert.

Most complete compilation known of newspaper records of 1859-1870 pertaining to activities along the road: Ramstetter, James K.: *Life in the early days.* This book is available at the Golden Feed Mill.

Guy Gulch Wagon Road

Ab. 2.75 miles long. Traversed the lower region of Guy Gulch to connect with the Clear Creek Canyon Wagon Road on the S and the Gregory Road on the N.

S/b Ralston Buttes and Evergreen quads.
S21-28-27-34-35, T3S, R71W Ralston Buttes.
S35, T3S, R71W Evergreen.

(See Guy Gulch <u>in</u> Drainages for more about the road though this gulch. Also see Clear Creek Canyon Toll Gate <u>in</u> Toll Gates.)

Ralston Creek Toll Road

Ab. 13 miles long. Traversed the length of Ralston Canyon to connect with the Cheyenne Road (the Golden-Boulder Road) on the eastward plains and the Gregory Road at Cold Spring.

S/b Ralston Buttes Quad.

Mule-drawn freight wagon on the Ralston Creek Toll Road.

Historical accounts are rare. (See Ralston Toll Gate <u>in</u> Toll Gates.)

EDITORS' NOTE: There is a possibility that:

1) the 7-mile house shown on Burt and Berthoud's map, and

2) the Cold Spring (the Colo. Transcript, Feb. 28, 1861, describes the Ralston Toll Road as "following up Rallston creek to the old road at the Cold Spring seven miles this side of Gregory."), and

3) Michigan House (the toll-road authorization describes the route as from "Tucker's Canon or nearest and best route to Michigan House in Cold Springs Valley")

are one in the same location: W of the foot of Junction (Michigan) Hill.

It should be pointed out that there was also a Michigan House at the E foot of Michigan Hill. Bayard Taylor dined there, as did others. But Ralston Creek junctioned with the Gregory Road on the W side of Michigan Hill, which argues for Cold Spring Valley, along with the Michigan House of the toll-road authorization, being on the W side.

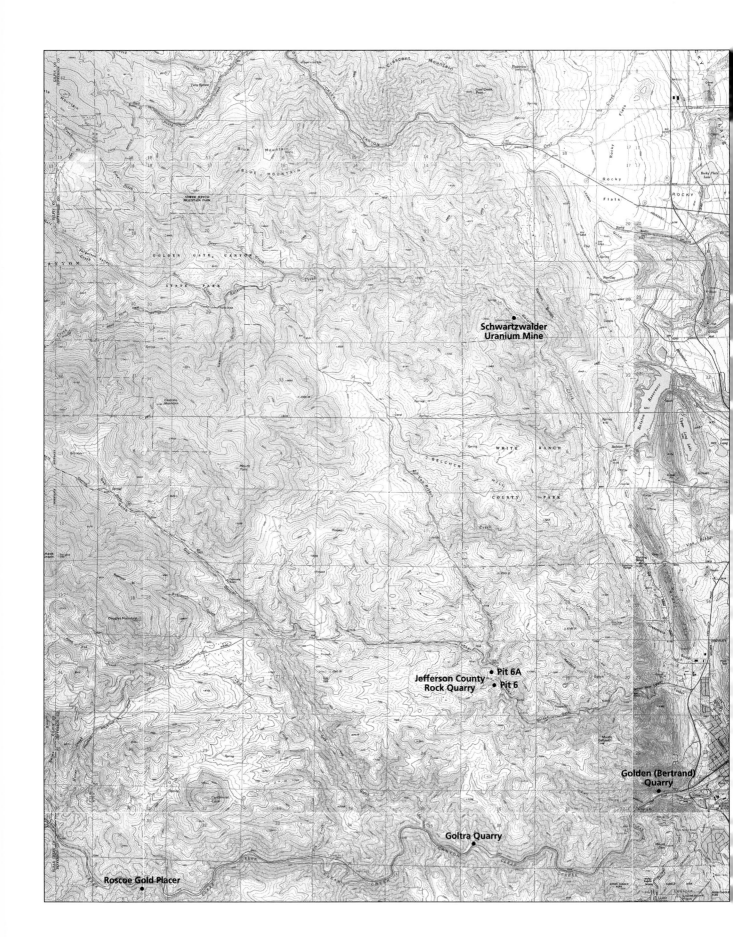

Schwartzwalder
Uranium Mine

Jefferson County
Rock Quarry
• Pit 6A
• Pit 6

Golden (Bertrand)
Quarry

Goltra Quarry

Roscoe Gold Placer

Mines

Despite high hopes and exaggerated claims, the labor and money spent during the 19th century in the search for gold and silver and copper far exceeded the rewards. Experienced miners claimed that a gold belt crossed the mountains in the viciniy of Golden. Geologists insisted that large deposits of free-milling ore existed beneath the streambeds, washed down through the ages. Every new strike was attended by hundreds of claims being staked out nearby.

Common wisdom had it that the deeper the mine the richer the ore:

> "[December 25, 1880] There is no doubt but that there is plenty of mineral in the foot-hills around Golden, but it has always been believed by old prospectors that it was at a considerable depth. However, from reliable information now in our possession, it is certain that in the spring Golden will experience a mining boom that will make her one of the No. 1 camps in Colorado. Whether this will be a silver boom or gold boom, or some other metal boom, there is no doubt that a superhuman effort will be made to extract that metal in the spring.
>
> As to further evidence of the richness of at least a portion of the mines near Golden, it might be well for those coming here…to closely observe only the fine carbonate-stained specimens on exhibition in nearly every part of the city, but also the beautiful rich nuggets of quite fantastic appearance worn as watch charms, which suspend from the vest charms of gentlemen all more or less interested in mines now being worked."
>
> (Source: Jefferies, Marguerite, *Mineral mining activities from 1875—*: typed manuscript stamped "Jefferson County Museum, Old Court House, Golden, Colo.")

Many a kingdom was lost it was thought, and indeed, who will ever know? for want of more and better equipment.

On the other hand, not everyone kept the faith.

"There is not a single good reason for the admission of Colorado [for Statehood]. Indeed, if it were not for the mines in that mountainous and forbidding region there would be no population there at all. The population, such as it is, is made up of a roving and unsettled horde of adventurers, who have no settled homes there or elsewhere, and are there solely because the state of semi-barbarism prevalent in that wild country suits their vagrant habits. There is something repulsive in the idea that a few handfulls of miners and reckless bushwhackers should have the same representation in the Senate as Pennsylvania, Ohio and New York."

(Source: Wagenen, T.F.V., 1926, *Views on the Admission of Colorado in 1876:*
Colo. Mag., v. 3, no. 3, p. 87.)

In 1892 gold was discovered at the entrance to Clear Creek Canyon. The *At Last Found Mine* yielded $50 to the ton on the surface. A company consisting chiefly of Golden businessmen sprang up to finance the mine. Anxious to give it a thorough test, their first act was to let a contract to sink a shaft 100 feet. Apparently the shaft went not a foot further. The May 20, 1893, Industrial Edition of the Golden Globe makes no mention of gold mining in the vicinity of Golden. Perhaps the *At Last Found Mine* was the last hurrah for gold mining in the valley.

By the start of the 20th century it was the far less glamorous deposits—albite, bertrandite, bismuthinite, bismutite, beryl, feldspar, garnet, mica, muscovite, topaz, tourmaline, and samarskite—that were providing, but barely, a living for would-be bonanza kings. Golden Gate Canyon is pockmarked with small, crater-like holes that remember their efforts.

The nod for the biggest money-maker goes to uranium, the major source of mining revenue in the 1960s and 70s. Aggregate could surpass uranium, but aggregate production has a problem that earlier mining ventures did not—a population better educated as to the environmental damage inherent in mining. As a result, the crushing of the bedrock has not gained the foothold in the RBQ that it has elsewhere.

Goltra Quarry

N of Clear Creek and E of Guy Gulch at the entrance to Huntsman Gulch ab. 2.8 miles above Tunnel No. 1.
S/b Evergreen Quad.
S35-36, T3S, R71W.
Elv. ab. 6150'.

This quarry is the result of major scarring caused by road building. The purpose of the road was to open an area in a remote region of the Elk Creek drainage to aggregate mining:

In the fall of 1987, Jeffco Commissioners authorized a 4-lane, million-dollar-plus driveway off U.S. Highway 6 in Clear Creek Canyon on ground owned by Chicago businessman O. R. Goltra. The driveway was to be constructed by the county in exchange for aggregate.

Driveway construction cratered the mountainside, and in October forty citizens' groups representing more than 5,000 members united to oppose the road under the banner *Canyon Defense Coalition.*

Goltra Quarry at the broken foot of the Huntsman in Clear Creek Canyon. Photographed 1991.

April 1988: Goltra submitted a plan to open a 320-acre, 75-year, multimillion-ton quarry called the Sheep Mountain Quarry to be located at or near S27, T3S, R71W, RBQ. The Sheep Mountain Quarry was to have access roads to both Clear Creek and Golden Gate Canon and result in 700 truck trips per day, 24 hours per day, six days a week.

May 1988: A fissure opened ahead of the driveway being built to the proposed quarry. The fissure was dynamited, but instead of collapsing on itself, the fissure widened to reveal a crystal cave. Citing concern for investigators, the cave was ordered destroyed by Jeffco Commissioners. (See Crystal Cave in Caves).

November 1988: Jeffco Commissioners shut down construction of the Clear Creek Canyon driveway one day before the general elections. Governor Roy Romer, on seeing the crater-like destruction from the air, called the driveway a gravel pit.

September 19, 1991: Jeffco Planning Commission by a 5-to-2 vote recommended approval of the Sheep Mountain Quarry.

In 1992, bowing to citizen pressure, Jeffco Commissioners voted 2-to-1 to reject the Sheep Mountain Quarry.

The driveway that goes nowhere is one of two quarries in existence downstream of the forks of Clear Creek. The other is the old Golden (Bertrand) Quarry at the entrance to the canyon (See Pit 24).

Jefferson County Rock Quarry, Pit 6 and Pit 6A

The aggregate was stockpiled at the entrance to Miller Gulch in Golden Gate Canyon. The quarry itself is located in a shallow ravine ab. 0.25 mile W of Miller Gulch.

S/b Ralston Buttes Quad.
S24, T3S, R71W.
Elv. ab. 7100'.

In the 1970s Jeffco Commissioners signed a series of contracts with landowner O. R. Goltra to extract gravel from the vicinity of Miller Gulch. The gravel was paid for, in part, with roads which were built through the property at county expense.

A rock crusher was set up. The rock in Pit 6 was mined out in the 1980s, and the land reclaimed.

January 1987: Jeffco Commissioners voted to open a 15-year, 20-acre, 2-million-ton quarry called Pit 6A, above Pit 6.

Pit 6A has not yet been opened, perhaps due to the cumulative effect of court suits brought in the late 1980s by citizens' groups and private individuals against the county and Goltra. However, the lease held by the county on this ground, at a cost in excess of $100,000 per year, extends into the 21st century.

Pit 24 (Quarry)

Exists only on paper. Proposed to encompass the old Golden (Bertrand) Quarry in Clear Creek Canyon on N side of Highway 6 ab. 0.5 mile W of the intersection of Highways 93 and 58.

Pit 24 was the dream of Brannan Sand and Gravel Company. Brannan purchased the 845-acre Warren D. Hall property in 1977 hoping to gain rezoning to re-open the old Golden (Bertrand) Quarry located on the property. The old quarry, encompassing approximately 16 acres, was opened in 1926 and mined intermittently until 1973 when Jefferson County officials closed it due to a geologic hazard—a scarp-potential rockslide area adjacent to the highway. The quarry supplied crushed rock to Lake McConaughy in Nebraska and eventually to highway construction through Clear Creek Canyon.

Brannan proposed removing the geologic hazard and extending the life of the quarry with a four-phase, 35-year mining operation beginning with open-pit mining followed by underground mining.

In 1979, a large citizens group called GASP, consisting of residents of Golden Gate Canyon and Golden with strong support from metro Denver, organized to oppose the mining plan.

July 11, 1979, Jeffco Planning voted to recommend denial of the rezoning application. April 13, 1981, in a 2-1 vote, Jeffco Commissioners denied the application.

What makes Pit 24 unique is the length to which Brannan went to educate the public and various government agencies as to the scope of the mining plan. Arguing that "a mining operation can be conducted in a metropolitan area if adequate safeguards are implemented to protect the environment," Brannan's exhaustive studies raised the bar on the application process and gained new respect for an industry everybody wants, but not in their back yard.

Roscoe Gold Placer

Three miles above Tunnel No. 3, this general vicinity.

S/b Evergreen Quad.
S6, T4S, R71W.

Placers pockmarked the banks of Clear Creek. The major placer below Forks Creek was at Rosco. In 1896-97 a group of miners attempted to work the gravels by hydraulic elevator methods but were unable to obtain sufficient water pressures.

> "In 1932 the Humphreys Gold Corporation built a **2,000-cu-yd-per-day** floating suction dredge on Clear Creek at Roscoe…this dredge was abandoned after about 1 month's operation. In 1933 it was converted to a floating washing plant, fed by a 1¼-cu-yd dragline. Both these operations had equipment to recover sulphide minerals lost in the tailings of the mills of the mining district upstream, as well as gold. It functioned effectively, but the amount of sulphide minerals in the gravels was found to be negligible. After 3 or 4 months operation, the second plant was also abandoned; and a portable washing plant, mounted on caterpillar treads and fed by two draglines, was installed. With two 2½-cu-yd draglines and a power shovel, the plant could handle from **3,000 to 4,500 cu yd** per day…in 1934-35, **498,429 cu yd** of gravel was mined on Clear Creek below Forks Creek; and in 1936, **612,144 cu yd** was mined on lower North Clear Creek. At the end of the 1936 season the plant was dismantled."
>
> (Source: Parker, Ben, 1974, *Gold placers of Colorado,* book 1 of 2 books: Quarterly of the Colorado School of Mines: v. 69, no. 3, July 1974, p. 77. Also see p. 76 for reference to 1896-97 hydraulic attempts.)

Schwartzwalder Uranium Mine

S side of Ralston Creek ab. 2 miles above Ralston Reservoir.

1965 Ralston Buttes Quad.
S25, T2S, R71W.
Elv. 6600'.

> "Uranium was being found abundantly near Ralston creek before 1875."
>
> (Source: Jefferies, Marguerite, *Mineral mining activities from 1875—:* typed manuscript stamped "Jefferson County Museum, Old Court House, Golden, Colo.").

There was little use for uranium then. But comes the hour comes the man.

Fred Schwartzwalder was born in Hornberg, Germany, in 1896. Stricken with rheumatic fever as a boy, he was sent to live with an uncle in Iowa. By the time two of his cousins came from Germany to attend the Colorado School of Mines, Fred was a married man with a family of his own. He moved to Golden, provided room and board for the cousins and went to work for the

Golden Brickyard. Eventually he landed a permanent job as janitor in the Golden schools for $200 a month.

A rock-hound bug caught from his cousins drove him to prospecting in the mountains. Rocks began filling up the corners of his yard. Christmas 1950 his four children pooled their money and bought him a Geiger counter. When a rock in the yard set it off, Fred recalled collecting the specimen on the land of Paul and Anna White.

COTTER CORP.

The surface facilities of the Schwartzwalder Mine as seen looking upstream to the N.

He negotiated an agreement to pay the Whites 15% of the gross proceeds of any minerals obtained from their land, and began driving a drift into the side of Indian Head Mountain. His pick, shovel, hand drills and a 12-pound sledgehammer had to be carried in by hand four miles to the site.

Seventy-five feet into the drift, after suffering heart attacks, surgery and cave-ins, Fred found a sizable pocket of pitchblende. A 15-pound sample assayed 0.48% uranium oxide. Encouraged, the Schwartzwalder family mucked the pitchblende out by hand, hauled it by dump truck to the railroad, and shipped it to Salt Lake City. In November 1953 Fred received a check for $12,000 from the Salt Lake City smelter. The Atomic Energy Commission stepped in. Professional miners were hired, and in 1954 Fred quit his janitorial job.

In 1957, health deteriorating, Fred sold the mine to Golden-Denver Uranium Company for $293,000. He and his wife bought dentures, a house and a new car and took a trip back to Germany to see the brother he'd left 46 years before. Fred's wife died in 1960. Fred lived on until 1965, spending his winters prospecting in Arizona.

(Compiled from: Bond, R. F., 1989, *The land persists:* Jeffco Hist. Com. contest entry.)

Cotter took over the mine in 1966. In 1976 a shaft deepening the mine to 2,000 feet below the surface was completed. December of 1986 production was curtailed due to lack of demand; however, exploration and development were continued. September of 1989 exploration and development were curtailed, and the mine was placed in a standby and maintenance status. On March 1995 limited and operation and development resumed at the mine. July 1996, after almost 10 years, production ore is once again being shipped from the Schwartzwalder.

(Compiled from: *Fact File:* Cotter Corporation.)

"What Uranium is Used For. The most common use of 'yellowcake' uranium is to create pellets for nuclear power plants. Uranium-based fuel pellets have the advantage of packing a lot of energy into a small mass of material. For example, a pound of refined uranium contains enough energy to produce the same amount of heat as 1,500 tons of coal or 300,000 gallons of fuel oil. Uranium is a clean fuel, creating useful energy for the production of electricity without the pollution generated by fossil fuels.

How the Uranium is Processed. After ore is mined from the earth, the uranium must be extracted from it. To do this, a mill like Cotter's Cañon City facility crushes and grinds the ore to liberate the mineral particles which hold the uranium. The ground ore then is leached to dissolve the uranium, and the resulting solution is purified and concentrated. This solution then is treated to produce a solid uranium concentrate called yellowcake. After converting the oxides to uranium hexafluoride gas, the fissionable portion—the part that can release the energy—is enriched and made into pellets for the fuel rods of nuclear reactors."

(Source: *Turning ore into energy:* Cotter Corporation pamphlet.)

Early miners. Oscar Dahlberg is believed to be the second from the right. Note the hat tossed over the dynamite box. It probably belongs to the photographer who, taking the picture, has his head under the camera's curtain.

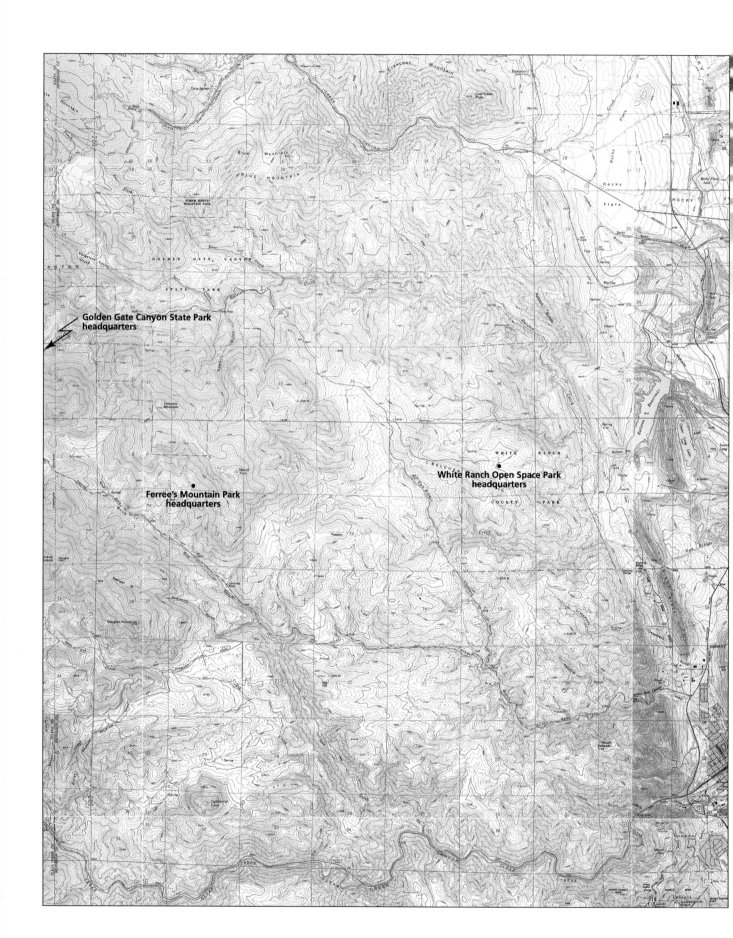

Golden Gate Canyon State Park headquarters

White Ranch Open Space Park headquarters

Ferree's Mountain Park headquarters

Parks

Ferree's Mountain Park

Near the top of the Guy Gulch drainage.

1948 Ralston Buttes Quad.
S5, T3S, R71W (headquarters).
Elv. ab. 8590'.

In the 1930s and 40s, and possibly earlier, Peter Ferree and his brother operated a nudist colony, community hall, and mountain park in the higher reaches of Guy Gulch. The community hall was a short distance above the 10-mile marker beside the road to the W. The buildings were further back in the trees. A large sign beside the driveway to the camp directed visitors to *Please honk horn.*

The park itself was at the head of Guy Gulch near the top of the E fork.

By making their hall and park available for community events the Ferree brothers remained respected members of the community. Although it was common knowledge that the purpose of the park was the opportunity to commune with nature in the buff, references to the nudist colony as such are as absent from the literature of the time as the nudists themselves were absent from view.

Golden Gate Canyon State Park

Second largest state park in Colorado.

At the headwaters of Smith Hill Gulch, Guy Gulch and Ralston Creek.
Black Hawk, Ralston Buttes and Tungsten quads.
Elv. 7200'-10,400'.

"The first lands that make up the Park were purchased in the early 1960s from the Ellison, Greenfield, and Gallagher families. The rest of the Park's now 14,000 acres were obtained from ranchers, the Bureau of Land Management, and the Colo. State Land Board.

The Park was opened to the public about 1965. Its headquarters are in a newly remodeled Visitor Center at the junction of Ralston Creek and GGC road (Route 46)—S35, T2S, R72W, BH Quad. It has seven stocked fishing ponds; ten picnic areas; one campground each for RVs and tents, tents only, and group tentsites; numerous backcountry shelters and campsites; and 12 hiking trails that together cover 35 miles. An effort is under way to rehabilitate several groups of the Park's abandoned historic buildings, which will then be used to educate visitors about the families who homesteaded in this area in the last half of the 19th Century."

(Source: Malcolm G. Stevenson, GGC State Park Historian.)

"Most settlers provided for their own needs and sold some of their surplus goods to nearby cites of Blackhawk and Golden. They grazed cattle (milk cows) on the lush mountain meadows, drinking the raw milk and selling it to nearby communities (until the government intervened with the new law against the sale of raw milk). Most families also raised chickens, some finding it profitable to sell the eggs. Farming was also prevalent: Fields of head lettuce and peas were harvested and 'put up' for winter storage or sold to markets. Ranchers cut the hay and pitched it by hand, selling it or storing it for winter use.

Hay rakes and other old farm equipment can still be seen here rusting away in the tall grasses, and some of the old log-hewn cabins throughout the park are relics of these settlers' early days.

Logging operations set up camps in the upper part of the park, cutting the much-needed lumber for the mines and growing towns. The timber was hauled by oxen to Central City or Golden.

'Sawmills were everywhere,' recalls Jeanne Jacobson who grew up near Dory Lake. Besides the sale of lumber, green trees were burned in large pits until reduced to charcoal and sold at smelters.

As the Prohibitionist era of the 1920s arrived, a new industry was created within the park boundaries, moonshining, the hottest item on the black market.

Moonshining was pursued with a zeal that matched the craze of the gold miners more than 50 years earlier.

The prohibitionist reign didn't last long. The moonshiners found their business falling off. Besides, the government men were finding and destroying their stills. This colorful era of history eventually died and life went back to usual.

(Much evidence still remains today in the park of the moonshiners: parts of old stills, barrel hoops and staves, broken crockery, and an old truck that has 'Smith's Breadwagon' painted on it. An old pair of shoes with chicken wire tacked to the soles was found—apparently they were makeshift snowshoes which left no tracks in the snow.)"

(Source: Cozine, Ken: private paper.)

The size of the park has recently been dramatically increased by the acquisition of the Green Ranch, approximately 3,000 acres of high mountain meadows and timber owned by Kenneth

TROY SCOTT PARKER

Centralia Peak as seen from the Bridge Creek Trail in Golden Gate Canyon State Park, looking E.

and Lela (White) Green. The Smith Hill Road crosses this ranch, most of which lies to the W of the road.

> George S. and Edna Hunt Green [parents of Kenneth and Malcolm] moved from Ludlow, Colorado, to the mountains NW of Golden in 1917, where they ranched for fifty years. In 1940 George was appointed to fill a vacancy as Jefferson County Commissioner and elected to the post twice more, serving ten years.
>
> (Compiled from: Wagonbach, Lorraine, 1997, *A Short Biography of George S. Green:* private paper for Jefferson County Historical Commission.)

"The decade [George Green] served the County was probably the most pivotal in its history…He implemented the first peace-time draft and was called to build the Remington Arms factory. The arms factory, now the Denver Federal Center, was successfully completed in little more than six months…

Completely dedicated to serving the County, George Green turned over the operation of his ranch to his son Kenneth and daughter-in-law Lela. The area he personally served was the mountains of Jefferson County where he was very conscientious about knowing each road and every road worker. This assignment was made more difficult by the manpower shortage of the war and the rationing of gasoline and tires. He was paid $100 a month.

Early in his political career, he anticipated the post-war growth of the County. The aging 1878 Court House, the original County seat, would no longer be adequate. Fiscally responsible through his tenure, he encouraged budgeting monies for a new edifice. The second Jefferson County Court House was completed in 1953 and served the unprecedented needs of the County for over 40 years.

...His dedication to community service did not cease after his death. Through the arrangements of his son and daughter-in-law, Kenneth and Lela, 2900 acres in Gilpin County of pristine Colorado beauty were deeded to the Golden Gate Canyon State Park with a provision that it be called the Green Ranch. The land he loved and cared for is his legacy to generations to come."

(Source: Wagonbach, Lorraine, 1997: untitled private paper for Jefferson County Historical Commission.)

Both the State Park and the Open Space Park now encompass ranch lands formerly owned by the Green and the White families.

"We worked and our folks worked too long and too hard to see the land turned into ugly subdivisions of ugly houses."

(Source: Lela White Green as quoted in *Commitment to the land—the story of the Whites and the Green.* This wonderful three-part article by Irma C. Wyhs appeared in the Fence Post, Dec. 1, 8, 15, 1997.)

KEN AND LELA (WHITE) GREEN COLLECTION

Ken and Lela Green on Ken's 85th birthday. Photographed October 1996. Kenneth Green was a veterinarian as well as a rancher. Those who could pay got a bill. Those who couldn't got the same good service, rain or shine, daylight or dark of night.

The Green Ranch is the largest and latest acquisition by Golden Gate State Park which, with over 14,400 acres, is now the second largest Colorado state park. Sixty-eight homesteads, claimed between 1868 and 1940, are within the park boundaries.

Golden Gate Canyon Youth Camp

Honor camp for juvenile offenders.

Across from Kriley Pond and up the hill S of the GGC Road.
S/b Blackhawk Quad.
S34, T2S, R72W. (Not mapped in this book.)
Elv. ab. 8500'.

Opened in 1965. Larry Johnson, Director.

The only fence was the one erected at the edge of the basketball court to prevent loose balls from rolling downhill.

Camp residents, nearly half of whom were employed full-time in nearby Golden Gate State Park, virtually built the park and its trails. They maintained and repaired buildings, cut down beetle-infested trees and bundled the wood for state parks and senior citizens who needed fuel, and removed debris from old trails and roads.

The camp had its own teachers, and the remainder of the campers were in school five days a week.

In the 1970s and 80s, as juvenile detention facilities in the cities became more crowded, the ranks of the low-risk campers at the honors camp were swelled by offenders who had committed more serious offenses.

This resulted in a change in policy which in turn resulted in the decision to close the camp in 1986.

(Source: Compiled from: Engler, Suzy, 1986, *Unique youth camp to close*: Colo. Transcript, May 29, 1986, p. 1, 3.)

The 20-acre facility has since been considered for outward bound programs, a boot camp, and a women's detention facility. It is currently the home of Discovery Camp and Conference Center, a privately managed Community Resources program.

White Ranch Open Space Park

Foothills NW of Golden.

Ralston Buttes Quad.
Elv. 6150'-7880'.
Over 4000 acres of land and 19 miles of trails.

Acquired and developed with revenue from the one half of one percent Open Space sales tax approved by the citizens of Jefferson County in 1972.

The ranch that gives this park its name was acquired in 1975 by Jeffco Open Space for $857,814.

Ninety-two acres of the Dry Creek drainage were added in 1976 for $497,925.

There are two parking lots. 1) West entrance: at the bottom of the White Ranch Road, S1, T3S, R71W, RBQ. 2) East entrance: N of Golden at W 56th Avenue and Pine Ridge Road, S8, T3S, R70W, GQ.

In 1881 James Bond homesteaded the flat meadow N of Belcher Hill. The Park headquarters are located here. Over the years Bond added to his homestead, eventually acquiring 880 acres. In

1905, Mary Elizabeth, James' daughter, sold the Bond Ranch to John and Lucy Andrist. In 1923 Paul Revere White and his brother, Claude, bought the ranch from Andrist. The Bond Ranch and land added to it by Paul became known as the White Ranch. The White family ranched here from 1913 to 1972. In 1975 Anna Lee, Paul's widow, transferred 3002 acres of the ranch to Jeffco Open Space.

(Compiled from: Bond, R. F., 1989, *The land persists:* Jeffco Hist. Com. contest entry. R. F. Bond is the great-grandson of James Bond.)

KEN AND LELA (WHITE) GREEN COLLECTION

Paul R. and Anna Lee White, for whom White Ranch Park is named.

In 1995 Jefferson County purchased 1,000 acres from Golden Properties, Inc., a division of Coors. This land lies to the NE of the White Ranch and includes an almost pristine canyon with critical bear habitat. There is also a striking waterfall, breathtaking buttes and rock formations, and a thriving stream habitat.

White Ranch Open Space Park is dedicated to the memory of Paul R. White.

Clear Creek Canyon Open Space

"Jefferson County commissioners have made it clear that Clear Creek Canyon will be an open space park by the end of the century.

Purchase of the Flynn site [184 acres for about $700,000 to keep development out of the south rim of the canyon and protect the 8-mile Beaver Brook Trail] would be the third major acquisition toward preserving about a 2-mile stretch of towering canyon lands and lower shelves between Golden and near the junction of U.S. 6 and Colorado 119.

On Aug. 1, Jefferson County made the first acquisition of 766 acres along the north rim of the canyon for $2.9 million from Chicago developer Ren Goltra. Goltra is the county's largest landowner, with 9,200 acres.

In October the county spent $2.5 million for 875 acres at the mouth of the canyon, north of U.S. 6 and west of Colorado 93."

(Source: Garnaas, Steve, 1995, *Jeffco Open Space closer to vision for canyon:* Denver Post, Dec. 15, 1995.)

The last block of land mentioned above was purchased from Brannan Sand & Gravel Company. The 875-acre shape roughly resembles the top half of a T-square and encompasses the lower region of Magpie Gulch (pioneer designation), the upper region of Indian Gulch (pioneer designation), Galbraith Mountain, and the land at the entrance to Golden Gate Canyon.

EDITORS' NOTE: For an excellent description of the Brannan purchase, see Brannan's 528-page proposal entitled *Pit 24 (Quarry)*. In addition to detailed mining plans, the book is a gold mine of maps and photographs interlaced with reports on climatology, vegetation, history, wildlife, etc., and has become a collector's item.

> "Clear Creek is *'Denver's Grand Canyon'*—the last largely undeveloped canyon system in the metro Front Range. Worthy of permanent park protection, the canyon west of Golden is rated by experts as 'a world-class landform' and 'unique' because of its incredibly deep, sheer gorge. It is the Front Range equal of the Royal Gorge and the Black Canyon of the Gunnison National Monument!...
>
> The Canyon is more than a monument of stone. It is still being carved by one of Colorado's most famous white-water rivers, flowing from the Continental Divide into the South Platte-Missouri River system. In its gorges, uplands, and streams, wildlife—black bear, mountain lion, bobcat, bighorn sheep, elk, deer, fox, coyote, marten, trout, hawks, and bald and golden eagles—still roam, swim, and soar within sight of Denver skyscrapers. Rare plants, fragile wetlands, and a range of ecosystems from near-desert to sub-alpine give it incredible diversity. It is rich in historical landmarks—from the first railroad though the Rocky Mountains to our earliest gold diggings, and in the prehistoric—from Indian camps, trails and sacred crystal caverns, even mastodon bones...
>
> Protection of the Canyon is off to a great start, with nearly 4,000 acres already set aside in open space..."
>
> (Source: Clear Creek Land Conservancy, Dec. 1995.)

In March 1999, Jeffco Commissioners agreed to purchase approximately 2,900 acres from the O.R. Goltra family trust to further preserve Clear Creek Canyon. The property is situated between Clear Creek Canyon on the south and Robinson Hill Road on the north and borders Guy Gulch on the west.

The ground, which includes Sheep Mountain and the Elk Creek and Mayhem Creek drainages, is not yet classified as a park. Until it can be classified as a park, it will remain closed to the public.

The total purchase price of $18.8 million includes a 79-acre parcel in Indian Gulch (a.k.a Magpie Gulch).

More recently, an adjoining 430 acres on Elk Creek were purchased from Hayes-Angell for $2,500,000.

EDITORS' NOTE: Four hundred thousand acres of open space are lost to development every year in the United States. Jefferson County's Open Space Program is a remarkable amalgamation of citizen action and government planning.

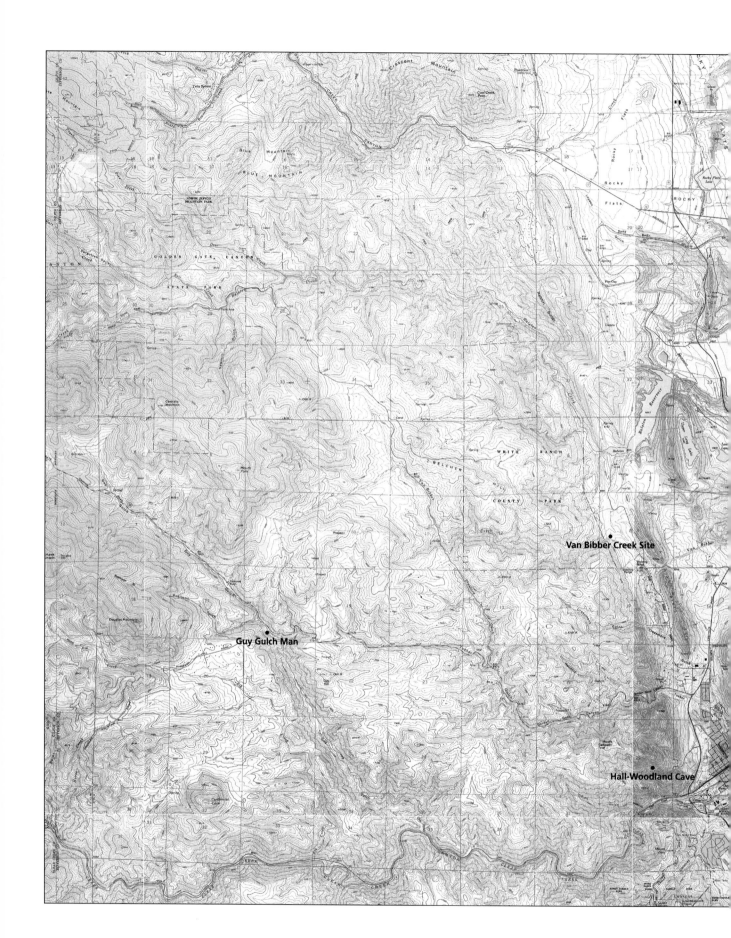

Van Bibber Creek Site

Guy Gulch Man

Hall-Woodland Cave

Prehistoric Sites

Guy Gulch Man

A prehistoric burial at the bottom of Guy Gulch ab. 0.25 mile S of that gulch's intersection with the Robinson Hill Road.

S/b Ralston Buttes Quad.
S16, T3S, R71W.
Elv. ab. 7350'.

The human burial was unearthed by road builders while digging a quarry in 1975. The bones were placed in a sack and the site destroyed. As a result, all contextual relationships were destroyed. No cultural materials were recovered. Later analysis of bone fragments by the Colorado University Department of Anthropology revealed that the skeleton was intact prior to being unearthed, and that the bone breakage was fresh.

The burial was that of a male, 30-35 years old, stature approximately 168.0 centimeters. The man is thought to date from the Woodland occupation, A.D. 700-1000.

(Compiled from: Nickens, P. R., 1977, *An isolated human burial of probable Woodland association from Golden Gate Canyon, Colorado:* Plains Anthropologist, v. 22, no. 76, pt. 1, p. 119-122.)

It is now against county regulations to destroy a grave site prior to thorough archaeological investigation.

Guy Gulch as it climbs N between the massive shoulders of Mt. Tom to the right and Douglas Mountain to the left. The Robinson Hill Road can be seen coming in from the W midway in the picture. Guy Gulch Man was buried on the flat this way from the Robinson Hill Road. Photographed 1991.

Hall-Woodland Cave

The cave accommodated an aboriginal occupation that dates from Woodland times. See Hall-Woodland Cave in Caves.

Van Bibber Creek Site

Open surface site on the S bank of Van Bibber, a.k.a. Dry Creek, where the creek exits the Front Range.
S/b Golden Quad.
SE¹/4 of S8, T3S, R70W.

Ancient man's living quarters. Three cultural zones were found, representing time spans ranging from 190 B.C. through A.D. 900.

> "…reported in 1956 by Mr. Richard Van Horn, a geologist for the United States Geological Survey, when he noted a distinct layer of charcoal exposed in the south bank of Van Bibber Creek…"
>
> (Source: Nelson, C. E., 1969, *Salvage archaeology on Van Bibber Creek,* in Southwestern Lore: Colo. Archaeological Soc., v. 34, March 1969, no. 4, p. 85-106.)

The exposed charcoal occurred about 13 to 17 inches below the creek bank. A sample collected from this level for further study yielded a side-notched projectile point fashioned from quartzite, and the base of an second side-notched point fashioned from obsidian.

Several factors threatened the site: a portion of the bank had been cut away by high water, 75 percent of the area had been bulldozed into the creek, and a small earthen dam had taken its toll. As a result, it was decided to excavate the site immediately.

This salvage excavation began February 10, 1967. Only undisturbed areas were studied. Also, care was taken not to excavate too close to the creek bank so as not to invite further erosion. Careful study revealed three different levels of occupation, the deepest (190±145 B.C.) between 20 and 35 inches deep.

The detailed, well-illustrated 22-page article offers a glimpse of our long-ago neighbors who may have originated in the Southwest, drifting northward in splinter groups into the San Luis Valley, over Poncha Pass and along the Arkansas River into South Park. From here the waters of the South Platte would have led them north and east out of the mountains into the foothills region.

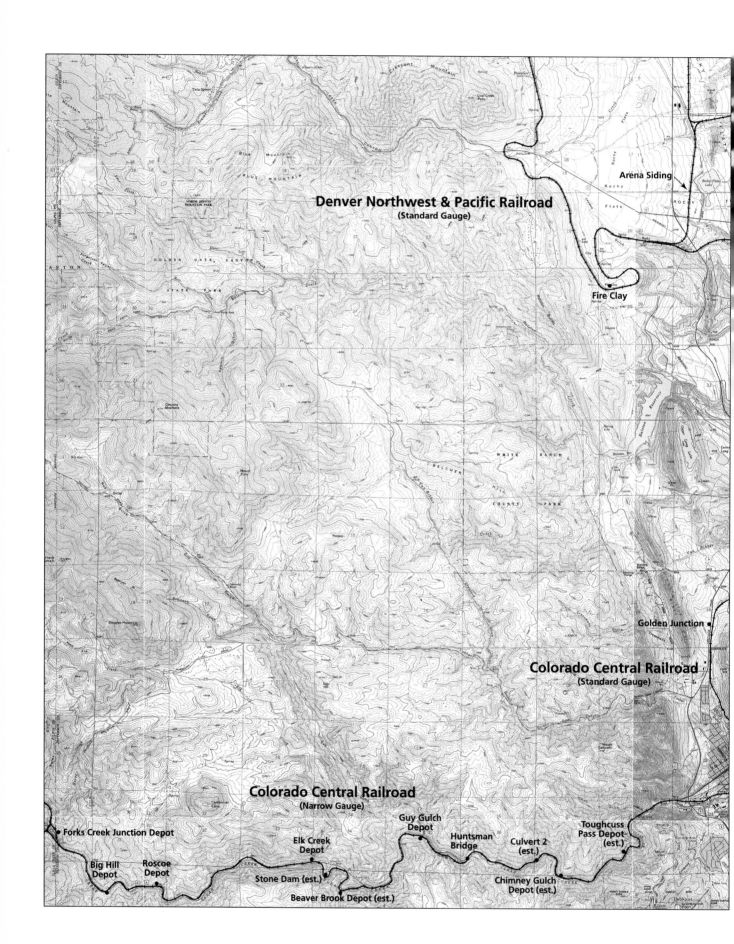

Arena Siding

Denver Northwest & Pacific Railroad
(Standard Gauge)

Fire Clay

Golden Junction

Colorado Central Railroad
(Standard Gauge)

Colorado Central Railroad
(Narrow Gauge)

Guy Gulch
Depot

Forks Creek Junction Depot

Elk Creek
Depot

Huntsman
Bridge

Culvert 2
(est.)

Toughcuss
Pass Depot
(est.)

Big Hill
Depot

Roscoe
Depot

Stone Dam (est.)

Beaver Brook Depot (est.)

Chimney Gulch
Depot (est.)

Railroads

Colorado Central, Clear Creek Canyon
NARROW GAUGE

"Work on the Col. Central R. R., West Division, will be put through now in a short time with vigor. C. C. Welch has contracted to do the grading to a point just beyond Guy Gulch, nearly 6¼ miles, of which ¼ mile is already completed. The remaining 6 miles require a great deal of work, perhaps the heaviest part of the work upon the whole route to the forks of the Creek. The work to be completed by spring."

(Source: Colo. Transcript, day missing, 1871.)

"The roadbed is ready for track as far as Big Hill Station, twelve miles from the Golden depot…about half a mile E of Washington Street… Track laying commenced at the depot Monday, July 22 [1872].

Track laying reached the Forks of Clear Creek Sunday, September 15th… The first load of pay freight came down Clear Creek Saturday, Sept. 21. There were no tunnels on this twelve miles of railroad and the creek was crossed but twice. There were hardly a hundred consecutive feet of straight track. Maximum grades were four per cent, or over 200 feet rise in a mile. Maximum curvature was 33 degrees.

The whole line was an engineering experiment."

(Source: Davis, E. O., 1949, *Building Colorado's first mountain railroad*: Colo. Mag., v. 26, no. 4, p. 298-305.)

"[Clear Creek Canyon] twists and turns marvelously, and its stupendous sides are nearly perpendicular, while farther progress is to all appearance continually blocked by great masses of rock and piles of snow-covered mountains.

Unfortunately, its sides have been almost entirely denuded of timber, mining operations consuming any quantity of it. The narrow-gauge, steep-grade railway, which runs up the canyon for the convenience of the rich mining districts of Georgetown, Black Hawk, and Central City, is a curiosity of engineering. The track has partly been blasted out of the sides of the canyon, and has partly been "built" by making a bed of stones in the creek itself, and laying the track across them. I have never seen such churlishness and incivility as in the officials of that railroad and the stage-lines which connect with it, or met with such preposterous charges. They have handsome little cars on the route, but though the passengers paid full fare, they put us into a baggage-car because the season was over, and in order to see anything I was obliged to sit on the floor at the door. The singular grandeur cannot be described."

(Source: Bird, Isabella, 1873, *A lady's life in the Rocky Mountains:* New York, G. P. Putnam's Sons, pp. 220-221)

"There are two passenger trains daily between Denver and the mountain cities, running narrow gauge cars... An observation car is run in the tourist season on all trains. [From Golden] the train is divided into two sections, one goes to Central and the other to Georgetown, but run over the same track until they reach the forks of Clear Creek, thirteen miles from Golden."

(Source: Crofutt, G. A., 1881, *Crofutt's grip-sack guide of Colorado:* Omaha, Neb., Overland Pub. Co., p. 40.)

"[July 22nd 1880]. Went on excursion to Idaho Springs through Clear Creek Canon...The scenery through this Canon is grand, sublime, while at the same time it is awful. To think that a R. Road could be built at all through such a place looks beyond the ken of human ingenuity.

One continuous serpentine course of 25 miles following the course of the Creek, crossing the same some dozen times, winding around huge Boulders, running under Cliffs, shutting out the light of the sun, thence again going through the same ordeal again; and on, on, until we arrive at the Springs, a rather nice little Town, strung out in a narrow valley, say 200 yards wide between the mountains.

...On our return trip to Denver...we left Idaho with Breaks on and steam all off. For 25 miles we sped down through the Canon at a rate that made my head giddy, often dodging for fear of coming in contact with some huge Boulder on some short curve, of which there were hundreds.

To describe the Rocky Mountains such as looms up from this Canon is entirely beyond my ability with the pen to do."

(Source: *Colorado as seen by a visitor of 1880:* Colo. Mag., v. 12, No. 3, May 1935.)

"[Observed while riding to Black Hawk around 1880] We pass a heavily loaded freight on its way to the mines and mills. Soon after we meet one equally heav-

This picture is notable for the enormous talus slope below the rock cliff to the right. By studying the skyline, can you tell where this section of track was?

COLORADO DEPARTMENT OF TRANSPORTATION

ily laden speeding to the valley by the simple power of gravitation. Let us see what they carry. The one ascending has among other items a car-load of salt, from Great Salt Lake, which came via the Union Pacific all this distance, and is now being taken to the great smelting works above, to perform its part in separating the metals from the ore. Another car bears hay from valley meadows to mountain stables. Mule-power is a grand lever up there, and can't be perpetuated without hay. Then there is an immense steam engine and mining machinery occupying another car. There will be thousands more before the ore channels are all developed, for mining is in its infancy here. Other cars are loaded with tons of flour, beef, groceries, vegetables and mining supplies of every nature. And this is only one train. Sometimes there are two or three a day, and this continues every day in the year, for mining communities *produce only gold and silver.* Everything else must go to them though this narrow and ever-beautiful pathway.

Coming down on the other train there was what? *Gold from Central! Silver from Georgetown!* Here was business on a specie basis, sure enough, and the simplicity of the transaction renders comment unnecessary."

(Source: Strahorn, Robert, *To the Rockies and beyond.*)

By the 1920s the encroachment of the automobile was having its effect, passenger revenues were dropping and train trips through the canyon were being reduced. In 1921 the Colorado and Southern Railroad petitioned the public utilities commission for authority to further curtail passenger service on its Clear Creek Division. Vigorous protests were made by residents of Silver Plume, Idaho Springs and Georgetown.

R. I. P.

"...the first locomotive, the 'General Sherman,'
whistled in the Canon August 21, 1872,
and the last one whistled out July 8, 1941.
During the 69 years of operations this baby road carried millions of passengers and tons of freight.
It was for over 50 years the most popular one-day
railroad excursion trip in Colorado..."

(Source: Davis, E. O., 1949, *Building Colorado's first mountain railroad:*
Colo. Mag., v. 26, no. 4, p. 298-305.)

For an exciting ride back in time on the old CC, complete with great old photographs, read Hauck, C. W. 1972, *Narrow Gauge to Central and Silverplume, Colorado Rail Annual No. 10*, available at the Colorado Railroad Museum, Golden.

Bridges and Stops

Listed as encountered from Golden W through Clear Creek Canyon as far as Forks Creek. A caveat! Some stops, with no gulch nearby to anchor their history, may have evolved into more than one name. For example, the first timetable printed in 1872 shows the stops in this order: Golden, Toughcuss, Culvert 2, Guy Gulch, Beaver, Elk Creek, Stone Dam, Tahapi, Forks. But the handbill of 1874 makes no mention of Toughcuss, Culvert 2, Stone Dam or Tahapi.

Remember that not every stop had a depot. Stops were utilized as traffic demanded. With no one waiting at Huntsman's Ranch, for example, the little train whizzed on by.

Three bridges: Huntsman (a.k.a. Brown's) (a.k.a. Guy Gulch), Elk Meadow, and Forks Creek.

Toughcuss Pass
Named for Toughcuss, *i.e.*, Clear Creek Canyon.
Evergreen Quad

On the 1872 timetable in the handbill collection of the Colorado Railroad Museum, Toughcuss Pass is 14 minutes above Golden.

Toughcuss Pass as seen looking upstream in Clear Creek Canyon. The railroad is to the right. To the left, tacked onto the side of the mountain, is a water flume. The poles across the river in the foreground accommodated a plank footbridge. Locate the skyline and you will have located Toughcuss Pass.

COLORADO RAILROAD MUSEUM

Chimney Gulch Depot

Chimney Gulch opens S of the creek ab. 1 mile above Tunnel No. 1. Prior to highway construction there was a large meadow here. A tall, skinny rock formation at the entrance gave the gulch its name.

S/b Evergreen Quad.
S6, T4S, R70W.
Elv. ab. 6000'.

"First stop / 20 minutes / 3.2 miles W of Golden"

> (Source: CCRR Time Schedule No. 25, handbill, Oct. 26, 1874.)

"Maximum speed of narrow-gauge passenger trains…Golden to Forks Creek, 15 miles per hour…"

> (Source: 1904 Colorado & Southern Railway / Clear Creek District / Timetable.)

"Chimney Gulch is passed in three miles and Guy Gulch in another three. Between these two gulches are many old placer claims, but little has been done in them since 1859-60, when this was a busy camp. Two miles further is Beaver Brook…"

> (Source: Crofutt, G. A., 1881, *Crofutt's grip-sack guide of Colorado:* Omaha, Neb., Overland Pub. Co., p. 40.)

This may also have been the site of the *Culvert 2* stop listed in the first detailed CCRR timetable as 24 minutes above Golden.

Crofutt lists Chimney Gulch as 18 miles west from Denver; fare, $1.10.

Station no longer in existence, exact site unknown.

Culvert 2

S/b Evergreen Quad
Site and history unknown.

On the 1872 timetable, Culvert 2 is 24 minutes above Golden.

Huntsman Bridge

Between the entrances to Guy Gulch and Huntsman Gulch.
The first bridge in the canyon.
Named for Huntsman Ranch.

S/b Evergreen Quad.
S36, T3S, R71W.
Elv. ab. 6200'.

{Var. names: **Brown's Bridge, Guy Gulch Bridge.**}

"By Monday evening, July 24th, [1872] two and one-fourth miles had been laid and on August 7th tracks reached Brown Bridge, four miles from Golden. (This bridge was a through wooden truss about 100 feet long, the first crossing of Clear Creek.)"

(Source: Davis, E. O., 1949, *Building Colorado's first mountain railroad:* Colo. Mag., v. 26, no. 4, p. 298-305.)

Bridge no longer in existence. Numerous photographs of the bridge in the Hauck book, *Narrow Gauge to Central and Silver Plume,* give the viewer a good idea of its location.

Huntsman Bridge in Clear Creek Canyon as seen looking downstream.

Huntsman Bridge in Clear Creek Canyon as seen looking upstream.

Guy Gulch Depot

At the mouth of Guy Gulch.

S/b Evergreen Quad.
S35, T3S, R71W.
Elv. ab. 6200'.

(Source: 1942 Denver Mountain Parks Map.)

"On Monday, August 12, track-layers reached the bridge near Guy gulch, seven miles up the Canon, and still no locomotive…All the rail and most of the ties were hauled from Golden with horses, but this slow process now ceased as the locomotive 'General Sherman No. 2' arrived Monday night, August 19th.

The track materials were drawn up on flat cars by horses and often the driver and horses were allowed to coast back down to Golden of their own volition. They frequently rushed down at the speed of twenty miles an hour, gracefully and safely turning every curve."

(Source: Davis, E. O., 1949, *Building Colorado's first mountain railroad:* Colo. Mag., v. 26, no. 4, p. 298-305.)

"Second stop / 47 minutes / 6 miles W of Golden"

(Source: CCRR Time Schedule No. 25, handbill, Oct. 26, 1874.)

"Guy Gulch—Jefferson county, a small station…six miles west from Golden and twenty-one miles from Denver; fare, $1.40. Near are many evidences of placer mining, but little has been done since 1860."

(Source: Crofutt, G. A., 1881, *Crofutt's grip-sack guide of Colorado:* Omaha, Neb., Overland Pub. Co., p. 106.)

The entrance to Guy Gulch as seen from across Clear Creek. Photographed 1991.

Frequent washouts in the lower regions of Guy Gulch resulted in the Guy Gulch Wagon Road through the bottom of the gulch between the depot and the Gregory Road being abandoned for good. People living in Guy Gulch then walked over the eastward ridge to the Huntsman Ranch to catch the train.

Station no longer in existence, exact site unknown.

Beaver Brook Depot

Directly SW of Beaver Brook entrance.

S/b Evergreen Quad.
S3, T4S, R71W.
Elv. ab. 6400'.

(Source: 1942 Denver Mountain Parks Map.)

"Third stop / 59 minutes / 8 miles W of Golden"

(Source: CCRR Time Schedule No. 25, handbill, Oct. 26, 1874.)

"Beaver Brook, the first stopping place so far on this route…a small stream, comes in on the left, down a narrow canon, up which six miles distant, is located a saw mill in a perfect forest of timber. Near the station, away up on a projecting point of the mountain, 300 feet above the road, and almost overhanging it, is located a pavilion with a stairway leading to it from near the platform below. In the summer this place is a great resort for picnic parties from the valley below and the mountain town above…The scenery at this point is grand…"

(Source: Crofutt, G. A., 1881, *Crofutt's grip-sack guide of Colorado:* Omaha, Neb., Overland Pub. Co., p. 40.)

Crofutt lists Beaver Brook as 22 miles west from Denver; fare, $1.50. Not listed on the 1904 Colorado & Southern Railway / Clear Creek District / Timetable.

Station no longer in existence, exact site unknown.

Looking upgrade at INSPIRATION POINT, ELEV. 6840 FT. *just west of Beaver Brook Station. The spot takes its name from being a particular favorite for photographers because of the rock cribbing all the way around the curve, and the narrow defile between the canyon walls.*

OVERLEAF *Beaver Brook Depot, from* **Crofutt's Grip-Sack Guide of Colorado,** *1881.*

COLORADO DEPARTMENT OF TRANSPORTATION

BEAVER BROOK STATION, WITH PIC-NIC PAVILION.

miles east from Pueblo—fare forty cents— on the north side of the Arkansas River. *Tour 8.*

Beaver Brook—Jefferson county, is situated at the junction of a small creek, called Beaver Brook with Clear Creek, in Clear Creek Cañon, on the line of the Colorado Division Union Pacific Railway, twenty-two miles west from Denver, fare $1.50. It is a great resort in summer for pic-nic parties; the scenery is very grand and beautiful. *Tour 2.*

Beaver Creek—Fremont county, situated

Stone Dam

S/b Evergreen Quad.
Site and history unknown.

On the 1872 timetable, Stone Dam is 1 hour 3 minutes above Golden.

Elk Creek Depot

Directly NE of Elk Creek entrance.
S/b Evergreen Quad.
S34, T3S, R71W.
Elv. ab. 6600'.

(Source: 1924 Denver Mountain Parks Map.)

"Fourth stop / 69 minutes / 9 miles W of Golden"

(Source: CCRR Time Schedule No. 25, handbill, Oct. 26, 1874.)

"Elk Creek, a side track for passing trains, is reached, one mile above Beaver Brook, and we continue climbing up, up, between towering mountain cliffs…"

(Source: Crofutt, G. A., 1881, *Crofutt's grip-sack guide of Colorado:* Omaha, Neb., Overland Pub. Co., p. 40.)

Station no longer in existence, exact site unknown. The bridge here was called the bridge at Elk Meadow. This was the second bridge in the canyon. Numerous photographs in Hauck's book *Narrow Gauge to Central and Silver Plume* give the viewer a good idea of the location of the bridge.

Tahapi

S/b Evergreen Quad.
Site and history unknown.

On the 1872 timetable, Tahapi is 1 hour 15 minutes above Golden.

Roscoe Depot

Three miles above Tunnel No. 3 at the entrance of Mayhem Creek between Big Hill and Elk Creek stations. (The only drainage approaching this stretch of track from the N.)
S/b Evergreen Quad.
S6, T4S, R71W.

(Source: 1924 Denver Mountain Parks Map.)

Not listed on the 1874 railroad handbill. Station no longer in existence. Exact site unknown. Hauck's *Narrow Gauge to Central and Silver Plume,* however, does have a picture of the depot.

Big Hill Depot

One mile E of Forks Creek Junction.

s/b Squaw Pass Quad.
S6, T4S, R71W.
Elv. ab. 6800'.

(Source: 1924 Denver Mountain Parks Map.)

"Fifth stop / 1 hour 34 minutes / 12.5 miles W of Golden"

(Source: CCRR Time Schedule No. 25, handbill, Oct. 26, 1874.)

Last stop E of Forks Creek Junction on the Colorado Central Railroad.

Track completed to Big Hill, Aug. 31, 1872. The first train reached Big Hill Sept. 2, 1872.

(Compiled from: Davis, E. O., 1949, *Building Colorado's first mountain railroad:* Colo. Mag., v. 26, no. 4, p. 298-305.)

"Here the old Mt. Vernon wagon road comes down the mountain from the left… [A detailed description of the difficulties of the Mt. Vernon road follows.] Those who grumble at railroad charges, please take notice: the wagon road is still there—*try it.*"

(Source: Crofutt, G. A., 1881, *Crofutt's grip-sack guide of Colorado:* Omaha, Neb., Overland Pub. Co., p. 41.)

Crofutt lists Big Hill as 26 miles west from Denver; fare, $2.00. Station no longer in existence.

Forks Creek Junction Depot

14 miles W of Golden at the W entrance to Clear Creek Canyon.
Takes name from location at confluence of the north and south forks of Clear Creek.

S/b Squaw Pass Quad.
S36, T3S, R72W.
Elv. ab. 6820'.

This is the point where the Colorado Central Railroad divided NW toward Black Hawk and SW toward Georgetown.

Narrow-gauge track reached here Sept. 15, 1872. A bridge was constructed over each fork of the creek to make a wye connection.

(Compiled from: Davis, E. O., 1949, *Building Colorado's first mountain railroad:* Colo. Mag., v. 26, no. 4, p. 298-305.)

"Forks Creek, one mile further on, is the junction of the North and South Clear Creek. Here the route for Georgetown turns to the left, across the bridge, while

Forks Creek. The track to the left ran to Idaho Springs, the track to the right to Black Hawk. With its large Howe Truss bridge and a short tunnel, the Forks Creek wye enabled trains to switch engines and cargo to utilize both routes. As this picture was taken, the settlement's eating house and post office are behind the photographer. Until 1999, the modern highways crossed the creek at the same locations.

that for Black Hawk and Central keeps to the right. As we have always had a desire to do right, we will keep to the right awhile longer, and note the result."

(Source: Crofutt, G. A., 1881, *Crofutt's grip-sack guide of Colorado:* Omaha, Neb., Overland Pub. Co., p. 41.)

Crofutt lists Forks Creek as 28 miles west from Denver; fare, $2.15. The junction accommodated a train station, post office and restaurant. Some stonework is still visible above the water.

Where the forks of the creek meet is the common corner for Clear Creek, Jefferson and Gilpin counties, as determined by the 1902-04 State Survey.

Colorado Central, Golden Quad
STANDARD GAUGE

"We have noticed a camping party for several days on the bluff south of town, which, on inquiry, we found is a party of men getting out the timber for the railroad bridge across Ralston Creek, which point the graders have nearly reached."

(Source: Colo. Transcript, June 2, 1869.)

"We are informed by one of the engineer party that there are 28 teams now working on the grade of the Colorado Central near where the road crosses Ralston Creek. Some time has been lost during the late storm, owing to the difficulty in scraping through the mud. We believe the number of men and teams is to be considerably enhanced in a few days."

(Source: *Ibid.*)

"It is a busy scene down the grade of the Colorado Central R. R. Between thirty and forty teams are at work near the crossing of Ralston; a portion of them are at work upon the east side of that stream, where good progress is being made. The spring rains do not appear to have injured the grade in the least, but rather improved it. It appears to be thoroughly settled to place, and will be in fine condition for track-laying."

(Source: *Ibid.* June 20, 1869.)

"[Golden] now contains a population of 2,731…The shops of the 'Central' are located here, where most of their box, flat, coal and common cars are manufactured."

(Source: Crofutt, G. A., 1881, *Crofutt's grip-sack guide of Colorado:* Omaha, Neb., Overland Pub. Co., p. 104.)

"The Union Pacific Company…will build an elegant new depot this summer at the crossing of Washington avenue and Railroad street…

Golden is the terminus of the Colorado Central railroad, narrow gauge branch of the Union Pacific, and the transfer point. There are sixty employees of this company residing here permanently. The company does a large freight business, second to Denver only, in Colorado, on the Union Pacific system. There are sixteen daily trains, excepting Sunday. There is a switch engine and crew here all the time and between six and eight miles of switch track in the yards. The tracks run to three brick yards, two coal mines, two warehouses, paper mill, flouring mills, smelter, clay banks, glass works, etc. The property of the company at Golden consists of a fourteen stall round house, coal platform, store rooms, carpenter shop, paint shop, wrecking outfit, two depots, viz: Passenger depot

65 × 24 feet having two fine waiting rooms, office and baggage room, freight depot 150 × 40 feet, containing the offices of assistant agent, transfer clerk, warehouse clerk, yardmaster, roadmaster. On an average six million pounds of coal are transferred here per month."

(Source: *The Union Pacific R.R.* in The Golden Globe, Industrial Edition, May 20, 1893, p. 13.)

Churches Station

17999 West 60th Ave. (1 mile E of State Highway 93).
S/B Golden Quad.
NE1/4 of S10 and NW1/4 of S11, T3S, R70W. (Not mapped in this book.)
Elv. ab. 5750'.

{Var. name: **Water Board Place.** The Denver Water Board has owned this property since 1937 when the Ralston Reservoir was built.}

Described variously in early literature as a railroad station, a ranch, and a stage stop.

Charles Ryland writes of Captain Berthoud as having been "seen in the neighborhood of Churches (Ralston Creek) with a huge instrument surveying a road."*

*(Source: Ryland, Charles S., *The Energetic Captain Berthoud,* in The Westeners 1965, The Denver Brand Book, p. 93.)

A grant was awarded to the Arvada Historical Society for preservation of Churches Ranch. The historical survey report was written by Laurie Simmons and funded by the Colorado Historical Society. We are indebted to Marcetta Lutz of the Jefferson County Historical Commission for raising the following color from the extensive amount of research documents:

John C. Churches was born in Somerset, England, July 8, 1823, and died on August 12, 1910, in Jefferson County, Golden, Colorado. He married Mary Ann Colepriert about 1845. She was born in Somerset, England, September 13, 1817, and died May 16, 1889.

The Churches family came to America in the early 1850s and settled in Iowa and Milan, Missouri. John C. Churches traveled by ox team with Asahel Haines and John A. Higgins among others in the 1859 gold rush to Colorado.

(Compiled from: The Arvada Enterprise, Aug. 18, 1910, as quoted in *Arvada, just between you and me,* 1904-1941: Arvada Hist. Soc., 1985, p. 29.)

It is interesting to note that Churches father's name was John Churchouse. The surname was changed to Churches by the first family to settle in Jefferson County.

(Compiled from: Robson, Carolyn Churches, *Biography*, Arvada Hist. Soc. Collection.)

He returned to Missouri, and in the spring of 1862, John C. Churches' citizenship papers were filed in Milan, Missouri. Homestead records indicate that by 1868, Churches had built a stone house, stone barn, corral, two water wells, and a log barn. Patent for the land was issued

September 1, 1869. The Churches home was also used as a half-way house for travelers and their livestock on their way to the mountains.

(Compiled from: National Archive Records, Washington, D. C. Affidavit Required of Homestead Claimants, Acts of May 20, 1862, and June 21, 1866, signed December 21, 1868. John C. Churches Patent, No. 9, was approved and received May 11, 1869.)

Churches Station. Both buildings are still standing and are now owned by Jeffco Open Space.

The former Churches Station, photographed 1977. Note the original barn building behind the later-built silo. Ralston Buttes are in the background. Indian Head mountain (see arrow) is named from viewing it from this angle.

Realizing the necessity of water for farming and livestock, John C. Churches built an irrigation ditch out of Ralston Creek, which covered a distance of several miles and a reservoir in the area.

(Compiled from: Colo. Transcript, March 2, 1870. By Oct. 8, 1872, the Transcript reported that the project was almost completed.)

John Churches was the first Worthy Master of Enterprise Grange No. 25. He and his wife, Mary Ann Churches, also served in the Colorado State Grange and in Darden Pomona No. 1.

(Compiled from: Ogilvie, Caroline, *History of Enterprise Grange:* unpublished manuscript.)

In 1881 Mary Ann Churches, together with Mary A. Wadsworth of Arvada, were active in the Woman Suffrage movement. The women of Denver and the state at large were urged to attend meetings to discuss the social and political status of women "with a view to organizing a society through which they may help themselves and each other to self culture and self government for the benefit of society, their country and posterity."

(Compiled from: Rocky Mountain News, Jan. 15, 1881: captioned *A Call for a Women's Meeting*, p. 8, c. 3.)

Golden Junction

N of Golden near State Highway 93.

S/b Golden Quad.
S16, T3S, R70W.
Elv. ab. 6000'.

{Var. name: **Jones Siding.***}

(*Source: Scott, G. R., 1976, *Historic trail map of the greater Denver area, Colorado:* U.S. Geol. Survey Misc. Inv. Ser., Map I-856-G.)

"First stop / 15 minutes / 2 miles N of Golden"

(Source: CCRR Time Schedule No. 25, handbill, Oct. 26, 1874.)

"Two miles from Golden the summit is reached at Jones; here we find several coal mines and lime kilns, and on our left a long, narrow, high rocky ridge called the 'hog back,'…"

(Source: Crofutt, G. A., 1881, *Crofutt's grip-sack guide of Colorado:* Omaha, Neb., Overland Pub. Co., p. 37.)

Station no longer in existence, exact site unknown.

Ralston Depot

On Ralston Creek.

S/b Golden Quad.
S3, T3S, R70W. (Not mapped in this book.)
Elv. ab. 5748'.

"Second stop / 30 minutes / 5 miles N of Golden"

> (Source: CCRR Time Schedule No. 25, handbill, Oct. 26, 1874.)

"Ralston station will be an excellent point for shipment of coal from Boulder county… As a cattle depot it offers particular inducements, and the R. R. Co. intends to ship cattle from this station."

> (Source: Colo. Transcript, day missing, 1871.)

"At Ralston station a depot (frame) 16?×80 is being put up. Also a section house 20×30. The depot site is beautiful and promises to be a valuable way station."

> (Source: *Ibid.*)

"We are now on the down grade [from Jones] and shall reach Ralston in five miles from Golden…The creek, from which the station is named, is a small stream coming down from the mountains through a deep cut in the 'hog back' ridge…"

> (Source: Crofutt, G. A., 1881, *Crofutt's grip-sack guide of Colorado:* Omaha, Neb., Overland Pub. Co., p. 37.)

Station no longer in existence, exact site unknown.

Denver Northwest & Pacific [Denver & Rio Grande Western, now Southern Pacific]

STANDARD GAUGE

Crosses Coal Creek Canyon in S13, T2S, R71W, Eldorado Springs Quad.

Part of the Moffat Road built by David Moffat. The line was surveyed July-November 1902, work began December 1902. Track was completed from Denver to Mammouth, today's Tolland, on June 23, 1904.

The trestle crossing Coal Creek was 265' long and 60' high. In 1938 a flood washed out the road and damaged the bridge. A new bridge, with its current 40' span, was built 250' W of the old bridge.

(Compiled from: Brescia, Janice, *Coal Creek Canyon history:* Jeffco 1991 North Mountains Area Community Plan.)

The 1942 RBQ labels this line the Denver and Salt Lake. The 1948 RBQ labels it the Denver & Rio Grande Western.

The variety of names the railroads hold is due to changes in areas served and to changes in ownership.

Arena Siding

N side Leyden Gulch below Highway 72.
1948 Ralston Buttes Quad.
S20, T2S, R70W.
Elv. 6200'.

{Var. name: **Rocky.** (Source: 1965 RBQ.)}

A switch siding for the railroad.

Extensive clay mining was carried on in this area. The clay was hauled out on railroad cars.

Fireclay Stop

At the edge of the foothills between Ralston and Coal creeks.
1948 Ralston Buttes Quad.
S29, T2S, R70W.
Elv. 6400'.

Took its name from the red clay mines in the area. The clay mined here was sold to Golden Fire Clay and others. In 1940's two old frame houses were occupied by the railroad section foreman and his helper. Earlier quads show three houses.

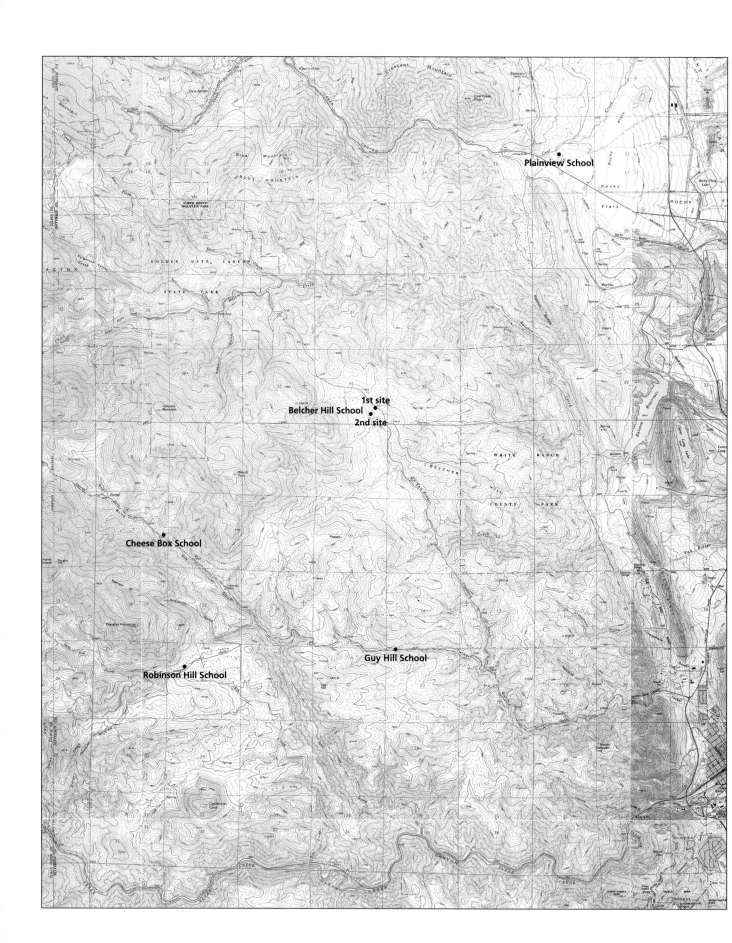

Plainview School

1st site
Belcher Hill School
2nd site

Cheese Box School

Guy Hill School

Robinson Hill School

Schools

GRADES ONE THROUGH EIGHT were taught in these one-classroom schools. Required subjects included reading, penmanship, arithmetic, history, geography, grammar and physiology. Music and art were also taught, depending on the skills and interests of the teacher. At Christmas the students performed a Christmas play for the neighborhood.

Hours were from 9 a.m. to 3:30 p.m., with one hour for lunch and two 15-minute recesses. Because the schools also served as the community center for social meetings, Sunday School services, and dances, the seats were not fastened down. Occasionally, when enrollment was low, several of these schools might be combined.

During the course of the school year a teacher might stay with several local families. How those children got to school, afoot or horseback, was how the teacher got there. A siege of bad weather could close the schools. When this happened, the only children lucky (or unlucky) enough to get their lessons were those pupils whose families harbored the teacher. Schools in the higher reaches of the mountain canyons opened in the summer and closed in the winter.

It is logical to assume that everyone in the host family benefited from an increase in reading, writing, and arithmetic skills. These families also received a small stipend from the State to offset the cost of lodging the teacher.

While the "old maid" country schoolteacher is a common stereotype, in reality the average teacher was under 21 years old, female, and soon married to one of the local bachelors.

In its later years Guy Hill had a teacherage. One of the teachers who lived in this small, one-room frame building hung red flannel long-johns on the clothesline to make it appear a man lived there. In time the teacherage acquired a telephone, which made Guy Hill the only school in the region to have its own telephone.

Where year(s) of service is not known, teachers are listed alphabetically. It is interesting that while both men and women taught in rural schools at the entrances to Coal Creek and Ralston Creek canyons, only two men's names have surfaced in the early RBQ schools: Ted Long, c. 1920, taught for a year in the first Belcher Hill School; Charles McFadden, c. 1893, taught in the old Coal Creek School.

Bay State School—District 10—Elementary

Located 3.6 miles N of the junction of Douglas Mountain and Smith Hill roads, and 1.2 miles S of the junction of Gilpin County Road 8 and Jeffco Road 69.

N side of road.
1942 Black Hawk Quad.
S11, T3S, R72W. (Not mapped in this book.)
Elv. ab. 8900'.

{Var. name: **Smith Hill School** from proximity to Smith Hill Road. The road was built by E. B. and N. K. Smith, c. 1869.}

Named for its first location in the Bay State Mining District before being moved to the Mountain House District. (See Macy Gulch <u>in</u> Drainages.) The name "Bay State" may have originated with miners from Massachusetts. Classes were held from May to October because of heavy winter snows.

One-story frame building. Peak roof, shingled. One entrance. One room, single desks, wood stove, rock chimney.

Surrounding area: well, coal shed attached to the school, outlying shed for horses, one outhouse.

The Green brothers, Kenneth and Malcolm, rifles in hand. Note the rabbit Malcolm is holding. It is easy to imagine the conversation that took place between the boys and the photographer. Smith Hill School as seen from the E is in the background.

Teachers: Betty Alexander, LaVerna Mitchell 1925-1928, etc. LaVerna, who rode horseback 4.5 miles each way from her home W of Golden Gate State Park on weekends, boarded a mile from the school at the Rudolph Ranch during the week. She was paid $90 per month.

Building burned, foundation remains.

(See: Wyhs, Irma, 1996, *The pioneer from Gap Road:* Fence Post, Monday, March 18, 1996, for more about La Verna Mitchell.)

Bay State School, in or after 1927.

Belcher Hill School—District 29—Elementary

1948 Ralston Buttes Quad.
S34, T2S, R71W.
Two different elevations in the 7800-7900' range.

{Var. name: **Drew Hill School** from proximity to Drew Hill.}

Takes name from Belcher Hill.

First site: The school was first built c. 1880 on the ridge beside the Drew Hill Road. A few foundation remnants may still be found. With its gable roof, narrow windows and board-and-batt siding, the weathered little building resembled a miner's cabin.

Teachers: Nellie Barron. Edith M. Culton. Helen Gurney. Miss Hart. Miss James. Cecilia Kelicott. Ted Long, c. 1920. Alice Maguire, c. 1919. Miss Sackley. Winifred White. *Et. al.*

> "The school was first built farther up the hill but the severe winds made it uncomfortable and sometimes downright dangerous. Tom Pearce gave permission for a school building to be put on his place and in 1900 the present building was constructed on the present site in the lee of a protecting rock ledge below the brow of the hill."
>
> (Source: Wyhs, Irma, 1994, *Ranch History*, compiled for Red School Ranch.)

At one time the little school was hit by lightning and severely damaged. This occurrence may have figured in the decision to rebuild it down off the top of the hill.

Belcher Hill School, first site on top of the ridge (beside Drew Hill Road on the ridge line across from today's Pearce Ranch sign).

Belcher Hill School, second site. Photographed 1994, abandoned and forlorn. The building is still in existence, but out of sight on private property.

Second Site: A new school was built down the slope to the W of the original school. This second site is 0.25 mile W of the W entrance to the White Ranch Park.

Teachers: Hazel Alexander. Alice Corbin. Virginia Gatchell, c. 1940. Ella Holmes. Cora Hudson, 1929—married Aubrey Ladwig. Alta Keene. Monroe, c. 1941-42. Lena Rittenhouse. *Et al.* (See Guy Hill School for more about Mrs. Monroe.)

One-story frame building, white with green trim, 24' × 30'. Shingle, 4-12 hip roof. One outside entrance. One classroom.

Surrounding area: small space to play ball, two outhouses, a coal shed, stable, and flagpole. There was no teacherage, but at times a trailer was pulled in.

Abandoned as a school in 1944, the building continued to serve as a community center. After the community hall at the mouth of Crawford Gulch was completed in 1953, the old school was used only for hay storage. Structural integrity intact and spruced up with a coat of red paint, the building served as the sales office for the Red School Ranch until 1997. Privately owned, it is opened now only for special occasions.

Belcher Hill School class picnic, about 1909. BACK ROW *Annie Boyle, Anna Maloney, Miss Hart (teacher), Rosena Maloney, Jack Boyle, Tommy Pearce, Margaret Boyle.* FRONT ROW *James Maloney, Teresa Boyle, Johnny Pearce, Emily Pearce.*

Cheese Box School—District 10

Located on the N side of the GGC Road ab. 1.4 miles above the 8-mile marker at the entrance of the drainage coming down from the N.

S/B Ralston Buttes Quad.

S7, T3S, R71W.

Elv. ab. 8000'.

{Var. names: **Crackerbox School, Matchbox School, Michigan Hill School (?).**}

The names reflect the long, narrow shape of the school.

Built in 1900, used until 1917.

Teachers: Ruth Williams—married Rudolph Bengson and when widowed married John Wikstrom. Swena. *Et al.*

One-story frame building. In the only picture known to exist, the building appears to be white.

Building gone. A few foundation remnants are clearly visible beside the highway.

Coal Creek School—Original—District 27

S/b Eldorado Springs Quad. (Not mapped in this book.)

Dated by local rancher Leavitt Booth as existing in 1893. A one-room log cabin. Children attended classes from May 1 through September 30 to avoid bad weather.

(Compiled from: Brescia, Janice, *Coal Creek Canyon history:* Jeffco 1991 North Mountains Area Community Plan.)

The old Coal Creek School, 1893.

ISABELLA (BENGSON) KOCH COLLECTION

LAVERNA MITCHELL COLLECTION

The legend written by Hilda Belcher on the back of this photo reads: "The old Coal Creek School taken summer of 1893. It is me in plaid dress and apron. Frank back of me. Gus Brumm next to Frank. Alvena sitting on ground with white dress. Chas McFadden, our teacher standing on left of us. James. Cocknen, The rest are the Bengsons and Terrys."

Columbine School

29280 Highway 72, Coal Creek Canyon. Located W of the road.

S/b Eldorado Springs Quad.

S9, T2S, R71W. (Not mapped in this book.)

Elv. ab. 7800'.

Built in 1916. In 1948 the building was sold and expanded into a private home.

(Compiled from: Brescia, Janice, *Coal Creek Canyon history:* Jeffco 1991 North Mountains Area Community Plan.)

Guy Hill School—District 10—Elementary

Located on the N side of the GGC Road ab. 1.5 miles above the Tucker/Crawford Gulch junction.

1948 Ralston Buttes Quad.
S14, T3S, R71W.
Elv. 7260'.

Takes name from proximity to Guy Hill.

Built between 1874 and 1876.

Closed in 1951.

Teachers: Ethel Finch, Hassie Lee McNight, *et al.*

Including: "La" Lorraine Spicer, c. 1815. Gladys Foster, c. 1920—married Ernest Ramstetter. Bertha Olson, c. 1925—married Otto Ramstetter. Muller, c. 1938. Delos James, c. 1940. Virginia Gatchell, c. 1941. Alice C. Maguire, c. 1944—married George Ramstetter. Vina Williams, intermittently for 20 years—married Henry Ramstetter. Crosby, c. 1946. Mullin, c. 1947. Wellman, c. 1948.

> "Guy Hill pupils are having a few days vacation due to the illness of Miss Gatchell. She contracted a very bad cold and was unable to return to school for a week with the exception of one day.
>
> The seventh and eighth grade students are studying hard for the county exams to be given next month. Mrs. Monroe says Belcher Hill School will probably be out the 16th of May."
>
> (Source: *"Static,"* April 1941. Subheading: "25 cents a year and worth twice that." A monthly newspaper sponsored by Lovell and Jeanette Johnson of Golden Gate Canyon. The first edition came out February 1941.)

> "Belcher Hill School and Guy Hill School will have their end of school program and graduation exercises Thurs. evening, May 15th. Jack Pearce and Martha Koch are the eighth grade graduates.
>
> Belcher Hill school picnic will be May 16th. Mrs. Monroe plans to teach the same school again next year.
>
> Guy Hill school picnic will be May 23rd. They are going to Buffalo Bill's grave."
>
> (Source: *Ibid.,* May 1941.)

One-story frame building. Outside dimensions 30.5' × 18.5'. Shingle roof. White w/green trim outside, light color inside. One outside entrance, anteroom and classroom. Two windows on each side of classroom, a window above outside door. Anteroom had closet, coat hooks, table w/water container. Classroom heated w/stove at front of room.

Graduating class at the Guy Hill School, 1910 or thereabouts. Note the rifles the boys are holding. It was common practice for mountain boys to carry a rifle on the long walks to and from classes. The boy second from the right is Walter Ramstetter. Walter died in 1911 after being kicked by a horse. This school is now in the Clear Creek Living History Park.

JIM RAMSTETTER COLLECTION

Guy Hill School class of 1945.
FRONT ROW, LEFT TO RIGHT: *Karol Ramstetter, Norman Crosby.* MIDDLE ROW: *Kenneth Ramstetter, Sam Nankervis, Charlie Ramstetter, Arlene Ramstetter, Jeannet Crosby, Betty Lou Nankervis.* BACK ROW: *Nora Buckman, grandmother of Sam and Betty Lou; Mrs. Crosby, the teacher and mother of Jeannet and Norman; Lue Ramstetter, mother of Karol.*

LUE RAMSTETTER COLLECTION

Surrounding area: swing and teeter-totter, two-door outhouse, stable. Eventually the stable was abandoned, and the students who rode to school kept their horses in the Buckman barn just up the road.

From 1876 through the 1920s graduation exercises were held in the Eight-mile House. In the 1940s a well was drilled. The subsequent well house/coal storage shed was later converted into a separate teacherage. (See introductory remarks.)

Guy Hill School. Photographed 1950, one year before its close in 1951. The small building in the foreground is the teacherage.

In April 1961, Victor Nelson bought the ground the school sat on, along with the school itself. Victor eventually sold the ground and school to Colorado School of Mines Professors Ramon Bisque and Franklin Stermole and their wives.

In 1976 Jo Ann Thistlewood, Mitchell PTA President, was approached by kindergarten teacher Verna Katona to work with the Mitchell Elementary School students on a centennial-bicentennial project. Jo Ann thought the kids wanted flags, what they wanted was to move the Guy Hill School from the canyon to Golden.

The Bisque and Stermole families supported the project with their donation of the school to the Golden Civic Foundation.

Involving the Golden community in the idea, Jo Ann and Verna coordinated the move—obtaining permission from the school board, securing labor and equipment, notifying the State patrol and Golden police, and raising money not only to move the building but to repair and repaint it.

(Compiled from: Jamieson-Nichols, Jill, *Guy Hill finds new home, once again:* Golden Transcript, July 12, 1996, p. 1-2.)

"It was an exciting day for Golden when the historic little Guy Hill School was moved from the mountains to the grounds of Mitchell Elementary School 20 years ago.

Verna Katona, kindergarten teacher at Mitchell Elementary, was driving around the mountains when she spied the original schoolhouse on the side of a hill up Golden Gate Canyon. The windows were broken and some of the side boards had been ripped off for firewood.

She knew the building wouldn't last much longer and dreamed of having it brought to Golden and restored by Mitchell students.

...Guy Hill will be moved from its present location on the Mitchell school grounds to the Clear Creek Living History Ranch at 11th and Cheyenne streets, where it will share honors with other early day structures."

(Source: Dempsey, Alice, 1995, *Guy Hill School to share history:* Golden Transcript, Nov. 23, 1995.)

In 1996 Guy Hill Schoolhouse was moved its fourth and final (but who can say for sure?) time.

"...Guy Hill School, the quaint little schoolhouse at 12th and Ford streets, will be moved to the Clear Creek Ranch Park in the wee hours of Monday, July 29.

It will join the 1860s-era Pearce and Reynolds cabins, which were moved from Golden Gate Canyon in 1994...

City Councilman Ed Ramstetter...remembers going to Grange meetings and Sunday school there. His grandfather and grandfather's three brothers all married schoolmarms that taught at Guy Hill.

A few years ago, his father told him the story of the school being moved to Crawford Gulch in the 1890s because there was more population there than in Golden Gate. Golden Gate residents made such a stink that it was quickly returned."

(Source: Jamieson-Nichols, Jill, *Guy Hill finds new home, once again:* Golden Transcript, July 12, 1996, p. 1-2.)

Mountain House School

Located on the S side of the GGC road 2 miles W of GGSP Headquarters. It is probably no accident that this site is virtually equidistant from the bottom of Junction Hill and the top of the Dory Hill junction. No foundation remnants.

1942 Black Hawk Quad.
S33, T2S, R72W. (Not mapped in this book.)
Elv. ab. 8500'.

Classes were taught in the summer, May through mid-October.

Teachers: Bertha (Olsen) Ramstetter. LaVerna Mitchell, 1929-1931. Hazel Vaughn. *Et al.* LaVerna was paid $75 per month.

"It was a perfect spring day. My partner and I had secured seats on top with the driver, and every minute and foot of the journey was a pure delight…Somewhere along the way we stopped for dinner. I recall a vigorous appetite and a generously loaded table of clean and wholesome food to satisfy it but the name of the station has passed from memory long ago. I also remember passing, in the middle of the afternoon, a little red school house among the pines and firs, all by itself, closed for the day, and with no signs in any direction so far as I could see, of homes that could supply the attending scholars, though all around it were the signs of constant usage. 'Where on earth do the children come from!' I exclaimed. 'Oh,' replied the driver as he flicked a fly off the ear of his nigh leader with the tip of his long whip lash, 'they dig them out from under the stones here and there.'"

(Source: Van Wagenen, Theodore, *Colorado:* Colorado School of Mines
Master's Thesis, Colorado Room Document M36-683.)

Van Wagenen was looking for a job (enrollment in the Colorado School of Mines came later) when he took the stage up the Gregory Road to Black Hawk sometime around 1871. By the time he stopped for dinner he had already descended Guy Hill. It is therefore a good possibility that the school he saw in the middle of that afternoon was Mountain House School. Of his journey's destination he writes:

"We stayed a month in Gilpin county and had a room in a boarding house in Mountain City, the connecting link between Black Hawk and Central…a long double file of unpainted wooden shanties [stretched] up the narrow and deep gulch, projecting here and there a few rods up into side gulches, and lining the one wagon road which could find a place for itself in the narrow bottom. On both sides rose the steep hills, even then [c. 1871] almost completely shorn of the fine forest that had covered them, and dotted with dumps, shafts and tunnel portals. It was a weird scene for one whose only conception of a mining region and mines had been gathered from pictures in books, which, by the way, were at that time illustrated almost exclusively by wood engravings of drawings of German mines."

(Source: *Ibid.*)

This location has great historical significance. Cold Spring is near here, as was 7 mile house.

Headquarters of the old Fred Mitchell Ranch above GGC State Park. The sign over the driveway reads MOUNTAIN HOUSE. *Behind the photographer in the timber is where the old Mountain House School was located. Directly ahead in the center of the photo is Bear Mountain, now referred to as Tremont. Photographed 1997.*

Plainview School

Entrance, Coal Creek Canyon, N of highway.
S/b Eldorado Springs Quad.
S18, T2S, R70W.
Elv. ab. 6500'.

Teachers: Helen Klumker, c. 1918. Helen was the daughter of Martin Klumker, who drove the Glory Hole Stage between Central City and Idaho Springs. Sadie Giberson, c. 1940. Mrs. Smith. Mrs. Lutz. Miss Zeigler. *Et al.* (See Tepee Rings for more on Sadie Giberson.)

Built in 1935 near Plainview. The school was used until May 1951. Beginning in the fall of 1951 area children were bused to Golden.

(Compiled from: Brescia, Janice, *Coal Creek Canyon history:* Jeffco 1991 North Mountains Area Community Plan.)

One room. An adjacent coal shed occasionally served as a bedroom for a snowbound teacher.

Rand's School House

On Ralston Creek.
Golden Quad. (Not mapped in this book.)

"The appointments until further notice will be as follows: Rev. J. Casto will preach every Sabbath evening in the [Baptist] church at Golden City, and every alternate Sabbath at 11 o'clock, at Mount Vernon, and every alternate Sabbath at 3 o'clock, p.m., at Rand's School House, on Ralston Creek."

(Source: Colo. Transcript June 30, 1869.)

"Below are reports of the teachers of the different schools in the Golden City District for the week ending Saturday, Mar. 19, 1870: ...*Ralston District*—Thos. O'Donnell, *Teacher*. Nearest perfect in deportment and recitation:

Masters—Julius W. Flinn, Sydney Flinn, David Ballinger, James Ballinger, F. E. Songer, Jasper E. Crosby, Geo. W. Churches, G. M. Trail.

Misses—Katie Howlett, Alice L. Crosby, Mary Harris, Rachel F. Trail, Mary J. Trail."

(Source: *Ibid*. March 23, 1870.)

Robinson Hill School—District 10—Elementary

Located on the N side of the Robinson Hill Road 0.25 mile E from its junction with Smith Hill Road.

1948 Ralston Buttes Quad.

S20, T3S, R71W.

Elv. 8000'.

{Var. name: **Douglas Mountain School** and **Mt. Douglas School** for proximity to Douglas Mountain. Located on S shoulder.}

Built c. 1885.

Teachers: Charlotte Branch, Vineta Hayne, *et al.*

One-story frame, white w/green trim, approx. 24'×30'. Shingle, 4-12 hip roof. Three windows on each long side. One entrance, one anteroom, one classroom. Large anteroom had coat hooks, shelf for lunch buckets, table w/water bucket. Classroom had double desks w/small inkwell in each corner. Heated by big pot-bellied stove w/brick chimney.

Outside: Teeter-totter, 2 outhouses, coal shed and stable attached, flagpole.

Bessie Tripp married Theodore Koch in the Robinson Hill School. The Bootens of the Centennial House brought a wagonload of lilacs from their front yard to decorate the school.

The building has been converted to a private dwelling and is now located at the junction of Smith Hill and Douglas Mountain roads. There are no known foundation remnants at the original site.

School—Name Unknown

10607 Twin Spruce Road. Located W of the road.

S/b Eldorado Springs Quad.

S9, T2S, R71W. (Not mapped in this book.)

Elv. ab. 7750'.

Now the residence of Judy and Jim Wenzel.

In the late 1800s the right side of the residence was a school house. A totally separate cabin adjacent to the old school may have housed the school teacher, miners and loggers over the years.

By 1920 a second structure had been built nearby the school. This was Twin Spruce General Store.

By 1941 the general store had been joined to the left side of the school house.

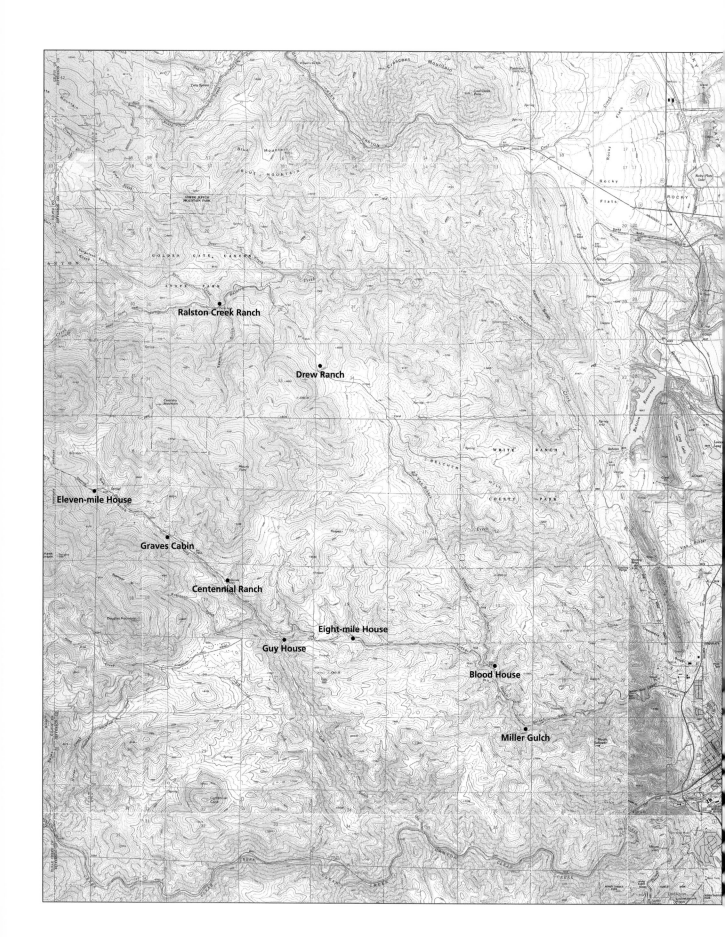

Ralston Creek Ranch

Drew Ranch

Eleven-mile House

Graves Cabin

Centennial Ranch

Eight-mile House

Guy House

Blood House

Miller Gulch

Stage Stops

EXCEPT WHERE NOTED, the stage stops were on the Gregory toll road. Stops thought to have been used mainly by freighters are also included and are indicated as such.

Blood House

On the N side of Tucker Gulch below its junction with Crawford Gulch.

S/b Ralston Buttes Quad.
S24, T3S, R71W.
Elv. ab. 6900'.

{Var. name: **5 mile house.** Only known reference:

> "Saturday, April 21st.—Fine morning. Started rather late, and took right hand road up a pleasant valley 2 miles to Golden Gate, a village of 26 buildings in all stages of completion. Entered mountains here, thru a toll gate, paying 75¢ per wagon. Travelled up gulch, cross a brook very often with muddy and steep banks. At 24th crossing, 2 houses; woman washing. Above 33, stopped for dinner, at 5 mile house from gate…"
>
> (Source: *Diary of a Pike's Peak gold seeker in 1860:* Colo. Mag., v. 14, no. 6, Nov. 1937, p. 213.)}

There is much freighter activity here, but no record of stages stopping. Lyman Blood and his wife Hanna homesteaded in this area and operated a dancehall and stage stop. All that remains of the original buildings is a chicken coop.

The old Blood house and barn, c. 1930, now known as the Nare Ranch. Note the WPA bridge under construction at the entrance to Crawford Gulch at left. The Nare family bought the Blood Ranch in the early 1900s. The barn burned in the 1980s. The house was torn down in the 1990s.

Centennial Ranch

At the entrance to Booten Gulch in Guy Gulch.

> *1965 Ralston Buttes Quad.*
> *S17, T3S, R71W.*
> *Elv. 7686'.*

{Var. names: **Booten House, Stone House.**}

There is no stop shown here on the 1860 Burt and Berthoud map.

The 1906 BQ shows *Centennial Ranch* with a cluster of buildings.

Daniel Booten squatted here with his sister in 1862 and built the stagecoach station referred to in diaries of the period. The house is at the junction of the original road to Gregory's with the Gregory toll road.

> In 1876 on this site Booten completed the house that now stands and called it Centennial House. The three-story structure has 12 rooms. The walls and partitions are 3.5 feet thick. In 1895 Centennial House was sold to Ernest S. Koch, the grandfather of George Koch, former Jeffco Sheriff.
>
> (Compiled from: *Colorado and Its People*, 1948: New York, Lewis Pub., p. 593.)

Centennial House, c. 1900. The man standing is Theodore Koch who owned the house at the time. His brother, Gus Koch, is on the white horse. The man to the far right is unknown. Note the wooden water tank beside the steps. This water was made available to all who passed by.

Ernest in turn sold the property to his son, Theodore who married Bessie Tripp and raised his family here. Theodore sold the property to his son, George, who lived here in the 1940s with his wife, Jeanette. Jeanette was one of the founders of the Columbine Ladies Club, which used the old Centennial bunkhouse as a clubhouse.

Churches Station

(See Churches Station under Colorado Central, Golden Quad <u>in</u> Railroads.)

Drew Ranch

N down over the summit of Drew Hill on the Drew Hill Road.
> *S/b Ralston Buttes Quad.*
> *S34, T2S, R71W. Elv. ab. 8085'.*

The 1906 Blackhawk Quad shows *Drew Ranch* with a cluster of buildings on both sides of the road. In addition to being the headquarters of the Drew ranch, this site was also a stage stop to change horses. The buildings are gone, only a few grassy humps remain.

Eight-mile House

Eight miles from Golden Gate City.
> *Stage stop, restaurant and dancehall.*
> *S/b Ralston Buttes Quad.*
> *S15, T3S, R71W.*
> *Elv. ab. 7450'.*

{Var. names: **Robinson and Baker House** (c. 1861). **Child's House** (opened with grand ball, 1868). **Hutchinson's Guy Hill Hall** (Capt. G. A. Hutchinson, 1896). **Snow's House** (Col. R. S. Snow, c. 1930). **George Ramstetter's Store,** c. 1930.}

The Burt and Berthoud map shows *8 mile house* at the head of Tucker Gulch.

> (Source: Burt, S. W., and Berthoud, E. L., 1860, *Quartz mining region of the Rocky Mountains:* Denver City, Rocky Mountain News Printing Co., map insert.)

Tucker Gulch was called Eight-mile Gulch. Thus was Eight-mile House advertised as being located at the "Head of Eight-Mile Gulch on the Central City Road." This house and the Guy House were the two most well-known stage stops on the road to Gregory's.

> "Snow on the hills all day, and down beside the road in P. M. Hauling very severe. At 37th crossing, White broke singletree. At 8 mile house, head of gulch, and 50th crossing of stream, camped for night. I slept in tent, with White's party. Enoch in house, others in wagon. A little snow fell in eve."

> (Source: *Diary of a Pike's Peak gold seeker in 1860:* Colo. Mag., v. 14, no. 6, Nov. 1937, p. 213-214.)

Remodeled by Hiram Heath in 1868:
> "**A GOOD HOUSE—Mr. Heath, at the Childs House,** head of Eight-mile gulch on the Central City road, has his new house completed and nearly ready for occupancy. It is the best house upon the road, and one of the best in the Territory. It is just in the right place, and will be a convenient and good stopping place for the mountain travel. We understand it will be opened shortly with a

Historic Eight-mile House as it looked in 1923. The whole of the upstairs was a ballroom. It boasted two pianos, a baby grand and an upright. Dances were held well into the 1930s. The entrance to Koch Gulch is in the upper left hand corner of the photograph.

grand ball, which we hope to see largely attended. Mr. Heath is a popular land-lord, and we shall be glad to see him in his new house, in which his area of free-dom will be greatly enhanced."

(Source: Colo. Transcript, Dec. 16, 1868.)

The 1906 Blackhawk Quad shows a house here but no legend.

In 1918 the body of a man buried up-right was discovered during excavation for a silo. (See Eight-mile House Site <u>in</u> Burial Sites—Historic.) The silo is still standing. The unidentified man was laid to rest in the Golden Cemetery.

Of the stage-stop era, the chicken coop, out of sight behind the house, is the only surviving structure. The Eight-mile house was torn down in 1962.

Eight-mile House. Photographed 1952. At one time the county public road crossed from one side of the creek to the other on the bridge in the foreground.

Eleven-mile House

Eleven miles from Black Hawk.

S/b Ralston Buttes Quad.
E of the summit of Michigan Hill.
S12, T3S, R72W.
Elv. ab. 8500'.

{Var. name: **Michigan Ranche, Michigan House.** One of two houses so called. See Michigan House.}

Burt and Berthoud show *11 mile house* S of the road above the Gulch Gulch drainage.

(Source: Burt, S. W., and Berthoud, E. L., 1860, *Quartz mining region of the Rocky Mountains:* Denver City, Rocky Mountain News Printing Co., map insert.)

"The descent [down Guy Hill into Guy Gulch] looked dangerously steep; but our driver, with locked wheels went down on a trot, passing two ox-teams with wonderful skill. The valley we now entered was greener and fresher than the first, and with a tolerably level bottom, along which we bowled to the Michigan House, where dinner awaited us,—an excellent meal, at one dollar and fifty cents. The water was unsurpassed in coolness and agreeable flavor."

(Source: Taylor, Bayard, 1867, *Colorado, a summer trip:* New York, G. P. Putnam & Son, p. 53.)

The 1906 quad shows a house to either side of the road but no legend. References to *11 mile house* are rare.

Four-mile House

Four miles above Black Hawk.

S/b Black Hawk Quad.
S?, T2S, R72W. (Not mapped in this book.)
Elv. ab. 9200.

Burt and Berthoud show *4 mile house* at the top of what is today called Fourmile Gulch not far from where Dory Hill Cemetery is now located.

(Source: Burt, S. W., and Berthoud, E. L., 1860, *Quartz mining region of the Rocky Mountains:* Denver City, Rocky Mountain News Printing Co., map insert.)

References to this house are common; however, none have been found to describe the house in any way.

Graves Cabin

In Guy Gulch two miles upstream from the foot of Guy Hill.

S/b Ralston Buttes Quad.
S7, R71W, T3S.
Elv. ab. 8000'.

> "Sunday, 22nd.—Fair most of day; a few spits of snow. Left camp rather late, and doubled teams up ridge. Descent quite long and steep. Thence some 2 miles up another gulch, on Fair road, to Graves' cabin*, 12 miles from Gate."
>
> This cabin erected by Linus Graves in 1859 became the headquarters for most of the party during the next month."

> (Source: *Diary of a Pike's Peak gold seeker in 1860:* Colo. Mag., v. 14, no. 6, Nov. 1937, p. 214.)

*Two miles up Guy Gulch would have placed the cabin where the Swena house was later built. (See Settlement.) The Graves cabin was not a stage stop. That it was a stop for freighters is reflected in the traffic itemized in the above diary. Later diary entries by our gold seeker indicate he is working on the toll road, perhaps to shore up his meager gold findings.

Guy House

In the bottom of Guy Gulch 0.25 mile downstream from the Robinson Hill junction.

1906 Blackhawk Quad.
S16, T3S, R71W.
Elev. ab. 7400'.

To get a sense of the location of Guy House, compare the following photograph with the photo of the burial site of Guy Gulch Man <u>in</u> Burials.

Colo. Transcript advertisement, June 2, 1869.

Colo. Transcript advertisement, March 23, 1870.

Early pictures show numerous large, white frame buildings. The original stage stop was operated by John C. Guy. The Guy House offered guest rooms, a bar, and a large dining area. Out

JIM RAMSTETTER COLLECTION

1880. John Guy's House in the bottom of Guy Gulch, seen looking N up the gulch.

buildings included a blacksmith shop and barns for extra teams. Coaches heading east and west stopped here for dinner. Extra teams were kept here.

(Compiled from: Ramstetter, James K., 1996, *Life in the early days*.)

On October 5, 1861, J. C. Guy sold the Guy House and property supposed to contain 160 acres, together with several other 160-acre claims, to J. G. Hendrickson for $1500.

(Compiled from: *Jefferson County Records, Book A*, p. 199. Opened January 6, 1860. Eli Carter, Recorder.)

"**GUY HOUSE / H. M. Howell, Proprietor.** / THE GUY is the best hotel between Central and Denver. It is situated fourteen miles from Central. The coaches stop at it for dinner each way. Accommodations are good, and the table is supplied with everything in the market."

(Source: Colo. Transcript advertisement, May 20, 1868.)

"P. O. WANTED.—Our citizens in the vicinity of the Guy House claim to be very much in need of a Post-office at or near that station. There are some sixty or seventy people settled around there that would be accommodated by it, and we presume a petition sent to the proper office would accomplish the end desired, especially as the coaches run past there daily, and the changing of the mail there need be of no extra expense to the government or the Stage Company. A petition forwarded to our attentive delegate would doubtless receive his early attention."

(Source: Colo. Transcript, July 8, 1868.)

The 1906 Blackhawk Quad shows no house here. Few foundation remnants remain today.

Junction Ranch

On the W side of Michigan, a.k.a. Junction Hill, E of the road.

One of the old Junction Ranch buildings still stands W of the road immediately beside the GGC and County Road 7 junction.
1942 Black Hawk Quad.
S1, T3S, R72W. (Not mapped in this book.)
Elv. ab. 8542.

{Var. names: **Junction House, Junction Branch.**}

This is where the Enterprise Toll Road, opened in 1860, reached the Gregory Road. The Junction House, run by J. Boutwell, shows up on the 1866 Map of Gilpin County. (See Donald C. Kemp's *Colorado's Little Kingdom.*)

However, Junction Ranch was not the commencement point for the Enterprise Toll Road as outlined in the 1861 Act. That honor goes to "the Michigan House in Cold Springs Valley," which was upstream from the bottom of Junction Hill.

Michigan House

A stage stop that may have been in the vicinity of the old Mountain House School. If so, this would be another name for the 7 mile house.

1942 Black Hawk Quad. (Mountain House School)
S33, R72W, T2S. (Not mapped in this book.)
Elv. ab. 8500'.

{Possible var. name: **7 mile house.**}

The Gregory Toll Road authorization describes the route as from "Tucker's Canon or nearest and best route to Michigan House in Cold Springs Valley." Michigan House may have been at the cold spring itself, which is believed to have been at *7 mile house*, or simply in the valley, perhaps a short ways upstream from where the Ralston and Gregory toll roads would have junctioned.

Miller Gulch

Freighters stopped here.
  (See Drainages.)

Ralston Creek Ranch

At the junction of Nott and Ralston creeks on the Ralston Creek Toll Road.
  1948 Ralston Buttes Quad.
  S29, T2S, R71W.
  Elv. 7653'.

{Var. name: **Strang's Dude Ranch.**}

This is the only stage stop identified within the canyon itself. References are rare.

Operated in the 1930s and 40s as a tutoring ranch by Stephen and Elaine Strang and sons Bart and Mike. A brochure put out in 1939, the Strang's 9th season as the Ralston Creek Ranch, reads in part:

> "The ranch is about 8000 feet up in the Colorado Rocky Mountains, thirty miles from Denver and fifteen miles northwest of Golden. We have 1450 acres of creek-bottom, upland pasture, and heavy timber, with five and one-half miles of three streams running through the property. From the time it was homesteaded, about seventy years ago, it was operated at a cattle ranch until 1931, when the first dude came sniffing up the canon. All our neighbors are cattle ranchers, and we are insulated from the outside by eight miles of unlikely road that leads nowhere, so that we feel as remote as the Gobi Desert, through we can get to Denver in a little over an hour if we have to. There are trout in the streams, and deer, elk, bear, and coyotes up in the timber.
>
> At this altitude the air is clear and dry, and the sun shines hard all day. But the shade is cool, and you use blankets every night. The climate has proved helpful in many cases of asthma and hay fever…
>
> Ours is a ranch, not just a Dude Ranch. We breed, break, and market our own saddle horses…Our own small herd of cows provides our milk and much of our beef. We raise our hay and as much garden stuff as can be grown at this altitude…
>
> Our prime recreation is, of course, riding. You may never have mounted a horse before, but here you will do it naturally, as the obvious means of getting from place to place. Everyone has his own horse, chosen to fit his experience and ability. We have a swimming pool and a rifle association and a tennis court and a ranch paper…
>
> In the evening there is singing around the piano; bridge beside the log fire; and talk. Moonlight rides are popular, and Saturday nights there is a dance at one of the mountain villages or squaredancing at the school-house…"

Burrowes "Buzz" Hunt was one of the tutors. (See Geoffrey Gulch <u>in</u> Drainages for more about Hunt.)

"Mellerdramer" at Strang's Dude Ranch. From Strang's Dude Ranch brochure, c. 1938.

The Ralston Creek Ranch house and several outbuildings burned in 1960s. The ranch, including the remaining large red barn, is now encompassed by the Golden Gate State Park.

Ralston House

"INTERESTING TO FREIGHTERS.—The Ralston House, which has just been opened by Mr. S. Foshee, at the Cheyenne crossing of Ralston creek, is the place for freighters and other travelers to and from the mountains and Cheyenne to stop. The long trains of hay-wagons will find this just the place to spend the night. Mr. F. has plenty of excellent and warm stable room, and will always be prepared to furnish hay and grain, as well as food, for travelers, at very reasonable rates."

(Source: Colo. Transcript, Jan. 6, 1869)

"**Ralston House,** / Near the Cheyenne crossing of Ralston Creek, /**Spencer Foshee, Proprietor.** / GOOD STABLING, HAY AND GRAIN FOR / stock. Meals furnished at all hours. It is the intention of the proprietor to make his house a comfortable and agreeable stopping place. Patronage solicited."

(Source: *Ibid.* Advertisement, Jan. 6, 1869)

Ralston House was located in the immediate vicinity of where today's Indiana Street crosses Ralston Creek, as was Ralston Crossing School House (not included in this work).

Robinson House

S/b Black Hawk Quad.

According to Jefferson County records, Book B, p. 214, in 1862 Oliver Graves sold Daniel Moore one-half interest in a toll road leading from Robinson House at the head of Seven-mile Canyon up the main road to the Gregory diggings.

QUESTION: Where was Seven-mile Canyon? In 1861 a toll road was built through Ralston Creek Canyon from the prairie to the vicinity of the Golden Gate Park Headquarters, approximately seven miles, where tolls were collected on roads coming S from Boulder and E from Dory Hill. Is Ralston Creek Canyon the Seven-mile Canyon talked about here?

QUESTION: Where was Robinson House and who was Robinson? The man involved with *8 mile house*? The man who named Robinson Hill?

EDITORS' NOTE: Oliver and Linus Graves (of Graves cabin) were brothers from Bloomington, Illinois. Oliver settled in Arvada where his decendents still live.

Seven-mile house

Seven miles from Black Hawk in the immediate vicinity of Mountain House.

1942 Black Hawk Quad. (Mountain House School)
S33, R 72W, T2S. (Not mapped in this book.)
Elv. ab. 8500'.

{Possible var. name: **Michigan House.**}

7 mile house appears on the 1860 Burt and Berthoud map high in the Ralston Creek drainage.

(Source: Burt, S. W., and Berthoud, E. L., 1860, Quartz mining region of the Rocky Mountains: Denver City, Rocky Mountain News Printing Co., map insert.)

References to this house are rare.

Mountain House School was here, directly S of the road.

As was also Cold Spring, often referred to as seven miles this side of Gregory. The Colo. Transcript of Feb. 28, 1861, describes the Ralston Toll Road as "following up Rallston creek to the old road at the Cold Spring seven miles this side of Gregory."

Smith Hill Stage Station

Top of Smith Hill.
S/b Black Hawk Quad.
S10, T3S, R72W. (Not mapped in this book.)
Elv. ab. 8752'

{Var. name: **Smith's Ranche.**}

Takes its name from the hill it stands atop. The ranch was purchased in 1917 by George S. and Edna Green and became known as the Green Ranch.

COLO. HIST. SOC.

Smith Hill Stage Station. The road up Smith Hill divides today as it did when this picture was taken: the trace off to the SE comes out on Robinson Hill, the NE fork (just out of sight toward the photographer) comes out in Golden Gate Canyon at the old Junction Ranch.

Stage Stop (name unknown)

30410 Highway 72, Coal Creek Canyon.
S/b Eldorado Springs Quad.
S4, T2S, R71W. (Not mapped in this book.)
Elv. ab. 7800'.

Served as a stagecoach stop, inn and dance hall. Included a stable for horses and a veranda porch for socializing. The building is now a private home.

(Compiled from: Brescia, Janice, *Coal Creek Canyon history*: Jeffco 1991 North Mountains Area Community Plan.)

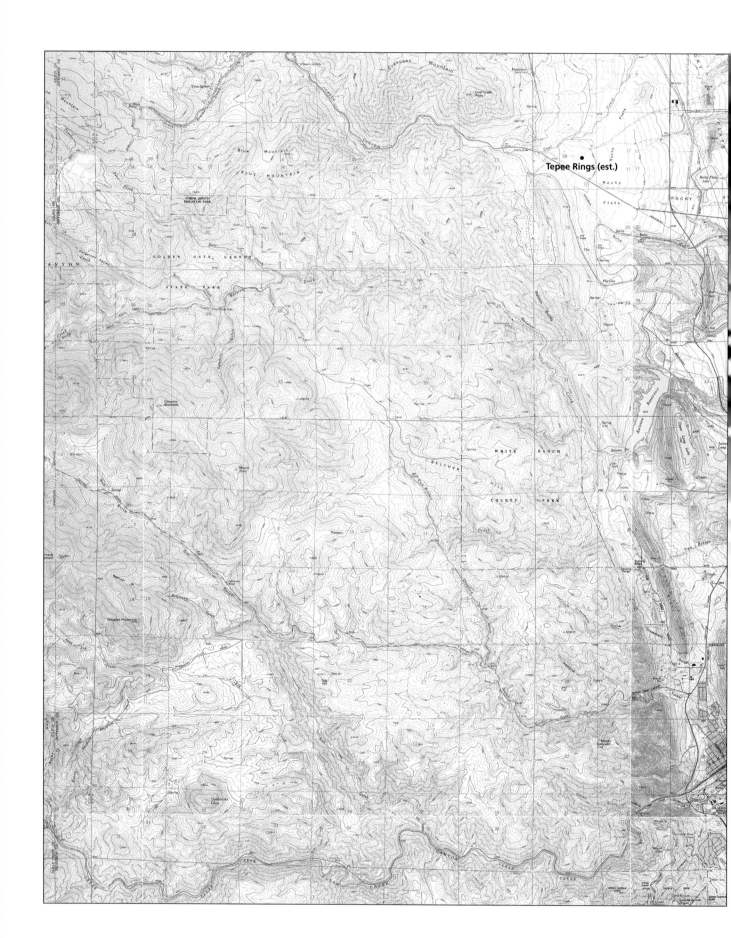

Tepee Rings (est.)

Tepee Rings

Entrance, Coal Creek Canyon, N of highway.
S/b Eldorado Springs Quad.
S18, T2S, R70W.
Elv. ab. 6320'.

"Her name was Sadie Giberson. Back in the forties she taught grade school in a small building at the base of Coal Creek Canyon south of Plainview. She was interested in American Indians and passed that interest on to her students. She often took them to a nearby area where there were several rings of boulders, the unmistakable remains of tepee sites. As part of their outing, the students searched for arrowheads and collected flint shards while she talked of the former inhabitants.

…the boulders were all but buried by decades of blowing soil. I thought of how they must have looked to Sadie and her young friends in the forties. I visualized the Indians rolling the rocks back off of the fringes of hide when they moved their camp. We found evidence of at least six tepees.

The rings of rocks are as large as 14 or 16 feet in diameter, suggesting that when moved back into place they ringed a tepee of 10 or 12 feet in diameter…there were springs nearby, probably the most compelling aspect of the camp location…The rocks used in these rings indicate that winds were certainly a major factor in construction. They are fairly large and close together. We would guess that this was a small temporary camp site. The nearest existing tree was some eighty paces distant but there was evidence that other trees may have been closer a hundred years ago.

In a brief search we found no flint shards or pottery fragments."

(Source: Bisque, Ray, 1995, *Tepee rings found:* Mountain Messenger, July 1995, p. 17.)

"The tepee rings that we wrote about in the July 1995 issue of the Messenger are very close to the newly purchased Open Space near Plainview…

Turn off 72 on to the Plainview road and drive one tenth of a mile to the old corral just east of the road. Park and follow the road east. You will pass one Ponderosa on your left, then two on your right. When you have gone three tenths of a mile (500 yards) the road disappears and there will be a ditch on your left (north). Cross the ditch and start looking. There are ten rings in an area of less than an acre…

As you are leaving you might want to walk north on the Plainview road to Coal Creek and see the foundation of the old Plainview school where Sadie Giberson held classes."

(Source: Bisque, Ray, 1995, *Tepee rings:* Mountain Messenger, May 1996, p. 6.)

In January, 1999, City of Boulder Open Space paid $8.75 million for 1,500 acres of undeveloped tall- and short-grass prairie located on the NW corner of Colorado 72 and 93. The purchase encompasses 1,100 acres of Jewell Mountain and 400 acres of the old Van Vleet ranch. In saving this sweeping beauty from development, Boulder Open Space has also saved the tepee rings.

Coal Creek Peak at the E entrance to Coal Creek Canyon. The tepee rings are behind and to the right of the photographer on the lift of land known as Jewell Mountain.

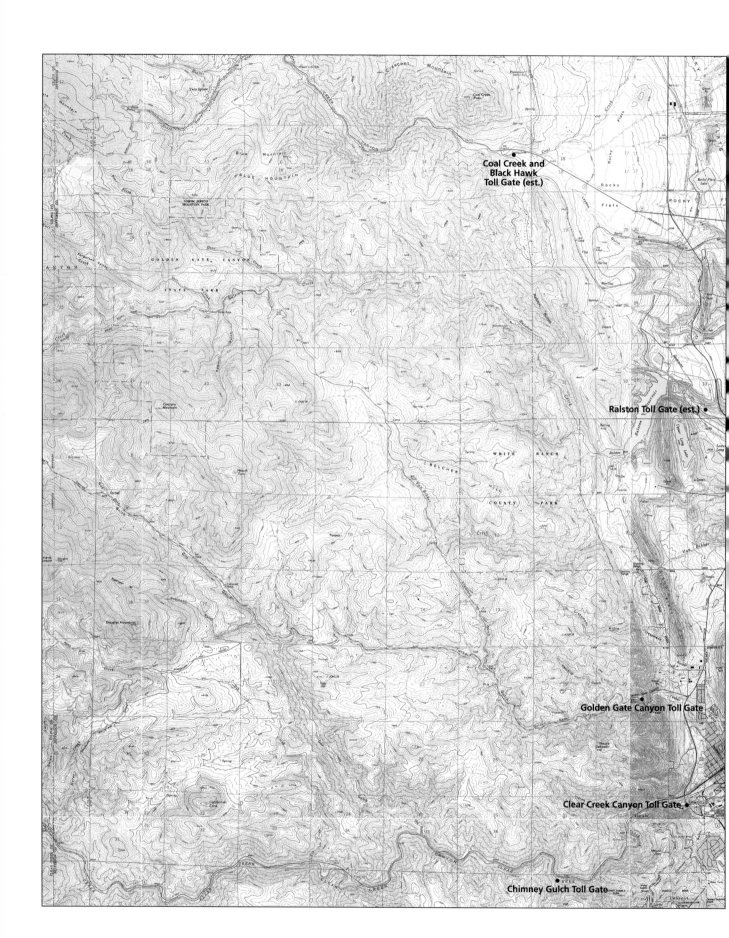

Coal Creek and
Black Hawk
Toll Gate (est.)

Ralston Toll Gate (est.) •

Golden Gate Canyon Toll Gate

Clear Creek Canyon Toll Gate •

Chimney Gulch Toll Gate •

Toll Gates

ALL TOLL GATES WERE STAGE STOPS, but not all stage stops were toll gates. The toll gates have their own place in history.

Chimney Gulch Toll Gate

(See Chimney Gulch <u>in</u> Drainages.)

Clear Creek Canyon Toll Gate

E entrance to canyon. Exact site unknown.
S/b Golden Quad.

W. A. H. Loveland was a road builder. He engineered roads north, south, and east of Golden. But where he longed mightily to go was west. His repeated reconnaissance of Clear Creek Canyon convinced him he had no choice, once he reached Guy Gulch with a road, but to swing N up through Guy Gulch to the Gregory Road. Toward that end he organized the Clear Creek and Guy Gulch Wagon Road Company in 1863.

On March 8, 1864, Loveland received legislative authorization for his wagon road company "to operate parallel with and to cross Golden Gate Gregory Road."

(Source: Ridgeway, Arthur, 1932, *The mission of Colorado toll roads:* Colo. Mag., v. 9, no. 5, p. 164.)

On the E end of the line tolls were collected at the entrance to Clear Creek. By the time Loveland reached Guy Gulch with his wagon road, he had lost interest in quitting the canyon. Even so, he built the road through Guy Gulch up to the Gregory road as planned.

The toll road through Clear Creek Canyon to the forks washed out repeatedly and was even abandoned for several years, but Loveland, who could hear a railroad knocking on his door, persevered.

"The Central City line had the great advantage over the others of not being troubled by hostile Indians. It was, however, hindered in its operation for a few months of the year by bad roads and cold weather. During the fall and winter of 1863 there was more difficulty than usual. Deep snows made it necessary to replace the wheels of the coaches with runners, and the 'sleighs' could not keep up the speed of the wheeled coach. During the following winter a coach upset at Clear creek. An inexperienced driver let the rear wheels drop into a deep rut covered with snow. The coach was hurled fifteen feet into a gulch, and the driver and one passenger were badly injured. In may 1864 it took two days for coaches to go between Denver and Black Hawk. On may 28 both westbound and east-bound coaches were halted on their trips. During a violent storm some of the horses had become exhausted and some had died. The next mail, two days later, was carried by buggy. Fresh livestock was sent from Denver and daily service was resumed the following week."

(Source: Frederick, J. V., 1940, *Ben Holladay, the stagecoach king*: Calif., Arthur H. Clark, p. 136.)

Coal Creek and Black Hawk Toll Gate

The toll road was approved by the Colorado Territorial Session of February 2, 1866, to follow the creek through Coal Creek Canyon.

"A wagon road is being constructed up Coal Creek, in this county, by Mr. George Rand and others, which it is claimed will save both distance and grade over the present traveled road by way of Golden Gate."

(Source: Colo. Transcript, June 30, 1869.)

Wagons paid 60 cents at the mouth of the canyon and another toll in Black Hawk at the foot of Dory Hill.

In 1883 the Jeffco Commissioners voted to survey the road and appointed an overseer to maintain it.

(Compiled from: Brescia, Janice, *Coal Creek Canyon history*: Jeffco 1991 North Mountains Area Community Plan.)

"After a flood washed out the road in 1894, the commissioners paid laborers $1.75 a day to rebuild it. The road followed the creek and was maintained by residents hired to grade it with a team of horses and a plow. A line of rocks, pushed by these plows, can still be seen today north of Highway 72 at the mouth of the canyon."

(Source: *Ibid.*)

Golden Gate Canyon Toll Gate

Inside the canyon at the bottom of Quartermile Gulch 0.8 mile W of State Highway 93.

S/b Golden Quad.
S20, T3S, R70W.
Elv. ab. 6200'.

Remnants of the rock foundations are visible under the grasses.

A bronze plaque on a granite stone beside the highway immediately W of the old toll house foundation reads:

GOLDEN GATE TOLL ROAD
SHORT CUT TO GREGORY DIGGINGS
OPERATED FROM 1860 TO 1871
OWNERS
ALFRED TUCKER & ELISHA DUNCAN
DEDICATED BY
DAUGHTERS OF COLORADO
MAY 12, 1938

View looking NW into the lower region of Tucker Gulch. The old bend in the creek directly ahead accommodated the toll house. Tolls were taken here to make it easier to prevent travelers from slipping by the gate. The shallow dip above the bend is Quartermile Gulch. Photographed 1981.

The bronze plaque commemorating the Golden Gate Toll Road. Photographed 1991.

The monument was first erected at the entrance to GGC on the N side. The same road-widening program that made it necessary to remove the monument from the canyon entrance also resulted in the curve of road upstream above the old tollhouse foundation being abandoned. The abandonment left room for the stone to be erected at its current location near the foundation. While here, the plaque was stolen, leaving its stone barefaced for several years. Eventually the plaque reappeared as mysteriously as it vanished, attached in place as if never having gone away.

The Golden Gate and Gregory Road Company received authorization August 15, 1862:

> "An act to incorporate the Golden Gate and Gregory Road Co. by Alfred Tucker, Elisha Duncan and J. Bright Smith. The main line of said road shall extend from the east line of the town of Golden Gate, by way of Golden Gate, through Tucker's Canyon, on the line of the now traveled road or by the nearest and best route to a point at or near the Michigan House in Cold Springs Valley. Authorized to collect following tolls:

Wagon and one span of horses, mules or oxen 65 cents each. Each additional span 15 cents. Horseback 10 cents each. General livestock 5 cents head. Sheep 1 cents head. Tolls shall be unlawful in case of those attending funerals or worship."

(Source: Acts of the Territorial Legislature, in Ramstetter, James K., 1996, *Life in the early days*, p. 13.)

The *Mountaineer* commended Daniel McCleary for his public spirit in passing 447 teams loaded with mining machinery free over his road during the 1860 season.

(Compiled from: Brown, Georgina, 1976, *The shining mountains:* Gunnison, Colo., B&B Printers, p. 141-142.)

"Saturday, April 21st.—Fine morning. Started rather late, and took right hand road up a pleasant valley 2 miles to Golden Gate, a village of 26 buildings in all stages of completion. Entered mountains here, thru a toll gate, paying 75 cents per wagon."

(Source: *Diary of a Pike's Peak gold seeker in 1860:* Colo. Mag., v. 14, no. 6, Nov. 1937, p. 213.)

"…soon reached Golden City, did not stop but went on and soon came to Golden Gate (everything has the name of gold but I have not seen any yet) where we had to pay toll on the road. After leaving the gate we traveled up a canon seven miles when we found ourselves at the top of a high mountain where we took dinner after which we went down the Mountain that was so steep that I expected to see the whole apparatus go *end* over *end*. there were rocks in the road as big as a hoss (a great road to pay toll on), which we lifted the wagons over."

(Source: *H. J. Hawley's Diary, Russell Gulch in 1860,* ed. by Lynn I. Perrigo: Colo. Mag., vol. ?, p. 133.)

"My grandfather purchased the lower ten miles of the toll road from Tucker in 1867, and operated it for about 14 years. My father [Frank J. Bond] passed his boyhood there.

Practically all the traffic into a mining community of 30,000 passed over the road…The toll for a wagon…was one dollar. A rider paid ten cents and a walker five cents. All Indians passed free by treaty rights.

The walkers, and often the riders, tried to avoid paying toll by cutting across the steep mountains near the toll gate at the foot of Tucker Gulch, where my grandfather had built his house and lived. But there was no escape for the wagons…

There was actually no graded road. The wagon tracks mostly followed the bottom of the creek, which was usually dry or nearly so. Only the impossible obstructions were removed, and getting a heavily loaded wagon over the rocks in the creek bottom was strenuous work. At more than one place, where the road bed sloped steeply with the hillside, long poles were kept stored which would be tied underneath a wagon, extending out on the low side of the road, so that men could lift on the poles and prevent the wagon from overturning on the sidling trail.

Roadwork was required after each flood to make it passable again. High spots were provided where wagons could be stopped when a flash flood was expected."

(Source: Bond, Fred C., 1974, *It happened to me, an American autobiography:* p. 9 and 10, unpublished. Fred's son, Robert F. Bond, used this paper as the basis for his work published in 1989 entitled *The land persists.*)

Fred Buckman bought the Gregory Toll Road from James Bond.

James Bond owned and operated the lower ten miles of the toll road from 1869 to 1883. In 1883 he sold the road to Fred Buckman and with his toll earnings bought the secluded 880-acre ranch on the E side of Belcher Hill that became the nucleus of what is today the White Ranch.

(Compiled from: Wiberg, R. E., 1978, *James Bond restless pioneer,* in Empire Mag.: Denver Post, Oct. 29, 1978, p. 22-27.)

"…our route is north along the base of the mountains, with Table Mountain on our right. The first mile is up a heavy grade and brings us opposite what was known in the early days as Tucker canon, at the entrance of which was Golden Gate. Through this 'gate' and canon a wagon road was constructed in 1859, and, until the completion of the 'Central' though Clear Creek canon, the stages, mails, express, freight teams and 'pilgrims' for the mining towns in Gilpin and Clear Creek counties passed through the gate and over this road, the tolls from which varied from $16,000 to $24,000 per annum, above all expenses."

(Source: Crofutt, G. A., 1881, *Crofutt's grip-sack guide of Colorado:* Omaha Neb., Overland Pub. Co. p. 37.)

In the beginning the toll road through Tucker Gulch ran in and out of the creekbed. Emigrants counted at least fifty crossings. As erosion began to take its own toll, the toll road inched its way uphill to the S. The best defined piece of old road to the N of the creekbed (and this may have been a side road that left the Gregory road to access the mountain up through the draw to the N) is directly upstream from Logan's Sandpit. (See Potpourri.)

(See Golden Gate City in Cities for a description of the fight over the toll road.)

Ralston Toll Gate

E entrance to Ralston Canyon. Exact site unknown.

S/b Golden Quad.

> "A new road to the Gregory mines is being opened, up Rallston creek. From this city the route is by the Arapahoe road to a point beyond Clear Creek, then diverging to the north it passes above the Table Mountain and enters the range four miles north of Golden City, then following up Rallston creek to the old road at the Cold Spring seven miles this side of Gregory. It is said to be an excellent route."

> (Source: Colo. Transcript, Feb. 28, 1861.)

The 1906 BQ shows the road through Ralston Creek. On the W side of S26 the blue ink that indicates the road fades and then resumes. Is part of the road gone, or has tracing the river's serpentine course temporarily undone the scriber's pen?

Hilda Belcher, a young girl in the early 1900s, talked of taking a wagon down Ralston to Golden. Today Ralston Creek Canyon with its high jumbles of boulders in the creek bed gives no hint of ever having accommodated a wagon. Except for the press of wheels here and there, sheltered by dark, old trees in a bend of river.

Items of Interest

The Columbine Club of Golden Gate Canyon

On November 8, 1936, nine prospective members met at the Guy Hill School to organize a Home Demonstration Club under the leadership of Miss Jeanne Warner, Jefferson County Agent.

Mrs. John Gilfillan
Edna Green
Ethel Hall
Jeanette Koch
Bessie Koch
Manetta Morris
Vina Ramstetter
Bertha Ramstetter
Mary Termentozzi

The club quickly grew to over thirty members. The purpose was to create better homes and communities. The emblem was the Colorado columbine. The official song, "Sweet Columbine," was sung to the tune of "Battle Hymn of the Republic." Meetings were held the third Wednesday of each month, beginning at 11 o'clock and closing at 3:30 p.m. Meetings were held in the members' homes, in school houses, and in the Centennial Ranch bunkhouse. The bunkhouse burned in 1997.

The minutes reveal a wide range of activities from petitioning the County Commissioners for road repairs, to gathering Bundles for Britain. Flood sufferers were aided. Flowers were sent to the sick. In times of sorrow, sympathy was expressed with cards and food. Four dances were given throughout the year. A community picnic was organized every July, complete with prizes and free lemonade. Food baskets were given to poor families at Christmas time. A yearly Christmas program was held for the community.

Meetings also dealt with the personal needs of club members, from learning how to select the best values in shoes, hosiery and clothing, to the curing of foot ailments and improved posture through exercises. Recipes were tried out, and the rules of table setting and etiquette learned. Nutrition came in for a great deal of consideration, as did home decoration.

Papers were read and discussed. Nineteen-thirties topics included: Leather, Washington and Lincoln, Furs, Tea and Coffee, Child Welfare, Candy, First Aid, Wood, Cellophane, and Syphilis.

In 1938 the Club's community activities included:

> "March 12, 1938—Benefit Box Social at Ferree's Hall for our unfortunate neighbors Mr. and Mrs. John Gulliksen, whose home was completely destroyed by fire. $55.00 was raised and each club member donated or collected food, clothing and household articles for them. One of our club members, Mrs. Larry McCarthy, cared for the stricken family in her own home until others members of the family came for them.
>
> April 9—A one-act play, "Cheese It," was prepared and given for the community at the Mt. Douglas School House.
>
> July 11—A community party featuring "Old Time Dances" was held at the Mt. Douglas School House.
>
> October 29—A fancy dress party was given at the Mt. Douglas School House with prizes awarded for the best costumes. We wish to mention here that most of our community parties are free, given to show our appreciation for what the community gives at our benefit affairs."

Old minutes recall other scenes long lost to memory:

> "Hunting season ended rather disastrously for Otto Ramstetter last Monday, when a cow was killed in the barn by a long distance shot."
>
> The high winds of last week did considerable damage in the neighborhood, upsetting hay stacks, putting the telephone lines temporarily out of condition and completely demolishing the barn full of hay belonging to Joseph Jully…"
>
> Everyone probably knows about the flood—about Gus Koch's pickup being washed away, 6 of Dick Johnson's cattle and 1 of Green's calves are gone."

In February 1941 Lovell Johnson and Manetta Morris began publishing a little newsletter called *Static*. These chatty newsletters are very rare.

> "****Fred Pearce has been off work the past week. He hurt his knee when he fell several feet and hit his leg on a box car down at the clay pits.
> ****Gilfillan's sold their cows. They thought ten cans of Columbine Milk would be enough till they got to town again. But Lo! it snowed, so they couldn't get to town. Black coffee and no breakfast food for several days. Mrs. Crowell finally

came to the rescue, but that is a long way to go for milk. If anyone knows of a milk cow for sale, give [Mrs. Gilfillan] a ring.

****Don and Rose Stewart and Iris Bennett have the measles."

The Columbine Club is still active, although on a much smaller scale.

Golden Gate City

Rocky Mountain Herald, April 30, 1860:

"Friend Gibson:—As you kindly offered to allow me to occupy a small space in the first issue of your valuable paper, I will give you a short history of the progress and prospects of Golden Gate and vicinity, which will doubtless be of interest. Golden Gate is improving rapidly and extensive preparations are being made to command the mountain trade, which we can do as soon as we have the goods to supply the demand. Judge McWhite is completing a large business house, which he proposes to occupy, with a large stock of miners' supplies, which he will sell as low as they can be had anywhere in the country. Buddee, Jacobs & Co. are fitting up a large Storage and Commission House, where they will always have on hand a large supply of Groceries, Provisions and Miners' supplies, which they will sell at lower rates than they can be bought anywhere in the whole country. All wishing goods sold on Commission, and wishing quick returns, will do well to leave them with Buddee, Jacobs & Co. at Golden Gate.

S[?] & Vandiver will also have on hand a large stock of Groceries, Provisions and Miners' supplies and are now prepared to receive storage goods on commission and ranch stock of all kinds. Preston & Bros. have opened the Gate City Hotel, and are prepared to give the traveling public the best accommodations the country affords. Capt. Golden is progressing rapidly with Gar[?] Hotel, which is thirty-two by forty feet, three stories, and will be completed by the first of July. The Capt. has also just finished the finest barn in the whole country, which will be a good accommodation to freighters, it being sufficiently large to accommodate loaded wagons and teams.

Esq. Mills is completing a large business house, which is to be occupied by Judge Bacon, of Iowa, in the wholesale Grocery and Provision business. Mr. Fletcher of Quincy, Ill., is expected in a few days with his family and a stock of goods. Also, Col. J. S. Rogers with a large stock of goods. Several large frame buildings are now under contract, and will be finished as soon as possible.

Golden Gate is positively the best natural business point in the whole Territory, being situated immediately at the foot of the mountains, at a point where goods can be hauled with as little expense as any other point in the Territory, and at a point where mountain traders can save at least fifty cents per hundred in transportation, and two days time in every trip from the mountains to purchase goods, and at the entrance of one of the best mountain roads in the known world, leading to the largest, richest and most extensive Gold Region as yet discovered in the whole Rocky Mountain range. It has the concentrated travel of the whole country from every direction of the Plains.

A route has been discovered and will soon be laid out, and a road opened from Golden Gate to the Park. It will be a magnificent road, with plenty of good grass and water, distance from Golden Gate only 40 miles.

A brick yard has just been established at Golden Gate, and the proprietor will soon be able to furnish the best of brick and promptly fill orders to any amount. Preston and Golden are prepared to furnish the world with lime the country affords at the lowest rates, they have five large kilns and will fill orders at short notice.

The surrounding country is settling up rapidly. Farms and Ranches have been opened on almost every quarter section. I shall do my best to send you a long list of subscribers from Golden Gate, and wishing the *Herald* success, I remain yours truly,

W. G. Preston
April 30, 1860"

EDITORS' NOTE: In which direction "the Park" was "only 40 miles" from Golden Gate is unknown.

John H. Gregory and Thomas L. Golden

John Hamilton Gregory rang up the curtain on the richest square mile on earth by boldly going where no man had gone before with a miner's pick. And plucking from the heart of the wilderness the golden rock that forever put an end to the charges that the Pike's Peak gold fields were a hoax.

Thousands followed where Gregory led, hurrying up his amazing trace, singing his praises. All that remained for him to do was name his gold camp Gregory City and proclaim himself mayor.

Instead he hired three hands to help him dig.

By the turn of the century the slight, wiry red-haired and full-whiskered gold miner from Gordon County, Georgia, was all but forgotten. The last remaining mine he owned in Colorado Territory, the *Discovery Claim* on Quartz Hill, was taken away from him by a decree in chancery in 1864. His road up the face of Enter Mountain vanished under the grasses, and with it, all memory of the road itself.

For saving the bacon of town promoters and making bonanza kings out of would-be miners, Gregory got his name on a mining district in a two-mile long, narrow, crooked gulch fouled by mine dumps. His camp and the 8740' peak to the east are named after an Indian, or possibly a horse thief. Denver is named after General James W. Denver, Governor of Kansas Territory, who never visited the gold fields. Gilpin County takes its name from Major William Gilpin who arrived in Denver in 1862, three years after Gregory trudged up frozen Clear Creek toward his date with destiny.

Where Gregory was born, where he died, if he had a wife to mourn him all her life, if his children they were brave—no one knows any more.

In those wild and crazy heydays of long ago, John Hamilton Gregory should have hired a public relations firm and got his picture taken.

(And weren't they gamblers all, those goldseekers, and wouldn't it bowl him over to see his gulch now, still aglitter in the middle of the night, still sucking them in like moths to the light?)

Tom Golden is our Renaissance Man.

An energetic, hail-fellow-well-met, said to have been born August 18, 1811, in Knox County, Kentucky, Tom wore many hats and all of them well.

He came to Clear Creek in 1858 to pan gold and stayed to promote a town. He and partner Samuel Curtis laid out Arapahoe City and surrounded it with a 10-mile square mining district, of which Golden was elected recorder. He also provided the new city with meat.

When John Gregory found gold high in the wilderness and engineered a trace straight up the face of a mountain, Tom laid out another town at the base of the new road and called this town Golden Gate City.

Realizing a better route to the new diggings would have to be found, and not wanting it found elsewhere, Tom and partner Dan McCleery opened a road through Eight-mile Canyon to link up with the Gregory road in Guy Gulch. In Golden Gate City, busily engaged in the commission business, Tom was the first merchant to advertise prices in the region. In short order he built a 3-story hotel and a large freighters' barn. And took a bride, Miss Fletcher of Nevada City.

What Tom thought of a rival camp's adopting his name no one knows. But it was too good a name not to use. The word *Golden* gladdens the heart. The town promoters at the entrance to Clear Creek Canyon, embracing *Golden* without the *Gate,* proclaimed themselves a bigger and better supply town. Unfortunately for our busy entrepreneur, this proved true, so true.

Two cities, a state park, and a canyon have been named after Tom. But there is no known photograph of him, no knowledge of where exactly he came from, and none whatsoever of where he went.

In the end the same mists that obscure John Gregory obscure Tom Golden. And perhaps for the same reasons. Perhaps both thought that having once caught that high tide in the affairs of men called gold fever, they could do so again somewhere else. They misjudged their place in history, they had no way of knowing that for them there would never be another Cherry Creek with its many splintered paths to fame and fortune.

Two letters written by Thomas L. Golden:

1) Letter written January 6, 1859, from somewhere near Arapahoe City:

> "I am in the gold country near Cherry Creek, and I assure you there is gold here, and plenty of it. I have discovered mines that will pay $20 per day; I have not mined much yet, on account of the weather being too cold to work, but am preparing sluice lumber to commence operations early in the spring.
>
> ...Game is in great abundance. I have killed fifty-four deer, six mountain sheep, and a large panther.

The Indians are thick here. We apprehend danger from them. They have sent us word by some of their chiefs, to quite their country, but we think we can stand them a rub, as we have 700 white men here. We have laid out a town by the name of Arapahoe City, after the aborigines. We have also laid off a mining precinct, ten miles square, of which I have been elected recorder."

(Source: Hafen, L. R., ed., *Colorado and Its People*: v. I, p. 164.)

2) Letter written June 23, 1859:

"I presume you have heard discouraging news from here lately by men that have not reached the mines, that have got discouraged and turned back, and turned others back that no doubt would have got here and at this time been making money.

I am in the mines called Gregory's Diggings, 30 miles in the Mountains on a small tributary of Vasquers Fork, about 42 miles west of where Cherry Creek empties into Platte River. We are working what are called 'leads' running through the Mountains, these 'leads' are among the quartz rock and average two feet in width and are from one to three miles in length. Some men are here taking out three hundred dollars to the sluice, others not so much; it is reported among the miners here that the Illinois Company is taking out to the sluice an average of five hundred dollars. The men here are generally satisfied to stay and work. There are a great many purchasing claims on these heavy 'leads' and pay weekly as they take it out. They generally make a contract to pay half they take out every week until the claim is paid for. The thoughts of climbing through the Rocky Mountains 30 miles to get to the mines sends a great many back after they reach the base of the Mountains. All we have to say to the returning emigrant to the States is to stay in the States, and we will bring the gold there. We ask no one to come here and would have been glad had they stay at home. We are getting our supplies from [New] Mexico before the Spring emigration got here and were satisfied that we would make our fortune by Fall, and return to the States, but the men that has been humbuged so are crowding us now and in fact are making the most money.

Yours, Thos. L. Golden"

The Lost Diary

The following 1928 Denver Post news clipping is in the Bessie Brown papers.

The subheading incorrectly states that the diary was written by John H. Gregory. The text makes clear that the diary was written by Albert Dean.

Dean's diary is the most detailed eyewitness account known of John Gregory's actions prior to his discovery of gold in the mountains on the north fork of Clear Creek. It is the only account known that speaks of Gregory's not being alone when he found the lead that resulted in his return to the north fork. It is the only account known that describes the engineering of what would become the first road to Gregory's.

18 *The Post Phone—MAin 2121*

STARVATION ALMOST CHEATED MINER OF FIRST RICH GOLD LODE

Fascinating Account of Early Prospecting Days in Colorado Disclosed on Yellowed Leaves of Old Diary Written by John H. Gregory.

(By L. A. CHAPIN.)

That John H. Gregory, the man who made the first important discovery of gold in Colorado, was without provisions and nearly starving shortly before he located the lode which still bears his name and brought him what in those days was a small fortune is disclosed in the yellowed leaves of an old diary which has never before been made public.

The diary was written during the winter of 1857-1858 by Albert Dean, one of the first hardy gold seekers to make the long and dangerous trek across the plains from Iowa.

It is now in the possession of C. R. Dean of Plymouth, Kan., a grandson of the pioneer.

Telling as it does of the first important discovery of gold in this part of the west and describing in detail how old Fort St. Vrain and Fort Lupton were constructed, it will furnish historians with a wealth of new material upon which to work.

**DIARY READS LIKE
CONTINUOUS NARRATIVE.**

Thanks to Mr. Dean of Kansas, The Denver Post prints below for the first time some of the more interesting passages from the diary. No dates are given as the diary reads for the most part like a continuous narrative:

"Several days have passed since we left O'Fallon's bluffs. We reached the South Plat (the pioneer Mr. Dean had no way of knowing the river was properly spelled Platte) but did not ford it. Have kept along the south side of the river.

"Ran into one squad of Cheyennes but they were friendly and wanted to trade. We swapped off a pint cup of sugar, one of salt and one of coffee for some moccasins, the saddles of an antelope and some dried buffalo meat.

**INDIANS MIX SUGAR,
SALT, COFFEE AND MEAT.**

"They took this stuff and emptied it into a three-gallon kettle along with some buffalo meat and water and put it over a fire to cook. We didn't stay to see how they liked the mess. . . .

"We camped a night each where St. Vrain's fort and Fort Lupton used to be. The sod walls are still standing, three feet thick and well preserved. On the northwest and southeast corners of these forts turrets were built about eight feet above the main walls which were about twelve feet high.

"The forts were about 150 feet square. The turrets were about ten feet in diameter and floored with split logs and a cannon appeared to have been mounted there.

**SPANISH TRADERS
BUILT EARLY FORTS.**

"Some old Spanish traders must have built them. Bunks made of split poles are still in place. One fort is built nearly opposite from where the Cashlapoo (Cache la Poudre) empties into the Plat; the other about twenty miles farther up the river....

"We arrived at the mouth of Cherry creek on Saturday and moved up the creek about a mile, where we found eighteen men camped. They have lived there all winter in dugouts and tents. Today, Sunday, we made them a visit. They seemed to look on us with suspicion and would not talk much, but said they are laying out a townsite.

"They have stakes driven everywhere and intend to hold the ground as claims. We think they have found something. . . .

**CUT DOWN TREES
TO FEED STOCK.**

"It has turned cold and a 10-inch snow is on the ground. There is no grass for the stock so we took them over to an island in the river where several cottonwoods are standing and cut one down for them to feed on. We have even fed them our 100 pounds of hardtack as well as all the grain we brought with us. . . . .

"We have been snowed in for three weeks. Every few days Bill or I would cut another tree for the stock. They have done well for the kind of feed they have been getting. The men camped here say they have prospected up Cherry creek and have found some gold, also up the Plat and Clear creek, but so far have not made any real find.

"They showed us two or three ounces of gold which they have taken out this winter. We tried our hand at panning and found a few specks of gold. We are all excited.

**LOCATED ON PRESENT
SITE OF GOLDEN.**

"The snow has disappeared here and we are going to move up on Clear creek a few miles and see what we can find. . . .

"We located between the two table mountains about a mile down the creek from where it comes out of the mountains. (Where Golden is now located.) We are doing fair, about $3 a day per man. We think we will be able to do much better as soon as we get our long-toom and sluiceboxes in shape.

"I hear some new arrivals are coming into Auraria. That is the name of the new town started on Cherry creek. It is located on the west side. I hear that some Georgia miners have come in and commenced sluicing just above where we first panned out a few specks of gold on a sandbar in the Platte and that they are doing well.

**WORK IN ICE WATER
UP TO KNEES.**

"The leader of this party is Green Russell. We think this gold we are getting comes from higher up in the mountains and as soon as we can we are going up to look for it. This work we are doing now, in icy water to our knees all day and for $3 and $4 a day, is not what we had planned on or came after.

"Doc (a Dr. Casto) and I have made a survey on top of these mountains for several miles along the creek. It is not safe to go up yet, for these deep gorges are full of snow.

"Doc went down to Auraria today to send some letters of his and mine to the states and found some letters for each of us which had been forwarded from Fort Kearney with some gold seekers who had just arrived.

"We are feeling fine tonight. First mail since we left home!

"A man by the name of Gregory wandered into our camp today just as we were getting ready to eat. He said he was very hungry and wanted to get dinner with us. Doc told him our supplies are running low and we hardly have enough for ourselves, and told him he had better go back to his own party—Green Russell's.

"He said he didn't believe he could make it back as he hadn't had a bite to eat since the day before and was feeling pretty weak. I got off my stool and told him to help himself. After he finished his meal he told us he is washing with a rocker about four miles below us and is getting about $6 a day. He wanted us to sell him a little flour and bacon.

GIVES VENISON TO HUNGRY MINER.

"We would not do this, but I gave him a big slice of venison, which he appeared glad to get.

"Gregory was back again today, saying he was about starved. We gave him another meal. He says he has spent considerable of his life mining in Georgia and he thinks this float gold we are getting comes from farther up the stream.

"If one of us will only furnish ten or fifteen days' rations and go with him, he is sure he can find the source of this gold.

"This morning was fine and Bill decided to go with Gregory into the mountains. They took about ten days rations and started off. We are surely hoping they will be successful. . . .

RICH LEAD FOUND BACK IN MOUNTAINS.

"Gregory and Bill came back today. Gone eleven days but they were successful in their hunt. They brought back some fine specimens of shot-like gold and say they have discovered a very rich lead. They say it is about thirty miles back into the mountains. We will have to wait about ten days before we can get our stuff thru to the new discovery.

"We are getting located on our claims. When Bill and Gregory came out they tried to pick a way we could get our wagon thru and had blazed a trail on the trees. When the snow was all gone, some of these marks were thirty feet from the ground where the snow was packed into the gullies.

"We are busy sawing out some lumber to make sluiceboxes and getting some logs cut to make a house. The creek is still freezing nights and the ice makes it very hard to do much yet in the way of mining. It is now the spring of 1858. If all goes well we will have quite a little work done before winter sets in again. . . .

DENVER SPRANG UP RAPIDLY.

"Auraria is building up fast and so is the new town on the east side of the river, which has been named Denver. Two portable sawmills have now come in and located up in the timber. They are getting $100 a thousand at the mills for lumber and $150 at Auraria. A stage line has been established, leaving St. Joe once a week for Cherry creek. It also brings in mail and a postoffice has been established.

"Very few of the newcomers now are gold hunters. Gamblers, etc., are about all that come in. The building of the town is the big thing. Everyone that came in is sold a town lot, if possible. The Denver side of the creek has the postoffice. A bridge has been built over Cherry creek."

Sadly, it is impossible to examine the original material for authenticity. Albert Dean's diary has vanished. Hence we will never know whether the error in the third paragraph from the bottom is Dean's or the typesetter's.

Letter written from Golden City, 1870

The following letter was found within a wall of the Lewis and Dorothy Cannady home at 906 Washington Avenue in Golden.

"golden, City, Col
July, 23, th/ 70,

Dear Brother
It is with pleasure that I take My pen in hand to inform you that I am well att this time I was in the Rockey Mountins last 5 days and knits I was in among the Rockey Mountin Bar and wolfs I had Stack wold to mak fares in 4 Sids So as to keep them from eateing alife. Mrojes thaut I was gone up tho they lef me to go after food for thir self and i left to you beet yor lif that was a bar hunt go way bar hunts that is my last time for me to go you beet

Well James I am in town to day but that is beeter then I expected yesterday ever.Body thought i was gon up for good tho I was in luck you beet I never Saw So meney come to See a horse wrais as Came to See me My (?) Jane was the first one to See me Come this was all glad to hear My Story of make ing fiers to drive annimales off from my Self go away bar hunting that is my last you beet your lif They caim in 2 feet of me i killed 7 bar and 4 kiots I praid five days and throwed fier five knits

I am halling ties for the Rail Road the C.C.P.R.R. That is the naim of this Road that is in 12 miles of golden. as Soon as hit Comes the first man wants My house and lot he can have hit and I lave Collorado. I am A Comeing to the Stats to get My Self good wife this thing of Cooking is agoing to Play by December and I am a comeing to old Mizsouri that is the Stat for me My Self

Wm. M. Couch"

As William writes, his handwriting takes on a wonderful flourish. He signs the letter several times and appears to be starting it again. Perhaps he is still celebrating his recent brush with death. On the back of one of the pages is the address
"James Couch
Clinton
Henry Co
Mo"
This was called "backing" the letter. Letters were folded and the address written on the blank side. Although the manufacture of envelopes began 1839, the practice of "backing" continued throughout the 19th century.

The 1879 Golden directory lists a Wm. Couch as a saloon keeper. Can this be the same William Couch who prayed five days and throwed fire five nights?

The Seeds of Death

"There are many unwelcome truths in the following communication of Dr. Floyd, of [Golden], to the State Board of Health at its recent second annual meeting, but we reproduce it in the hope that the authorities of the town may see the necessity of waking up to the necessity of doing their duty. We believe, at a recent meeting of the Board of Trustees the town constable was instructed to enforce the ordinances regarding the running at large of hogs. On Thursday last we counted thirteen, of various sizes, between our office and the Colorado Central depot. Will our town authorities read Dr. Floyd's indictment carefully, and have a little 'Get-up-and-get' about them...

Here is the doctor's bold and outspoken charge...

To the State Board of Health:

...There is no board of health in existence. Our 'authorities' think it unworthy of them to look after so small a thing as the sanitary condition of their town.

Dead animals are taken to the mere outskirts of the town limits, and there left to decompose or be eaten by the dogs.

There is no law enforced in regard to privies or sinks. The privies are mere holes in the ground—at the option of the parties— and when they become full, the house is removed and the stinking mass covered with a few inches of earth. The slops, from the outhouses and kitchens, are allowed to run as the incline from the house may be, to the street or alley. Clearings from stables are thrown into vacant lots or back alleys.

In many parts of town the accumulation of bones from butcher shops and kitchens are collected by dogs to many hundreds of pounds, and, I can say to pass one of these places during hot weather, is sickening.

Our drinking water is derived from wells. Their depth depends upon the dip of the clay bed upon which it is found. All wells under ditches are more or less affected. In portions of town, some of the wells are not to exceed ten feet deep, and in very wet weather rise to within a few feet of the top. In many places these wells and privies are not to exceed thirty feet apart...

S. T. Floyd.
Golden, January 2, 1878"

(Source: Colo. Transcript, January 30, 1878.)

Waterspout

Follansbee, Robert, and Sawyer, Leon, 1948, *Floods in Colorado:* U.S. Geological Survey Water-Supply Paper 997:

"In the eastern foothills region, usually below an altitude of about 7,500 feet and extending for a distance of about 50 miles east of the mountains, is a zone subject to rainfalls of great intensity known as cloudbursts…At times the intensity is so great as to make breathing difficult for those exposed to a storm…

A flood resulting from a cloudburst rises so quickly that it is usually described as a 'wall of water.' …The earliest recorded cloudburst—called at that time a waterspout—occurred in Golden Gate Gulch, July 14, 1872. The 'wall of water' was described as a 'perpendicular breast of 10 or 12 feet.'

…The account of this flood as given in the Rocky Mountain News of July 16, 1872 [is as follows]:

Those who have ever witnessed a waterspout will bear testimony to its appalling nature. One of these curious phenomena occurred on the Central Stage road in Golden Gate Gulch, 4 miles above the town of Golden, on July 14 about 4 o'clock. People residing in that vicinity report having seen, just above the higher mountains, numerous dense clouds, from which a conical pillar resembling condensed vapor, was seen to descend, and almost simultaneously a deafening peal of thunder was heard.

Mr. Jack Virden [and family] had been to Golden and were returning home in a double carriage and had reached the point indicated above, when the waterspout dispersed. * * * Presently a violent commotion, with confusion of sounds like the tumult of the elements, was heard high up in the mountains. Then came a tremendous torrent of water, bearing trees and boulders, and calculated to astonish and terrify by its magnitude, force, and violence. The horses, seeing that they were to be sacrificed to the prodigious volume, took fright, and shying to one side upset the carriage and all occupants were pitched into the bottom of the gulch. In an instant, as it were, and before they could recover their feet, the wave, with a perpendicular breast of 10 or 12 feet, was upon them and licked them up like the sands of the gulch. Mrs. Virden clung to her husband, and he, by miraculous chance, got hold of a limb and held fast until the flood subsided."

Little Known Facts About Lesser Known Things

In 1912, eighteen-year-old Bessie Mae Brown gave up the opportunity to study the violin under world-renown artist Mademoiselle Dupree to marry Peter Nare and live in Golden Gate Canyon, where she taught piano and violin to local children.

As a young man in Golden Uncle Paul Eiselstein bet a friend he could drive to Blackhawk faster up the railroad track than the friend could drive there through Golden Gate Canyon. Uncle Paul won the bet but said it like to jarred all his teeth out.

The row of trees along the N side of the highway at the entrance to Golden Gate Canyon represents a generous gift of time and money from the family of Hi Kilgore who founded

Ramparts. Many more trees have died and had to be replaced than have lived, but still the Kilgore family persists in returning to the land this gentle reminder of bygone days.

Mary Termentozzi, who grew up in Guy Gulch, told of reaching into the hens' nests and finding rattlesnakes coiled under the eggs for warmth.

The last major flood in the canyon was in 1965 when all the trees and bushes were scoured out of the bottom of Tucker Gulch.

Guy Hill was the most difficult height of land between Denver and Black Hawk for the ascent and descent of loaded wagons.

Horace Greeley filed the first eyewitness account by a major newspaper correspondent of the Gregory Road. But the account was eclipsed by reports of Greeley's having fallen off his mule in Clear Creek and being fished out of the drink by his unmentionables.

In the fall of 1859 Golden Gate City was the second largest settlement in the county with a population of over 100 persons.

In 1843 Rufus B. Sage gave the first written account of the valley that is now Golden, describing a crystal clear river that meandered through a rich bottom land attended by forests averaging a mile wide.

Prior to 1864 travel through the bottom of Clear Creek Canyon was possible only by foot and only after ice formed. Imagine that dark icy corridor made bumpy with layers of frozen ice and flanked with magnificent plumes of frozen water descending the tributaries.

Bands of horses, both Indian and emigrant, turned loose or runaway, roamed the countryside at the turn of the century. Ten-year-old Dan Thatcher, riding with his older brother through a little band of wild horses, saw a horse with a rotting saddle on its back.

Folks would ride for miles in a buggy or horseback to go to a dance, dance all night and not go home until there was daylight for the horses to see by.

During Prohibition the hills were full of stills operated by the landowner or by outsiders who rented the land and/or owner's teams and wagons to haul the moonshine. Moonshining was risky business. Men lost their homes and went to jail if caught.

Ralston Creek was full of beaver ponds, as were Guy Gulch and the larger drainages in Crawford Gulch. There is no record of beaver ponds in Tucker Gulch. Gone with the beaver are the large groves of aspen that occupied the countryside. Their scarcity is due partly to clear cutting for fields, and partly to the control of wildfires. Aspen grow more quickly than needle trees, but needle trees live longer and, where not destroyed by fire, slowly but surely crowd the aspen away.

Walter Ramstetter and Herman Hoffmeister, sons of homesteaders Henry Ramstetter and Casper Hoffmeister, respectively, died in separate instances after being kicked by horses. Walt was seventeen, Herman was eleven.

Jim Ramstetter reported spruce trees in Clear Creek Canyon as big around as wagon wheels. Timber men called these big trees "water spruce." In the 1940s, men working during the winter months to replace the railroad with a highway told of bulldozers uncovering large balls of rattlesnakes.

Golden Gate Canyon is the first rural community in Colorado to successfully initiate a downzoning of its land to save the past for the future.

Potpourri

Apple Trees

Early settlers planted apple trees and lilac bushes. While lilac bushes are still common, the little apple orchards have given way to new roads and old age. A few of the survivors easily visible from the public road are:

1) A lone apple tree on the W side of the Crawford Gulch Road 0.7 mile S of its junction with Drew Hill Road. From this apple tree W toward Douglas Mountain affords an excellent overview of the route of the original road to Gregory's as it ascended the valley toward the pass between Dry Creek and Guy Gulch.

2) A lone apple tree beside the GGC Road 1.6 miles W of its junction with SH 93. Due E from this apple tree is Hartzell Hill with its narrow piece of old road. This apple tree is the sole survivor of Ed Geery's orchard. Ed's house was across the road to the N and several hundred yards upstream.

3) Three apple trees W of the GGC Road directly below its junction with Crawford Gulch. These trees are on the old Blood homestead, now the Nare Ranch.

> "Ed Blood has the finest apple crop we've seen in many a day. Ed left a sample lot at the office during our absence for which he will please accept our thanks."

> (Source: Colo. Transcript: Sept. 23, 1896.)

4) Four apple trees N of the GGC Road ab. 1.5 miles above its junction with Crawford Gulch. This is the foundation of the old Guy Hill School.

5) A small lone tree immediately at the E entrance of Rye Gulch.

6) A lone tree N of the Smith Hill Road ab. 1 mile above its junction with the Robinson Hill Road. This the old Kolin ranch (the Blanchard homestead).

Daniel Boone Rock

Ab. 1.1 miles S of the junction of the Crawford Gulch/Drew Hill roads, and ab. 300 yards above the Crawford Gulch Road to the E on private ground.

S/b Ralston Buttes Quad.
S2, T3S, R71W.
Elv. ab. 7100.

The unusual rock formation is ab. 20 feet high. When viewed from the E, it resembles the profile of a man wearing a coonskin cap. The rock was a popular subject for early picture takers. It is now obscured by trees.

John Pearce, early rancher and former owner of the property, named the rock.

Daniel Boone Rock, c. 1900. The rock was a favorite subject for picture takers.

WIKSTROM COLLECTION

Golden Gates

Two ruined columns, their bases easily visible above the E entrance of GGC.

S/b Golden Quad.
S20, T3S R70W.
Elv. ab. 6150'.

Pioneer landmark. The rock columns put the word "Gate" in Golden Gate Canyon. One column held a large rock which resembled a flat hat. The columns were described as tall.

When the road was moved out of the creekbed uphill to the N, local residents requested that iron rods and heavy wire be used to hold the columns in place during the blasting. This was not done, and vibrations subsequently toppled the lower column and partially destroyed the upper column.

The bases of the shattered rock columns that named Golden Gate Canyon. Photographed 1997.

TROY SCOTT PARKER

Limbed Trees

Because cows in winter like to nibble on pine needles, and turpentine in the needles can cause birth defects and abortions, ranchers often chop or saw off the lower limbs of pine trees in the pastures where they winter their cattle. The best known examples of this practice are on the old Pearce ranch (now part of the Red School Ranch) W of the Crawford Gulch and Drew Hill roads.

Old ponderosa shorn of its lower limbs to prevent the pine needles being nibbled on by cattle in the winter. Photographed 1997.

Logan's Sandpit

Below the GGC Road, 1.5 mile above its junction with SH 93.
S/b Ralston Buttes Quad.
S20, T3S, R70W.
Elv. ab. 6300'.

In the early 1900s Elmer Logan dug a place beside the creek bottom where the creek waters, when high, deposited sand. The sand thus collected was sold. The high ridge to the N is the ridge along which thousands trudged on their way to Gregory's before the toll road was opened through the gulch.

The Lost Rifle

In 1995, while hunting the west ridge of Sawmill Gulch on Mt. Tom, Jess Wayne found an old Model 94 Winchester rifle lying on the ground beside a pine tree. The rifle was loaded and half-cocked. The weathered wood was swollen over the bands that held it to the iron.

The sun was shining, the woods were dry.

In that other time, the time when the rifle arrived on the mountain, who carried it? Did it slip from the tie that held it on a saddle? Was it left propped against the tree? What was the weather like then? Was the mountain full of snow and fog? Was it cold and getting dark?

Rifle lost on Mt. Tom. Photographed 1995 in Jess Wayne's yard.

Old Fenceposts

The oldest fenceposts in the region are pitch posts. They show distinct signs of having been in a fire and often have 2-inch holes bored through them. The mystery is, where did they come from? what were they used for prior to being planted in the ground?

Old pitch post on a fence line. Note the square nails. These old posts commonly have two 2-inch smooth holes bored through them at right angles to each other. Photographed 1996.

Old Stone Corral

In Guy Gulch 0.10 mile upstream from the Robinson Hill junction, up on the hill to the E, chinked between rock outcroppings, are the remnants of an old stone corral. This is the upper portion of a corral built before the turn of the century. The lower portion may have enclosed the creek, as the public road at that time passed W of the creek.

Rock Piles

In the 1950s countless small fields throughout the region were abandoned in a reflection of changing times in the marketplace. These old, overgrown fields can be identified by the rocks piled at the perimeters and/or within the field itself. Locate a pile of rocks, small enough as a rule to be carried by hand, and somewhere nearby is the edge of a furrow.

DON STEWART COLLECTION

Putting up oat hay on the Maloney homestead. Note the women's long skirts. It couldn't have been easy to clamber onto the wagon, nor to pile the hay. RIGHT TO LEFT: *Vernika Maloney, daughters Anna and Rosena, and friend Chris Mester.*

Telephone Trees

Pine trees in the path of the telephone line were commonly pressed into service. S of the GGC Road across the creek immediately above Miller Gulch is a wonderful example—an old pine tree with a crossarm for holding telephone wires.

Work on a telephone line for the Guy Hill district was started in 1912. The line operated until sometime in the 1960s. Shares in the Guy Hill Telephone Company sold for a dollar apiece. Ranchers whose land the line crossed were expected to donate labor and trees and to keep the line upright.

Telephone tree. Photographed 1981. Look for this tree across the creek and approx. 500 yards upstream from the flat below the Crawford Gulch/GGC road junction where the county piles its gravel.

Gus Koch purchased twenty shares of Guy Hill Telephone Company stock on February 25, 1924.

Warm-air hole

Belcher Hill Trail, White Ranch Park.
S/b RBQ.
S7, T3S, R70W
Elv. ab. 7200'.

A small hole in the earth where warm, damp air escapes. The hole is easiest to find in cold weather. Early-day travelers on the Belcher Hill Road stopped here to warm their hands. The site is unmarked.

Ways and Means

The good old days were the hard old days. Game became so scarce that hunters searched for days just to find a track to follow. "I wasn't very old, and I'd have to tail along after my sisters and brothers and carry the bucket and knives and a rope all the way out and back. It wasn't much fun, and I never cared much for hunting after that." – *Charlie Ramstetter*

The hills were full of garden farms and dairy farms. The biggest fields were the pea fields. "We got 3 cents a pound, and folks prided themselves on how fast they could pick. Rose Marie Ramstetter and I were the fastest. Rattlesnakes were a big problem, sometimes they'd even chase you." – *Mary Gulliksen*

One of the drop-off points for illegal whiskey was out near the old brick yard. "Two of my uncles were headed that way one night with a load of moonshine. There wasn't any moon and they were on that old road through Deep Gulch and looking up at the stars, at the different formations, when the wagon dropped a wheel into a ravine and they lost the whole shebang." – *Martha Koch*

Everybody was afraid of the revenue agents. "One night Allgood was hauling moonshine off Blue Mountain when he saw a string of car lights coming down Junction Hill. He rolled the barrels off the wagons and broke them, unharnessed the horses and threw the harness into the bushes and turned the horses loose, and hurried home before the agents come up on the mountain looking for him. Inside the house, friends and neighbors yelled "Happy birthday, Billy! Surprise! surprise!" – *Nora Buckman*

There was a lot of money bet on the 4th of July horse races. Folks wanting a longer race would take their horses onto the pastures across the road from the course laid out at the picnic Next to Strangs' Thoroughbred race horses the local horses looked like plow horses, but they were fast and used to dodging rocks over unfinished surfaces. "I saw Ollie [Koch] beat Steve Strang in one of those long races with that big black horse called Sailor." – *George Shephard*

"When I was little, my dad showed my older brother and me how to bump cows. He said mom was a school teacher and didn't know how to do those things, and he was pretty sick and wouldn't get well. I didn't pay a lot of attention then, but when he died, I remembered quick enough. We'd bump those cows, and when the calf got so big, we dry up the cow and quit milking her." – *Rose Marie Ramstetter*

Settlement

The Lyman C. Blood homestead deed. This rare document carries the original signatures.

The Homestead Act

The Act of Congress approved 20th May 1862, **"To secure Homesteads to actual Settlers on the Public Domain."**

That law provided that any U.S. citizen, or person with the intention of becoming a citizen, who was the head of a family and 21 years or older, could gain title to 160 acres of land after five years continuous residence on the land and payment of a small ($26 to $34) registration fee. Or, if the homesteader so desired, the title could pass into his hands after 6 months' residence and payment of the minimum price of $1.25 an acre. Satisfying the residency requirement was called "proving up."

The residency requirement, printed on the *Notice of Allowance,* reads:

> "NOTE: Residence on a homestead must be established by the entryman in person within six months after allowance of entry—otherwise forfeiture may result. An application for extension of the above period can not be entertained unless it be shown that, upon attempting to establish residence, the entryman was actually prevented, by climatic hindrances, from so doing within the required time. Such application can be made when final proof is submitted or in case contest is instituted against the entry, but can not be considered at any other time; nor can the entryman be excused by reason of climatic hindrances where by his own delay he allows such hindrances to intervene before undertaking to go on the land. Leave of absence can not be granted, for sickness or other cause, where the entryman has not established bona fide residence."

> (Source: *Notice of Allowance.* United States Land Office, Department of the Interior.)

In this part of the West, the Homestead Act applied only to even-numbered sections. Odd-numbered sections became the property of the Union Pacific Railroad as part of a 900,000-acre federal land grant made by Congress to encourage the railroad to lay track to the mineral-rich communities of the newly recognized territories. For homesteaders on odd-numbered sections, the terms of gaining title were similar to those spelled out in the residency requirement, except that these homesteaders purchased their land from the Union Pacific. *But they were not able to purchase the mineral rights.* Those were retained by the railroad.

The Homestead Act was officially repealed in 1934.

The *Blackhawk Quad, Colo. Edition of 1906,* shows the following houses in that portion of the quad now overlaid by the Ralston Buttes Quad. Whenever possible, where homesteads are known, the wife and children of the homesteader are listed using the earliest known spellings before the names became "Americanized." A good example is Vernika Maloney, page 244, who later spelled her name "Veronica." Known homesteads that do not appear on the 1906 quad are also included in this listing.

A caveat! The 1906 quad township descriptions vary from the RBQ. Use the RBQ to determine location.

For brevity, the following entries are listed by the first section shown on the legal description. When the quarter can not be determined, the half-section is used. To learn more about who homesteaded what, contact: National Archives, National Archives and Records Administration—Rocky Mountain Region, Denver Federal Center, Building 48, PO Box 25307, Denver, Colorado 80225-0307. Telephone 303-236-0817.

Helps barn on the Helps homestead overlooking Ralston Creek. This barn can now be visited in the Clear Creek Living History Park in Golden. Photographed 1981.

▦ T2S, R70W

S5, NW¼   Murphyville. At the E entrance to Ralston Creek Canyon. Several houses can be seen.

S6, NW¼   One house ab. 0.5 mile inside the E entrance to Ralston Creek Canyon.

S19, SW¼   O'Brien homestead, near the top of what is now called Blue Mountain Subdivision.

> "The original homestead cabin was built in the eighteen nineties by Jim O'Brien, an Irish settler. It was a three room log cabin served by a hand-dug well which still provides water one hundred years later."
>
> (Source: Bisque, Ramon, and Rouse, George, 1996, *Geology of the Blue Mountain Water District and Related History:* Golden, West by Southwest, p. 13.)

A wagon road up from the E entrance to Coal Creek Canyon passed by the O'Brien homestead to climb onto the backs of the mountains whence it proceeded W-NW through Sections 24, 23, and 14 (all in R71W on the RBQ). On the W side of Section 14, while on the high ground between Sections 14 and 23, the road divided. The northern fork dropped back into Coal Creek Canyon, reaching the river down a very steep ravine directly S of Crescent Mountain. The southern fork accommodated a string of houses in Section 22 to reach Ralston Creek.

S20, NW¼ Three houses on the prairie NE of Ralston Buttes. Not to be confused with Fireclay (S29), which does not appear on the 1906 BQ.

S30, SE¼ One house high on the E face of Ralston Buttes.

▨ T2S, R71W

S14-15 Three houses high in the Coal Creek drainage along the section line.

S19, NW¼ Nels A. Tallman homestead, 1889. Bachelor.

S19, SW¼ Anders Tallman homestead, March 20, 1882.

Anders' wife died in mid-ocean in 1871. The children, Anna, Nels, and John, met their father in New York. On December 15, 1876, shortly after starting his new homestead in what would eventually become Golden Gate State Park, Anders married Christina "Stena" Bengson.

Up Nott Creek ab. 1.5 miles above Ralston Creek. Several buildings. One appears to be in the NW¼ of Section 30.

(See Stevenson <u>in</u> Bibliography for Tallman family articles.)

WILDA (BENGSON) CORNELL COLLECTION

TROY SCOTT PARKER

TROY SCOTT PARKER

LEFT *Nels Tallman homestead in Golden Gate State Park. This site is on the State Register of Historic Properties.*
ABOVE *Ruins of one the Tallman homestead buildings. Photographed 1996.*

S20, S½   John Lindquist homestead. 1887.

S22   A string of houses along a road climbing out of Ralston Creek to the N. This road begins in a draw that opens on Ralston Creek ab. 1 mile below where Drew Hill Road meets Ralston Creek. The largest concentration of houses appears to be here. The road climbs N up this draw for ab. 0.5 mile, accommodating at least one more house. A short distance above this house it jogs over toward the NW across two more drainages. A short road 0.1 mile up the higher of these drainages reaches two more houses. The main road continues on across the corner of Section 15 to reach a high pass in the SW corner of Section 14, and a junction.

See Section 19, T2S, R70W, for more information on the road.

S26, SW¼   Helps homestead, 1875. James and Mary (McClinton). Children: one son known, Wellington.

Overlooking Ralston Creek from the S.

View looking N toward Ralston Creek from the shoulder of Songer Mountain. The Helps barn, center (see arrow), has since been relocated in the Clear Creek Living History Park in Golden where it was reunited with the Helps home moved from this flat into the Betty drainage some 80 years earlier before being moved to Golden in the 1990s. Photographed 1994.

James Helps immigrated from Canada…to Kansas in 1877. Tree rings established the construction of the Helps cabin…in 1878…
[James] mined in Bobtail Mine in Black Hawk and commuted on weekends to see his family, traveling the Dory Hill Road.

His mining career came to a sudden end when he drilled into an unexploded dynamite stick.

In later years, Helps was the county road supervisor and worked in construction. He built the family home at 21st and East streets. Another misfortune befell Helps when sunstroke blinded him three years before his death in 1936.

(Source: Gardner, Richard, 1997, *Holiday home tour:* Transcript, Nov. 14, 1997, p. 11.)

The Helps cabin on its new location on the Betty drainage. This picture looks to have been taken upon completion of the resurrection of the cabin, which John Pearce dismantled, numbering the logs as he went, and hauled on wagons from Ralston Creek. Note the upended barrel and scattered remains of what appear to be chinking material. The first man to the left is Tom Pearce, Sr. Sam Bowser is the man holding the hammer. The man on the far right is Tom Pearce, Jr. Next is Christina Wikstrom. The woman standing beside Christina in the dark dress is her mother, Martha Wikstrom. This structure is now located in the Clear Creek Living History Park.

John's Pearce's home, now in Golden's Clear Creek Ranch Living History Park, originally housed the Helps family on this site. The Helps barn has also been moved to the park.

S27, NW½ Nelson homestead, 1919. 160 acres. Carl S. "Charlie" and Christina. Children: Dorothy, Jeanie, Carl, Arthur, Elof Walter, Myron, Mary Ann, John. Home located in the bottom of Drew Gulch. Does not appear on 1906 BQ.

S28, NE¼   One house beside Ralston Creek to the N ab. 0.6 mile downstream of its junction with Drew Hill Road.

S28, SW¼   One house. At the N entrance to Geoffrey Gulch.

S28, SE¼   Two houses to the E and W of Drew Hill Road a short distance above its junction with Geoffrey Gulch.

S29 (center)   A cluster of houses at the junction of Ralston and Nott creeks. The Enos Macy homestead was here. 1891.
> Later occupants: Strang's Dude Ranch.
> *1942 RBQ Legend: Ralston Creek Ranch.*

S29, NE¼   Siverman homestead. 1892.

S29, N¼   Sylvester Nott homestead.
> Up Nott Creek ab. 0.25 mile above Ralston Creek.
> *1906 BQ Legend: Nutt Creek.*

S29, NW¼   Bengson homestead. Rudolph and Ruth (Williams). Children: Wilda.
> Up Nott Creek ab. 0.5 mile above Ralston Creek.

S32, SE¼   Timber town. Several houses in upper Sawmill Gulch on Mt. Tom.

Mt. Tom with its enormous black cape of ponderosa pine and red and blue spruce. Photographed 1984.

S32, SE¼   One-room cabin in saddle between Cabin Gulch and Sawmill Gulch. Built by bootleggers who made desultory attempts at digging a mine SW of the cabin on a higher slope of Mt. Tom. The mine was a front for the bootleggers' activities in the region.

Does not appear on 1906 BQ.

Bootleggers' cabin at the top of Cabin Creek, Mt. Tom. Photographed in the 1970s.

S34, NW¼   A cluster of buildings NW off the top of Drew Hill overlooking a north-slope basin.

1906 BQ Legend: Drew Ranch.

S34, SW¼   Boyle ranch.

SW off the top of Drew Hill high in the Betty drainage.

The ranch buildings burned to the ground in a fire that was visible in Arvada.

S34, SE¼   Betty homestead. The homestead that named Betty Creek. Upstream N of the Reynolds-Harry homestead.

In the big basin at the headwaters of Betty Creek E of the creek.

S34, SE¼   Reynolds-Harry homestead. Adam and Annie (Harry).

S of Betty Creek downstream of the Betty homestead.

Mrs. Annie Harry, a widow whose husband homesteaded here, married Adam Reynolds in Golden on April 4, 1901. Charles S. Staples, Justice of the Peace, officiated. Annie's children by her marriage to Harry: Gertrude, Hendrietta, Mary.

The Reynolds-Harry wedding certificate was found behind a framed picture in the home of Annie's daughter, Mary (Harry) Nelson in Crawford Gulch.

The Reynolds-Harry house, more commonly known as the Reynolds cabin, may now be seen in the Clear Creek Living History Park.

The Reynolds homestead in Betty drainage looking uphill toward the NW. The woman seated in the shadows is Annie Harry-Reynolds. The others are unknown. Photo by J. O. Jully, Jr., whose love affair with the camera resulted in a extraordinary collection of glass-plate negatives. Mr. Jully managed with his cumbersome equipment to document virtually every facet of life in Golden Gate Canyon in the late 1800s and early 1900s.

The remains of the Reynolds cabin in Betty drainage looking downhill toward the SW. This home may now be visited in the Clear Creek Living History Park in Golden. Photographed 1992.

EDITORS' NOTE: Park visitors are deeply indebted to Irma Wyhs, historian and writer, for her vision of the future that included such a park in the heart of Golden. And to Dr. Harvey Mozer, rancher, for his generous donations of the Reynolds cabin and the Helps house and barn. Were it not for the untiring efforts of these humanitarians, aided by a large cadre of believers, the Clear Creek Living History Park would not exist.

S35, S½   Songer homestead. Frederick and Martha. Eight children including Hallie and Myrtle.
Lower SE slope of Songer Mountain.

▨ T2S, R72W

S35, NW¼   Allgood ranch.

Two houses upstream of Golden Gate Park Headquarters.

"H. Miller is camping out at Allgood's ranch."

(Source: Colo. Transcript, Sept. 23, 1896.)

S35, NW¼   One house midway between the Allgood ranch and Park Headquarters.

▨ T3S, R70W

S5, NW¼   Glencoe. At the E entrance to Ralston Creek Canyon.
Several houses. Innundated by the waters of Ralston Reservoir in 1938.

S13, NE¼   One house.

S13, SE¼   Brown ranch.
In the big meadows on the back of the mountains N of Tucker Gulch and E of Crawford Gulch.

S18   Cressman homestead.
Bottom of Cressmans Gulch. Three houses strung out beside the creek in this section. The house 1.5 miles above the entrance is the Aubrey and Cora (Hudson) Ladwig Ranch.

S30, NW¼   Ed Gerry homestead.
In Tucker Gulch between Barnes wood road and Hartzell Hill. (See: Apple Trees <u>in</u> Potpourri.)
Does not appear on 1906 BQ.

⊞ T3S, R71W

S1, NW¼   Flinn home.

On the White Ranch in unnamed draw N of the upper parking lot.

In 1888 George F. Atto bought the Flinn farm and moved his wife, Mary, and seven children into the log-cabin home. While here, George built a 3-story barn from logs cut on the property. (The lower story rotted away and was removed by Paul White.) The barn, its upper two stories often pictured in park literature, is the only structure remaining. In 1906 George sold the farm to Fred F. Brackett. The farm was next sold to Torrence White, Jr., before being purchased by his brother, Paul White, Sr., in 1925.

The Flinn barn sans its lower story, as it appears to park visitors today.

S1 (center)   Bond homestead. 1881. James and Mary Elizabeth (Munshower). Children: Mary Elizabeth and James Wesley, Frank, Charles. (See Bond, R. F., 1989, *The land persists:* Jeffco Hist. Com. contest entry, for the story of the Bond family, the Atto family, and others who lived on what is now the White Ranch. Robert F. Bond is the grandson of Frank Bond and the great-grandson of James Bond.)

The White Ranch Park Headquarters is located in the old Bond clapboard-sided home.

S2, N½   Dillon winter home.

Located at the top of the section in the draw due N of Schrell Point.

S2, NE¼   Dillon summer home.

    High in a shallow draw that runs E into the White Ranch.

S2, NE¼   Community church.

    Ab. 0.25 mile above the Dillon summer home in the same draw that runs E into the White Ranch.

S2, SW¼   Wikstrom homestead, 1873. Lars and Martha.

    At the junction of Betty Creek with Dry Creek.

    Lars and Martha were married in Fort Dodge, Iowa, in 1869. Children: John, Mary Eureka, Anna Christina.

    Lars was born in Sweden in 1848. He died at his residence in Crawford Gulch in 1893. Martha was born in Sweden in 1840 and immigrated to America in 1866. She died in 1927 in Golden at the home of her daughter, Mary.

    This is where the original road to Gregory's turned W up the Dry Creek drainage to cross over the pass into Guy Gulch.

> "Blood Bros.' mill is now located at the Wickstrom ranch, and in a few days the manufacture of lumber will begin."
>
> (Source: Colo. Transcript, Feb. 10, 1896.)

The Wikstrom mansion. From left to right: 1) Ruth (Williams) Wikstrom, wife of 2) John Wikstrom; 3) unknown; 4) Christina Wikstrom; 5) the little girl with the hole in her stocking may be Wilda Bengson, the daughter of Rudolph Bengson, Ruth's first husband, who died of pneumonia; 6) unknown; 7) Oscar Dahlberg; 8) Martha Wikstrom (mother of John and Christina; grandmother of Oscar).

WIKSTROM COLLECTION

"A card party was given at the Wickstrom mansion Friday night."

(Source: *Ibid.*)

EDITORS' NOTE: "Wickstrom" was a common misspelling.

The Wikstrom mansion suffered the fate of many large wooden structures. Set ablaze by a kitchen chimney fire in February 1970, it burned to the ground. With it went a considerable chunk of early Golden history. Mary Wikstrom was married to Nels Dahlberg, a prominent figure in Golden's Swedish community who purchased the Goosetown Tavern from Casper Hofmeister (who homesteaded near James Helps in Ralston Creek). When Nels died, Mary and her son ran the tavern. The tavern was eventually sold to Sam Wayland, and the Dahlbergs moved back into the Wikstrom home, taking with them a large collection of memorabilia.

S3, NE¼   Pearce homestead. Thomas H., Sr.

E of Mt. Tom on the flat beside the road that ran W from Drew Hill Road up the W fork of Betty Creek to the timber town in S32 on Mt. Tom.

When Thomas' first wife died, he married Henrietta (Harry). Children: Minnie, Mabel, Gertrude, Florence, Emily, Tom, John, and Fred.

WIKSTROM COLLECTION

Thomas H. Pearce, Sr., homestead, 1909. From left to right: Oscar Dahlberg on horse, his mother Mary Dalhberg, and aunt Christina Wikstrom. Next to Christina are Margaret and Tom Pearce, Jr. John Pearce is on the far right. Tom and John were sons of Thomas H. Pearce. They married sisters Margaret and Susie Sparks.

The barns and outbuildings on the old Pearce ranch on the W fork of the Betty drainage. Thomas H. Pearce, Sr., homesteaded here. Two of his sons, Tom and John, lived here to old age with their families. Tom worked as road boss for the county, John worked on the land. Their homes are out of sight to the right. Tom and his wife and son lived in and added onto his father's house. John and his wife and four children lived in the old Helps cabin, moved here from Ralston Creek. Photographed 1991.

S3, SW¼   The 1867 Deane survey shows a sawmill here.

When the Gregory toll road was opened, a connecting road was built from the toll road through Koch Gulch to the original road.

At the top of this connecting road, in the immediate vicinity of the Jully and Maloney homesteads, is where this sawmill was located.

S4, NE¼   One house midway up Cabin Gulch on Mt. Tom. Walker homestead. Dick and Bess. Children: Buster, Ollie, Velma, Georgia.

S4, SE¼   Jully homestead. 1886. Joseph Otto and Elizabeth. Children: Joseph Otto, Jr.
            Under the shadow of Mt. Tom ab. 0.25 mile above the original road to
            Gregory's.

LEFT *Joseph Jully, Sr., homestead as seen looking N. Photographed Christmas 1919.*

ABOVE *The Joseph Jully, Sr., homestead nestled against the S shoulder of Mt. Tom as seen looking W. Photographed July 1997.*

DON STEWART COLLECTION

CAROLE LOMOND

S5, SW¼   One house high on the W face of Mt. Tom overlooking the Guy Gulch drainage.

S7, NW¼   Several houses beside the public road at the E foot of Michigan Hill.

S8 or S17   Swena house.
            The foundation is clearly visible N of the public road above Centennial Ranch.
            Does not appear on 1906 BQ.

S8 or S17   Cheesebox School.
            Above Centennial Ranch at the entrance to a drainage opening from N.
            Does not appear on 1906 BQ.

S8, SW¼   Several houses upstream from Centennial Ranch at the entrance to a steep,
            0.5 mile drainage off Mt. Douglas.

S9, SW¼   Koch Ranch. (Ernest, Jr.).
            In a meadow due S of the summit of Mt. Tom.
            Beside the original road to Gregory's on the pass between Dry Creek and Guy
            Gulch.

S9, SE¼   Baughman ranch.

In the same family since 1886 and still in agricultural production (see Jully homestead, S4), the Baughman ranch was recognized in 1990 as a Centennial Farm and Ranch of Colorado in a program co-sponsored by the Colorado Agricultural Department, the Colorado Historical Society, and the Colorado State Fair.

S10, NW¼ Maloney homestead. James and Vernika "Rony Maloney." Children: Anna, Rosie, Jim, Mary.

Situated on the original road to Gregory's, the Maloney homestead was at the terminus of two other heavily traveled roads:

1) A road that climbed Cabin Gulch to reach the timber town on the back of Mt. Tom.

2) The road that traveled E over the hill to the Gregory toll road.

As was common practice, the Maloney house and barns were burned to the ground in the 1940s to get them off the tax rolls.

The Maloney homestead, c. 1920, in the meadow below a S shoulder of Mt. Tom.

DON STEWART COLLECTION

S10, SE¼ Koch homestead. Ernest S., Sr., and Elizabeth (Snitker). Children: Matilda, Dorothia, William, Ernest, Theodore, August.

At the head of Koch Gulch beside the road connecting the Gregory toll road with the original road to Gregory's.

Ernest Koch, Sr., who peddled his vegetables in Central City, was known as "Cabbage" Koch.

"Miss Lizzie Hemberger spent several days at the Koch mansion."

(Source: Colo. Transcript, Sept. 23, 1896.)

"Jas. Nakivel and family, August Koch and wife, and Karl Ficht spent Sunday and Monday picnicing at Ernest Koch's place in the Guy Hill region. They report an excellent time, but didn't have an opportunity to kill a deer."

(Source: *Ibid.* Aug. 26, 1896.)

"During the severe storm of Friday evening last, lightning struck the home of Ernest Koch, of Guy Hill, tearing a hole through the roof, and breaking all the windows."

(Source: *Ibid.* Also see Burials for a storm casualty.)

Ernest Koch, Sr., homestead at the top of Koch Gulch. Photographed 1966.

S10, SE¼   One house in Koch Gulch due S of the Ernest S. Koch homestead. A two-story red brick house built around the turn of the century with bricks made on the site. This building is still standing and has recently received a new roof.

The Younger boys and their father shooting from stoop, December 25, 1919. Aiming rifles and standing attention with a rifle over the shoulder were common poses of the time and no doubt reflective of the Great War that ended in 1918.

Brick house on Ernest Koch, Sr., homestead at the top of Koch Gulch. Although the Kochs did not themselves encounter ghosts, people who later lived in their home, torn down in 1962, and in this brick house frequently spoke of things that went bump in the night. Photographed 1966.

The mysterious red brick house on the old Koch homestead. Many people have lived in this house, but no one knows who built it. The house has sweeping views to the S, including this view of Sheep Mountain.

S11, SE¼   Sam Bowser homestead. Bachelor.

           At the junction of Dry Creek with Crawford Gulch Road.

Sam Bowser homestead, about 1910. Christina Wikstrom is sitting on the chimney holding Oscar Dahlberg. Scratched on the glass negative is the legend, "When will Bowser return."

S11, NW¼   Three houses at the top of the basin on a W drainage of Dry Creek.

S13, NE¼   One house high in the S drainage of Dry Creek.

           Accessed by a road climbing out of Cressmans Gulch.

S13, SW¼   One house high to the W in the lower Crawford Gulch drainage.

           In October 25, 1890, Hannah Blood purchased from Le'once B. Delahoussaye, legal representative of Louis and Alexander Delahoussaye, 40.56 acres in the SE¼ of the SE¼ of Section 13. This ground was part of a large land claim aggregating 1361.12 acres entered by Louis and Alexander probably around the time of the gold rush to the Gregory Diggings.

           Hannah's purchase is near the original road to Gregory's (immediately W of Enter Mountain). (See Original Road to Gregory's <u>in</u> Historical Routes.)

           Louis and Alexander failed to satisfy their claim. They probably lost interest when substantial mineral deposits failed to be unearthed. As a result, Hannah was able to purchase her 40 acres for $1.25 per acre from the United States of America.

In January 10, 1891, Hannah Blood purchased 40 acres in the NE¼ of the SE¼ of Section 13, this time from John Berrois under conditions similar to those of the Delahoussaye purchase: Berrois had laid claim to land aggregating 526 acres which he failed to satisfy.

S14, NE¼ In later years this was called the Horn house. But it may have originally been the George(?) Forsberg homestead.

W of Forsberg Peak near the head of Crawford Gulch.

S14, SW¼ Guy Hill School. N of the public road in Tucker Gulch.

S14, N½ Theodore Koch homestead. Theodore and Bessie L. (Tripp). Children: George and Rose.

On the higher slopes to the W at the top of Thea Gulch in the Crawford Gulch drainage. The family later moved into the Centennial House.

Theo. Koch – 1910

Thea Gulch was named for Theodore Koch, homesteader. In his later years Thea worked for Adolph Coors.

S15 Ramstetter homestead. Henry, Sr., and Matilda (Koch). Children: Henry, Jr., George, Ernest, Otto, Walter.

Does not appear on 1906 BQ.

S15, SE¼   Grant ranch.

Beside the public road a short distrance upstream from the Guy Hill School. Later known as the Buckman ranch.

> In January, 1869, Thomas Grant advertised a new blacksmith shop in Golden City at the corner of "Washington Avenue and Garrison street, north of the upper bridge," and announced that "Having erected a large and commodious shop at this place, I am now prepared to do blacksmithing and repairing in all its branches. Horse, Ox and Mule shoeing, and all kinds of Agricultural work executed promptly and satisfaction guaranteed. Terms reasonable."

It may be that Thomas Grant and the Grant ranch in S15 are connected. This has also been called the Thornby ranch, but the source is unknown.

S15, S½   Eight-mile House.

Beside the public road on the E side of Guy Hill at the entrance to Koch Gulch. The 1867 Deane survey shows a sawmill here.

Colo. Transcript, Jan. 6, 1869.

The Grant Ranch, more recently known as the Buckman Ranch, at the entrance to Grant Gulch. Photographed 1951.

"A big time is booked for tomorrow night up at George Hutchinson's place on Guy Hill. There will be a social dance, with a profusion of eatables and drinkables on the side."

(Source: Colo. Transcript, Aug. 26, 1896.)

"The dance given by Capt. G. A. Hutchinson was a grand success. Fifty couples danced to the music of Prof. Albert Lintz' Central City Orchestra. A most enjoyable time was had by all who attended. Guy Hill was well represented."

(Source: *Ibid.* Sept. 2, 1896.)

"Al Naurch and his pard, 'Arizona Pete,' intend to give a dance some evening next week at Guy Hill Hall. Al told us to be sure to tell everybody to come, which we cheerfully do."

(Source: *Ibid.* Feb. 10, 1896.)

S16, SW¼   Guy homestead. John C. S side of creek downstream from Robinson Hill Road junction. *Does not appear on 1906 BQ.*

S16, NW¼   August Koch homestead. August Arthur and Isabella Cicilia (Bengson). Children: Basil, Claire, Howard, Betty, Della, Martha, William.

High in a Guy Gulch drainage N of Guy Hill.

The first telephone in the mountains was constructed between the Gus Koch (S16) and Joe Jully, Jr., (S9) households so that Kitty Jully and Belle Koch could visit.

S17, NE¼   A cluster of buildings in Guy Gulch at the W junction of the original road to Gregory's with the Gregory toll road. The 1867 Deane survey also shows something here. In 1872 the Colorado Central Railroad was advertising for 45,000 ties for use on its line from Golden to the mountain towns, and there was a large "tie camp" in Guy Gulch. Sixty-five people lived in the gulch and worked cutting timber for railroad ties. That camp and sawmill may have been here.

1906 BQ Legend: Centennial Ranch.

S19, NE¼   Crowell homestead. Ransom Amos and Alice G. (Loth). Children: June.

Crowell homestead, c. 1930s.

On Elk Creek at the junction of the Smith Hill and Robinson Hill roads. Later known as the Horn Ranch. Now called the Douglas Mountain Ranch.

S19, NW¼ Kolin homestead. 1901. Charles and Mary (Brothersen). Children: Helen, Lillian, Ruth, Oliver.

High on a S shoulder of Douglas Mountain overlooking Smith Hill Road.

S19, NW¼ Two houses 0.25 mile apart on Smith Hill Road.

The northernmost of these houses is the Blanchard homestead. Ole and Martha Kolin (parents of Charles Kolin, see above) brought the land from Blanchard. Martha planted the tall spruce trees in front of the house. She carried them from across the creek in her apron.

S20, NW¼ One house in a drainage running SE from peak of Douglas Mountain about 0.25 mile above Robinson Hill Road.

S20, NW¼ One house at the junction where Robinson Hill Road divides to accommodate ranches to the SE in the lower regions of the Elk Creek drainage.

S20, NE¼ Tripp homestead. (80 acres—the E ½ or the SE ¼ of Section 20) Edward Lory and Mary Jane. Children: Bessie, Edward, Jr., Mamie, Lena.

In the large, open meadows on the Elk Creek drainage.

S20, SE¼ Green ranch.

In the large, open meadows on the Elk Creek drainage.

S21 NW¼ One house on the Elk Creek drainage.

S21, SW¼ A. Tripp homestead. Bachelor.

On the Elk Creek drainage.

S22, ? Two houses. One on the Miller Creek drainage. The other on the high easterly shoulder of Guy Hill. One of these may have been the George Ramstetter homestead. In later years George was mayor of Central City.

No children.

The other house may have been the homestead of James Bond, who later homesteaded a second time on Belcher Hill. (See S1, T3S, R71W.)

S23, NW¼ Hawley(?) home.

Overlooking Tucker Gulch from the S in vicinity of Guy Hill School.

S24, NW¼ Harold Crawford(?) home.

Just inside Crawford Gulch on the N side of the public road.

S24 Blood homestead. 1873. (80 acres—the SE¼ of the NW¼ and the SW¼ of the NE¼ of Section 24)

Lyman C. and Hannah. Five children, including Edward and Art(?).

The main buildings were located in Tucker Gulch directly downstream of its junction with Crawford Gulch. This ranch served as a freight stop and as a community center.

"One day, Lyman was caught in a flash flood in the canyon, and badly injured. When his team of horses bolted and ran away, he crawled home, but died shortly of his injuries."

(Source: Dempsey, Alice, 1984, *Failed trade blocked papoose upbringing for Edward Blood:* Golden Transcript, July 26, 1984, p. 6.)

BESSIE (BROWN) NARE COLLECTION

Blood homestead, looking NW up Golden Gate Canyon toward the entrance of Crawford Gulch where the WPA is building the Crawford Gulch Bridge. Note dust plumes and rough grading from construction. Photographed ab. 1930.

The Nare Ranch, the grange hall and the county shop occupy a portion of the old Blood homestead. The old Blood barn burned in the 1990s. The house escaped the fire but was later demolished.

S24, SW¼ Nare Homestead, 1914. John H. (160 acres—the W½ of the NW¼ and the W½ of the SW¼, Section 24)

Known Children: George H. Nare.

The remants of the house are located 0.5 mile up Miller or Four-mile Gulch.

Miller lived at the entrance to Miller Gulch beside the public road in the 1800s. Whether he homesteaded here or just squatted is unknown. Also unknown is his connection with Four-mile House, which was here on the flat. The Four-mile House was a popular stop for freighters and travelers, but stages whizzed on by.

John H. Nare later homesteaded 80 acres in the NE¼ of the NW¼ and the NW¼ of the NE¼ of Section 24.

IL

020653

4—279

DEPARTMENT OF THE INTERIOR

UNITED STATES LAND OFFICE

Denver, Colorado,
(Place.)

November 14, 1914.
(Date.)

NOTICE OF ALLOWANCE.

John H. Nare,

Golden, Colorado.

Sir:

Your ___homestead application___, SERIAL No. ___020653___,
(Kind of application or entry.)

Receipt No. ___1400262___, for ___

___W½ NW¼ and W½ SW¼___, Section ___24___

Township ___3 S.___, Range ___71 W.___, 6th Principal Meridian,

containing ___160___ acres, has been this day allowed, subject to

your further compliance with law and regulations applicable thereto.

In correspondence relating to this entry, always refer to the

serial number.

Very respectfully,

_____, Register.

_____, Receiver.

6—1430

Approval of the Nare homestead application.

S25, SE¼   Ramstetter homestead. 1913. 160 acres. E½ SE¼, S25, and S½ SW¼, S30, T3S, R71W. Otto Albert and Julia A. (Allgood). Children: Elsie, Raymond, Ernest, Leona, Lois Jean, Virgil.

In the big basin at the head of Devil's Garden Gulch.

Otto later married Bertha Anne (Olson). Children: Rose, Gordon, Franklin, Arlene, Kenneth, Charles, Nora, Richard.

The Otto Ramstetter homestead at the top of Devil's Garden Gulch, 1960. Saulsbury Peak is the highest (leftmost) peak in the background. Photographed 1970.

S25, SE¼   Eldridge homestead. (?) and Hannah.

On the E side of the peak known locally as Eldridge, a.k.a. Crawford Peak.

S26, W½   A.(?) Saulsbury homestead.

On the E side of the drainage high in the draw between Taylor and Saulsbury peaks.

Does not appear on 1906 BQ.

S26, W½   Stafford home. Around the hill from the Saulsbury homestead on a SW shoulder of Saulsbury Peak.

S27, NW¼   Koch homestead, George. In the bottom of Guy Gulch due S of Guy Hill.

S28, NE¼   Tripp homestead. Anthony and Caroline Amanda (Terrill). Children: Anthony, Jr., Arthur, Belle, Cora, Florence, Grace, James, John, Katherine, Philmore.

On Elk Creek NE of Sheep Mountain.

S29, SW¼ Ballinger homestead.
Later occupants: Bingham, Edmond Clair.
At the N base of Sheep Mountain.
There is another house ab. 0.25 mile around the shoulder of the mountain to the W.

S30, SE¼ Two houses ab. 0.25 mile apart to NW and across the drainage from Sheep Mountain.

S31, N½ Mayhem homestead. High on the W slope of Sheep Mountain.

S31, NE¼ Gulliksen homestead. John.
High on a Clear Creek drainage W of Sheep Mountain. Ab. 0.25 mile from the above house, but not in the same draw.

S32, NE¼ Forest homestead.
High on a NE shoulder of Sheep Mountain.
A variety of minerals including fine beryl crystals were mined near here.

S35, N½ Frank Qualls homestead.
In the bottom of Guy Gulch due S of Saulsbury Peak.

S36, NW¼ Shephard homestead. Thomas Harris and Elizabeth (Body). Children: Ellen, Richard, Mary (or Mayme), Thomas Jr., Rebecca, Anna, Archibald, Emma, Albert, two unnamed infants.
In the higher regions of Devil's Garden Gulch downstream of the Otto Ramstetter homestead.

Cabin remains on Thomas Harris Shephard homestead in Devil's Garden Gulch. Photographed 1982.

▨ T3S, R72W

S12, NE¼   Two houses to either side of the public road up the E side of Michigan Hill.
One of these is the Ljungvall house.
This was the site of *11 mile house*.

Somewhere in Ralston Creek

"Our friend F. E. Hodges, of Ralston Creek, was unfortunate enough to lose his dwelling house and one of his granaries by fire on Saturday night last. The fire was discovered about 9 o'clock in the granary, and is supposed to have started from a match carelessly thrown among some sacks by Mr. Hodges' hired man, when getting feed for the horses. The granary in which the fire originated was consumed with some 2,000 pounds of chop feed, a valuable feather bed which was stored in it, and other articles. The fire was communicated to the house, which was also consumed, with a great part of the household goods. The dwelling house was a log structure, and not particularly valuable. Mr. H. sustains a considerable loss in property, and his family will be subjected to much inconvenience until another house can be built. He was in town on Monday purchasing lumber and materials for building."

(Source: Colo. Transcript, Jan. 30, 1878.)

Mile Marker Tour

THE GREEN MILE MARKERS along Golden Gate Canyon Road are here juxtaposed with nearby place names.

Mile 1   Entrance to Halfmile Gulch.

Mile 2   Directly N of the high ground known as Hartzell Hill, over which the early roads ran.

Mile 3   Ohman Mine. Abandoned uranium mine. The building beside the highway is the compressor house. The shaft, which crossed under the creek, is now collapsed. See photo on next page.

Mile 4   Queen Anne Mine. Abandoned uranium mine.

Mile 5   The old Grant ranch pastures are to the S.

Mile 6   Eight-Mile House was here beside the creek. The silo where the man was buried upright is here.

Mile 7   Douglas Mountain is directly to the W. The toll road switchbacks are directly across the draw to the S.

Mile 8   Junction GGC and Robinson Hill roads.

Mile 9   The original road to Gregory's and the Gregory toll road are now one. (They met at Centennial House.)

Mile 10   The foundation remains of Ferree's Community Hall are immediately above here on the W side of the road.

Mile 11   That portion of the wagon road up Michigan Hill known as Pole Hill is S of here.

The old Ohman molybdenum mine at mile marker 3 on the GCC Road. Photographed 1997.

Bibliography

Akal, Dorothy, 1989, *Questions about Golden Gate City always will remain:* Golden Transcript, Jan. 24, 1989.

Arvada, just between you and me, 1904-1941: Arvada Hist. Soc., 1985.

Bancroft, Hubert Howe, Works of: *History of Nevada, Colorado and Wyoming, 1540-1888:* San Francisco, 1890, The History Co., v. 25.

Bell, J. R., 1820, *The Journal of Captain John R. Bell, Official Journalist for the Stephen H. Long Expedition to the Rocky Mountains, 1820.*

Bird, Isabella, 1873, *A lady's life in the Rocky Mountains:* New York, G. P. Putnam's Sons.

Bisque, Ray, 1995, *Tepee rings found:* Mountain Messenger, July 1995.

_____ 1995, *Tepee rings:* Mountain Messenger, May 1996.

_____ and Rouse, George, 1996, *Geology of the Blue Mountain Water District and Related History:* Golden, West by Southwest.

Bond, Fred C., 1974, *It happened to me, an American autobiography:* p. 9 and 10, unpublished. Fred's son, Robert F. Bond, used this paper as the basis for his work entitled *The land persists.*

Bond, R. F., 1989, *The land persists:* Jeffco Hist. Com. contest entry.

Boulder Camera, 1945, *Toll roads in Boulder County and the pioneers who constructed them:* April 3, 1945.

Brannan Sand & Gravel Company, 1979, *Pit 24 (Quarry) Jefferson County, Colorado.*

Brescia, Janice, *Coal Creek Canyon history:* Jeffco 1991 North Mountains Area Community Plan.

Broad, Richard, Jr., *When Golden was the capital:* Colo. School of Mines Library, typed manuscript, Document 33792.

Brown, Georgina, 1976, *The shining mountains:* Gunnison, Colo., B&B Printers.

Brown's Gazetteer, 1860.

Burt, S. W., and Berthoud, E. L., 1860, *Quartz mining region of the Rocky Mountains:* Denver City, Rocky Mountain News Printing Co., map insert.

Byers, W. N., 1901, *Encyclopedia of biography of Colorado:* Chicago, Century Pub. Co., v. 1.

CCRR Time Schedule No. 25, handbill, Oct. 26, 1874.

Clear Creek Land Conservancy, Dec. 1995.

Ladies Columbine Club Notes, July 1941.

Colorado & Southern Railway 1904 / Clear Creek District / Timetable.

Colorado as seen by a visitor of 1880: Colo. Mag., v. 12, no. 3, May 1935.

Colorado in The Golden Globe, Industrial Edition, May 20, 1893.

Colo. Transcript, Feb. 28, 1861.

_____ Oct. 20, 1866.

_____ May 20, 1868.

_____ July 8, 1868.

_____ Dec. 16, 1868

_____ Jan. 6, 1869.

_____ June 2-16-20-30, 1869.

_____ July 28, 1869.

_____ March 2-16-23, 1870.

_____ day missing, 1871.

_____ Jan. 30, 1878.

_____ Feb. 10, 1896.

_____ Aug. 26, 1896.

_____ Sept. 2-23, 1896.

Cozine, Ken: private paper.

Crofutt, G. A., 1881, *Crofutt's grip-sack guide of Colorado:* Omaha, Neb., Overland Pub. Co.

Davidson, L. J., and Blake, F., eds., 1947, *Rocky Mountain tales:* Norman, Univ. of Okla. Press.

Davis, E. O., 1949, *Building Colorado's first mountain railroad:* Colo. Mag., v. 26, no. 4.

Deane, Cecil A., Surveyor General's Office, Denver, August 1867 map. T. III. S. R. L. XXI. W.

Dempsey, Alice, 1984, *Failed trade blocked papoose upbringing for Edward Blood:* Golden Transcript, July 26, 1984.

_____ 1995, Guy Hill School to share history: Golden Transcript, Nov. 23, 1995.

Denver Commonwealth, Sept. 3, 1863.

Denver Mountain Parks Map 1924.

The Denver Post, 1927.

_____ May 29, 1938.

_____ Friday, April 11, 1952, interview with rancher William Koch captioned: *Rancher Hiked up Peak to Crash Site Alone.*

_____ Friday, April 11, 1952, report by Al Nukkula captioned: *11 Die in B-25 on Golden Peak.*

_____ Friday, April 11, 1952, report by Thor Severson captioned: *Rescue Parties Take Out Bodies by Pack Horse.*

_____ *Ibid.*, captioned: *Wreckage Fails to Show Why B-25 Passed Lowry.*

Diary of a Pike's Peak gold seeker in 1860: Colo. Mag., v. 14, no. 6, Nov. 1937.

Diary of a journey to the Pike's Peak gold mines in 1859. Initials M.V.H.R.: Colo. Room, Colo. School of Mines Library, Document F-593-W5.

Engler, Suzy, 1986, *Unique youth camp to close:* Colo. Transcript, May 29, 1986.

Frederick, J. V., 1940, *Ben Holladay, the stagecoach king:* Calif., Arthur H. Clark.

Gardner, Richard, 1997, Holiday home tour: Transcript, Nov. 14, 1997.

Garnaas, Steve, 1995, *Jeffco Open Space closer to vision for canyon:* Denver Post, Dec. 15, 1995.

Garraty, John, 1966, *The American Nation, a history of the United States:* New York, Harper & Row.

Georgetown Courier, Oct. 7, 1913.

The ghost's gold, Denver Post, April 13, 1952.

Golden, in The Golden Globe, Industrial Edition, May 20, 1893.

Greeley, Horace, 1860, *An overland journey from New York to San Francisco in the summer of 1859:* New York, Saxton Barker & Co.

Hafen, L. R., ed., *Colorado and Its People:* v. I.

_____ 1941, *Pike's Peak gold rush guidebooks of 1859:* Clark Co.

_____ and A. W., eds., 1961, *Reports from Colorado—The Wildman letters 1859-1865 with other related letters and newspaper reports, 1859:* Glendale, Calif., Clark Co.

Hall, Frank, 1889, *History of the State of Colorado:* Chicago, Blakely Printing Co.

Handbill Collection, Colo. Railroad Museum.

Hanington, C. H. 1942, *Early Days of Central City:* Colo. Mag., v. 19, no. 1, Jan. 1942.

Harper's Weekly, Feb. 8, 1868.

Hauck, C. W. 1972, *Narrow Gauge to Central and Silverplume, Colorado Rail Annual No. 10:* Colo. Railroad Museum, Golden.

H. J. Hawley's Diary, Russell Gulch in 1860, ed. by Lynn I. Perrigo: Colo. Mag., v. (?).

History of Gilpin County in History of Clear Creek and Boulder Valleys: Chicago, Baskin, 1880.

Hollister, Ovando, 1867, *The mines of Colorado:* Springfield, Mass., Samuel Bowles & Co.

Jamieson-Nichols, Jill, *Guy Hill finds new home, once again:* Golden Transcript, July 12, 1996.

Jefferson County, in The Golden Globe, Industrial Edition, May 20, 1893.

Jefferson County Records, Book A. Opened January 6, 1860. Eli Carter, Recorder.

Jefferies, Marguerite, *Mineral Mining Activities from 1875—:* typed manuscript stamped "Jefferson County Museum, Old Court House, Golden, Colo."

Kemp, Donald, *Colorado's little kingdom,* map of Gilpin county.

Koch, Mary, 1978, *The lost highway:* Golden Transcript, Golden, Colo., Dec. 1, 1978.

Lake, Carlos, 1936, *The Kidnapping of Judge A. W. Stone,* in address given at meeting of Bar Association of First Judicial District, Denver, Sept. 23, 1936: Colo. Mag., v. 17, n. 1, Jan. 1940.

Morrison, S. B. 1860, in a letter written Sept. 16, 1860, to his brother, in *Letters from Colorado, 1860-63:* Colo. Mag., v. 16, no. 3, May 1939.

National Archive Records, Washington, D. C. Affidavit Required of Homestead Claimants, Acts of May 20, 1862, and June 21, 1866, signed December 21, 1868.

Nelson, C. E, 1967, *The archaeology of Hall-Woodland cave,* in Southwestern Lore: Colo. Archaeological Soc., v. 33, June 1967, no. 1.

Nelson, C. H., 1967, *The archaeology of Hall-Woodland cave,* in Southwestern Lore: Colo. Archaeological Soc., v. 33, June 1967, no. 1, p. 1-13.

_____ 1969, *Salvage archaeology on Van Bibber Creek,* in Southwestern Lore: Colo. Archaeological Soc., v. 34, March 1969, no. 4.

Nickens, P. R., 1977, *An isolated human burial of probable Woodland association from Golden Gate Canyon, Colorado:* Plains Anthropologist, v. 22, no. 76, pt. 1.

Norbeck, Carl, 1996, *Clear Creek Watershed Forum:* The Colorado Conservator, v. 12, no. 2, June 1996.

Ogilvie, Caroline, *History of Enterprise Grange:* unpublished manuscript.

George W. Parfet, his fine clay bed and business— sketch of his history, in The Golden Globe, Industrial Edition, May 20, 1893, inside cover.

Parker, Ben, 1974, *Gold placers of Colorado,* book 1 of 2 books: School of Mines Quarterly: v. 69, no. 3, July 1974.

Pettis, S. N., journal entry, Golden City, June 29, 1861, in *Letters of S. Newton Pettis:* Colo. Mag., v. 15, no. 1, Jan. 1938.

Pierce, John, Surveyor General's Office, Denver, Feb.10, 1867, map.

Place Names in Colorado, (G) and (R), in Colo. Magazine, which credits Smiley, Jerome C., *Semi-centennial history of the State of Colorado.*

Ramstetter, James K., 1996, *Life in the early days.*

Richardson, A. D., 1867, *Beyond the Mississippi:* New York, American Pub. Co.

Ridgeway, Arthur, 1932, *The mission of Colorado toll roads:* Colo. Mag., v. 9, no. 5.

Robinson, Joan, personal correspondence dated Sept. 2, 1996.

Robson, Carolyn Churches, *Biography:* Arvada Hist. Soc. Collection.

The Rocky Mountain Directory and Colorado Gazetteer for 1871: S. W. Wallihan & Company, Compilers and Publishers, Denver.

Rocky Mountain News, June 16, 1860.

_____ May 13, 1861: Evening Edition.

_____ Jan. 15, 1881: captioned A Call for a Women's Meeting, p. 8, c. 3.

_____ April 11, 1952: caption and front page photo by Morris A. Engle.

_____ May 16, 1988.

Russell, William, letter written from Gregory Gulch, Kansas, June 17th, 1859, in Spencer, E. D., 1966, *Green Russell and Gold:* Univ. of Texas Press, p. 117.

Ryland, C. S., 1965, *The energetic Captain Berthoud,* <u>in</u> The Westerners: Denver Brand Book.

Scott, G. R., 1976, *Historic trail map of the greater Denver area, Colorado:* U.S. Geol. Survey Misc. Inv. Ser., Map I-856-G.

Scott, Jacque, *Fiery goodbye to Indians' sacred hill:* Golden Transcript, date unknown.

Stevenson, Malcolm, 1996, GGC State Park Historian, misc. papers.

_____ 1996, *No more an old maid:* High Country Journal, Golden, Colo., April 1996.

_____ 1996, *Ruth:* High Country Journal, Golden, Colo., June 1996.

_____ 1996, *Adventures at the Tallman Ranch:* High Country Journal, Oct. 1996.

"Static," April 1941.

_____ May 1941.

Strahorn, Robert, *To the Rockies and beyond.*

Strange caves, Denver Times, v. 15, Dec. 4, 1983.

Taylor, Bayard, 1867, *Colorado, a summer trip:* New York, G. P. Putnam & Son.

United States Land Office, Department of the Interior. *Notice of Allowance.*

John Treffeisen, <u>in</u> The Golden Globe, Industrial Edition, May 20, 1893.

Van Wagenen, T. F., 1871(?), *Colorado:* Denver Public Library Western Collection.

_____ 1871(?), *Colorado:* Colorado School of Mines Master's Thesis, Colorado Room Document M36-683.

Villard, Henry, 1860, *The past and present of the Pike's Peak Gold Regions:* Princeton, Univ. Press.

Wagenen, T.F.V., 1926, *Views on the Admission of Colorado in 1876:* Colo. Mag., v. 3, no. 3.

Henry Wagner's Ranch, <u>in</u> The Golden Globe, Industrial Edition, May 20, 1893.

Wagonbach, Lorraine, 1997, *A Short Biography of George S. Green:* private paper for Jefferson County Historical Commission.

_____ 1997: untitled private paper for Jefferson County Historical Commission.

Wiberg, R. E., 1978, *James Bond restless pioneer,* <u>in</u> Empire Magazine: Denver Post, Oct. 29, 1978.

Wiley, Marion C., 1976, *The high road:* Bicentennial project of the Division of Highways, State Department of Highways, State of Colo.

Wyhs, Irma, 1994, *Ranch History,* compiled for the Red School Ranch.

_____ 1996, *The pioneer from Gap Road:* Fence Post, March 18, 1996.

Portraits in Time

A few of the portraits we've found—
portraits of people, of land, of place, and a way of life.

COLO. HIST. SOC.

Golden as watered by Clear Creek is in the foreground. In the background to the right is the southeast corner of the Ralston Buttes Quad. Aside from the obvious, this view is remarkable for what it says about Indian country. The old Ute trail, utilized by settlers, takes off up the draw to the extreme left. The Arapaho trail entered the draw to the right of the canyon (see arrow). From inside the draw the Arapaho trail swung onto the southward ridge and upward. Thus did the canyon divide the Nations in this part of the world. An uneasy truce at best.

The Ute owned the great trails across the mountains north and south of Clear Creek and traveled freely back and forth. The Arapaho, a johnny-come-lately to the eastern prairies, took poles and furs from the mountains but most likely did not tarry at the task. His trails into the mountains were few and far between. We are fortunate to know about this one.

In the latter part of the 19th century settlers reported Utes on the Golden Gate side of the canyon, but this probably had more to do with the excitement of the times than with any ceasing of hostilities between Arapaho and Ute.

It would be fun to know what was said when this picture was posed for. Jack Boyle is the man with the pistol. 1897.

Photographed in the Wikstrom yard, 1899. Sam Bowser is the "driver." Wheelbarrow rides were a common form of entertainment and spills were frequent.

Photographed 1904 on the Ernest Koch, Sr., homestead. Gus Koch shot the bear. Frank Termentozzi is on the left, Ernest Koch, Jr., Gus' brother, is on the right.

A liberated woman. Christina Wikstrom, 1918, sans sidesaddle. The furthermost building up the hill to the left is the chicken coop. This is the only structure still standing of the original Wikstrom homestead buildings.

Twelve-year-old Ed Tait, a violin student of Bessie Nare. Photographed 1925 in Bessie's front yard.

WIKSTROM COLLECTION

Darned old wind. The couple is unknown. Notice the girl's right boot turned just so,
and the bandanna around her hat.

WIKSTROM COLLECTION

Washday at the Wikstrom mansion, 1896.
Mary Wikstrom.

WIKSTROM COLLECTION

The wheelbarrow troupe, 1899. Sam Bowser
is the man riding. The others are unknown.
Note the ladder to facilitate forking hay off the
top of the stack.

South entrance to Coors, 1916. Note the Interurban electric trolley in lower left.

Looking S down Guy Gulch from Mt. Tom. Elk Creek Flats to the right in the distance.
Photographed 1973.

Serpentine Clear Creek from high in the Guy Gulch drainage.
The gulch swings left of the two humps, lower center, to reach the creek. Photographed 1975.

Douglas Mountain.

CROWELL COLLECTION

Back range seen from Stoney Point, W of Douglas Mountain. The point overlooks the top of Horse Creek, which accommodates Douglas Mountain Road.

Golden as seen from the summit of Galbraith Mountain. Photographed 1997.

Index

Maiden names are in *italics*.

About the Editors

CHARLES RAMSTETTER was born in the old *8 mile house* in Golden Gate Canyon. When he was seventeen, he joined the army to see the world. In 1979 he retired from the United States Air Force as a Master Sergeant and returned to the land where he is a fourth-generation rancher. His grandfather, Henry Ramstetter, Sr., married Matilda Koch, the daughter of homesteaders Ernest and Elizabeth Koch. His father, Otto Ramstetter, homesteaded between Tucker Gulch and Clear Creek Canyon, and was also a gold miner. His mother, Bertha, taught school in Mountain House and Guy Hill schools in the 1920s.

MARY RAMSTETTER grew up in Golden. Her father, Owen Francis Acers, was for many years Golden's only electrical contractor. Her mother, Geneva, did the payroll for all of Jefferson County in the 1940s. Mary retired from the Colorado School of Mines where she worked as secretary for the Humanities and Social Sciences Department. Her recently published novel, *Over the Mountains of the Moon,* about Mormon emigrants on the Oregon Trail in 1846, won the 1995 Columbine Award for Best Book of the Year and the 1997 Colorado Independent Publishers Award for Best Overall Design. *Over the Mountains of the Moon,* now in its second printing, was also nominated for the 1999 Mountain and Plains Booksellers Regional Books Award.

Together Charlie and Mary run a commercial cow-calf operation in Crawford Gulch. Their registered Colorado cattle brand, which is read by brand inspectors as C LAZY THREE, named their press. They have four children and two grandchildren.

C Lazy Three
PRESS

5957 Crawford Gulch ❧ Golden, Colorado 80403 ❧ Phone and Fax 303-277-0134

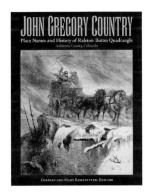

Available from your local bookstore, or directly from the publisher

John Gregory Country: Place Names and History of Ralston Buttes Quadrangle, Jefferson County, Colorado

Charles and Mary Ramstetter, Editors   ISBN 0-9643283-2-1
Softbound, 8½ × 11", 280 pages, nearly 200 photographs, quad and location maps, bibliography and index

An amazing collection of every scrap of history known to exist surrounding the first road through the mountains to the fabulous gold strikes in Blackhawk and Central City. Richly illustrated with photographs old and new, the book doesn't confine itself to the origin of place names, but ranges across the countryside to show how the dreamers who followed in Gregory's footsteps suffered and coped.

☐ Send one copy of *John Gregory Country* at the regular price of $24 plus $4 postage, total $28.

☐ Send two copies postage-free for a total cost of $48.

☐ Send three or more copies postage-free at a reduced cost of $21 per copy.
(_____ copies × $21 per copy)

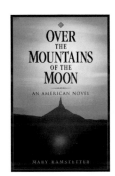

Available from your local bookstore, or directly from the publisher

Over the Mountains of the Moon: An American Novel

By Mary Ramstetter   ISBN 0-9643283-0-5
Softbound, 5½ × 8½", 496 pages, map and bibliography
*First Place Overall Design Winner—Best Design of a Novel
Colorado Independent Publishers Association, 1997*

Vol. I—A Seton-style narrative set in the West of the American emigrant in the late 1840s. A would-be trapper traps himself in a shadowy love affair. The first wife of a Mormon polygamist clings to shards of past happiness. A Fort Laramie bourgeois philosophizes about the Oregon Trail. Intrigue and betrayal, unexpected partings and surprising reunions pop up like dust devils. Plus dramatic river crossings, Indian captures, and dozens of well-drawn winners and losers from New York to New Mexico intermixed with true historic places and events—an irresistible, page-turning, history-rich experience from start to finish.

☐ Send one copy of *Over the Mountains of the Moon* at the regular price of $14 plus $4 postage, total $18.

☐ Send two or more copies postage-free at $14 each.

Down the Valley of the Shadows: An American Novel

By Mary Ramstetter   ISBN 0-9643283-1-3
Softbound, 5½ × 8½", map and bibliography
Available January 2000

Vol. II—The saga of *Over the Mountains of the Moon* continues. A timber man shoots two thieves and finds a brother he never knew he had. A painter with bad eyes attracts con artists with big eyes but no courage. A soldier in Fort Defiance, Arizona, hears a strange tale. The steady drumbeat of events makes for a fascinating, history-haunted story.

Available from your local bookstore, or directly from the publisher

☐ Send one copy of *Down the Valley of the Shadows* at the regular price of $14 plus $4 postage, total $18.

☐ Send two or more copies postage-free at $14 each.

DISTRIBUTORS: Baker & Taylor, Ingram, Books West

. . . and so the time has come to say goodbye

The man who kicked the bucket. Note the bucket in the background and the empty bottle close at hand. Even the dog is getting into the act.